Handbook of
Warehouse and Distribution Management
Forms and Reports

Handbook of
Warehouse and Distribution Management
Forms and Reports

James Lupis

PRENTICE HALL
Englewood Cliffs, New Jersey 07632

Prentice-Hall International (UK) Limited, *London*
Prentice-Hall of Australia Pty. Limited, *Sydney*
Prentice-Hall Canada, Inc., *Toronto*
Prentice-Hall Hispanoamericana, S.A., *Mexico*
Prentice-Hall of India Private Limited, *New Delhi*
Prentice-Hall of Japan, Inc., *Tokyo*
Simon & Schuster Asia Pte. Ltd., *Singapore*
Editora Prentice-Hall do Brasil, Ltds., *Rio de Janeiro*

© 1991 *by*

PRENTICE-HALL, Inc.

Englewood Cliffs, NJ

10 9 8 7 6 5 4 3 2 1

Library of Congress Cataloging-in-Publication Data

Lupis, James.
    Handbook of warehouse and distribution management forms and
reports / James Lupis.

      p.   cm.
    Includes index.
    ISBN 0-13-369968-4
     1. Warehouses—Management—Forms—Handbooks, manuals, etc.
2. Shipment of goods—Forms—Handbooks, manuals, etc. 3. Industrial
safety—Forms—Handbooks, manuals, etc. I. Title.
HF5485.L86 1991
658.7'8—dc20   91-31170
                                                     CIP

ISBN 0-13-369968-4

PRENTICE HALL
Business Information & Publishing Division
Englewood Cliffs, NJ 07632
Simon & Schuster, A Paramount Communications Company

PRINTED IN THE UNITED STATES OF AMERICA

This book is dedicated to my mother
Kathryn Gloria Lupis

WHAT THIS BOOK WILL
DO FOR YOU

The *Handbook of Warehouse and Distribution Management Forms and Reports* is an indispensable resource for executives, managers, and supervisors in the warehousing and distribution profession. This book details forms and reports vital to running an operation at top efficiency, and it provides excellent examples of essential interdepartmental communications.

Many companies with diverse backgrounds have contributed information and actual forms to be used in this book, to provide a complete and all-inclusive reference guide. The *Handbook of Warehouse and Distribution Management Forms and Reports* covers:

- Receiving and shipping documentation, and reports to monitor labor and productivity
- What forms are needed for import shipments and proper procedure for shipping overseas
- Forms and reports needed to maintain and control a customer return department
- Inventory and materials management forms and reports to maintain material flow and location control
- Production control and scheduling information that relates to warehousing and distribution
- How to process claims involving shortages and damages, including charts and checklists detailing claim procedures
- What forms are required to be filed with the Occupational Safety and Health Administration concerning employee illness or injury
- The Occupational Safety and Health Act
- Occupational illness or injury recordkeeping, including safety records, employee information forms, and safety checklists
- How to complete a Materials Safety Data Sheet
- What forms are required in the shipping of hazardous materials
- Hazardous materials and labels charts
- Emergency response and procedures charts

- Forms and checklists to maintain, plan, and schedule maintenance and repair operations more effectively
- Personnel forms and reports for hiring, evaluating, disciplining, maintaining, and terminating employees

Since warehousing and distribution involve many operations within an operation, the importance of proper documentation and procedures are vital to maintain control in an extremely hectic environment.

The *Handbook of Warehouse and Distribution Management Forms and Reports* provides hundreds of examples for the warehouse and distribution professional to improve the performance of your business.

ACKNOWLEDGMENTS

I would like to thank all my family, friends, and business associates who encouraged the writing of this book, and gave me the much needed motivation for its completion. A special thanks to my patient and supporting wife, Joni. To Prentice Hall for their interest in publishing this book, and in particular, to my editor, Ruth Mills, whose invaluable help brought me across the finish line.

Last, and certainly not least, I wish to thank the following people and companies who provided forms and information, to make this book an excellent reference guide for anyone involved in the warehousing and distribution field:

Bevis Custom Furniture, Inc.

Craft Communications

Ellie Brauner

Federal Express

Glendale Protective Technology

Jean Baldwin

Larry Zimmerman

Modern Materials Handling Magazine

National Institute of Occupational Safety and Health

National Safety Council, Chicago

N.Y.S. Dept. of Environmental Conservation

N.Y.S. Workers Compensation Board

Occupational Safety and Health Administration

Prentice Hall*

Rite Hite Corporation

Steven's Air Freight

---

* From the book *INVENTORY MANAGEMENT FACTOMATIC: A Portfolio of Successful Forms, Reports, Records, and Procedures,* by Robert S. Kuehne and R. Jerry Baker © 1978. Used by permission of the publisher, Prentice-Hall, Inc., New Jersey

Suffolk County Dept. of Health Services
Susan Schulman
Tops Business Forms
United States Dept. of Labor
United States Dept. of Transportation
United States Postal Service
V. W. Eimicke Associates, Inc.
Warehouse Executive
W.C. McQuaide, Inc.
William Poy
Yellow Freight System

CONTENTS

CHAPTER 9   SAFETY AND HAZARDOUS MATERIALS   193

Occupational Safety and Health Administration   193

CHAPTER 11   WAREHOUSE PERSONNEL MANAGEMENT   267

APPENDIX   UNIFORM COMMERCIAL CODE   321

INDEX   339

Chapter One

SUCCESSFUL WAREHOUSE AND DISTRIBUTION MANAGEMENT

During the past ten years warehousing and distribution have gone through tremendous changes. As American businesses restructured to maintain a healthy profitability in changing economic times, they discovered that warehousing and distribution played a vital role to their continued success. While previously they were considered a necessary evil, upper management has come to realize that the professional and successful management of these operations can very well be their company's profit margin.

During the 1980s, two events took place to change the way American businesses viewed warehousing and distribution. The first event was deregulation of the trucking industry. The Motor Carrier Act of 1980 promoted competition, with the hope that trucking companies would be "forced" to provide more efficient transportation services. This allowed shippers to negotiate rates and also made trucking companies more customer service oriented. This gave businesses the opportunity not only to distribute more cost effectively, but also to have better control over their distribution options.

The second event that took place was the implementation of the Japanese concept of "just-in-time" delivery. As American businesses realized they could no longer carry the high cost of inventory, they sought to operate with the least amount of stock possible. This put an increasing emphasis on materials management, which in turn put a greater importance on warehousing and warehouse management. The next ten years will continue to put heavy demands on the warehouse and distribution manager, as corporate strategy increases toward greater efficiency by way of automation and professionalism.

1

LOGISTICS

Webster's dictionary defines logistics as "the military science of procuring, maintaining, and transporting of material and personnel." This definition can be accurately applied to logistics and its meaning to warehousing and distribution. Logistics covers goods from the procuring process (planning and purchasing) to maintaining (receiving, storage, inventory control, etc.) and transporting (physical distribution).

Logistics planning and strategy have taken on a key importance in maintaining a tight cost control system. Corporate management of the 1980s discovered the many advantages of running a logistics program at peak efficiency and will continue to develop a world-class logistics plan. Warehouse and distribution managers will play an active role in planning and achieving the corporate goals necessary for their company's success.

COMPUTER SYSTEMS

Each year warehousing and distribution become more and more sophisticated as advanced technology improve these operations. As a warehouse and distribution manager, you must constantly upgrade your learning of new systems and equipment to ensure that you are running your department as productively as possible. (See Figure 1-1.) System integrators, automated storage and retrieval systems (AS/RS), automatic guided vehicles, automatic identification systems, and advanced computerized materials management are just some of the many options you have to reduce costs and increase productivity.

The successful warehouse and distribution manager of the 1990s will have to be experienced in advanced technologies that will dominate warehousing from the receiving process until the cycle is completed at the shipping function. The difficult decisions take place when matching a system with a particular operation. For example, in selecting an automatic identification system there are hundreds of various applications, but which would produce the best results? To determine this, you must combine a comprehensive understanding of the different applications, with knowledge of your own operation. Factors to be considered when purchasing any advanced technology system are:

- Corporate goals
- Feasibility of implementation
- Economic justification

Corporate goals must be determined in order to select the system that will best accomplish future objectives. If your company has a specific goal to improve inventory control, then you must evaluate a system with this in mind. When deciding on a bar coding system for the receiving department, keep in mind that it should have inventory tracking capabilities to coincide with the corporate goal. Choosing a system that confines bar coding only to the receiving process becomes counterproductive. Also, each system should have the capabilities to allow for substantial growth.

The next step is to determine if the system selected can be feasibly integrated with the corresponding department of operations. Will the application enhance procedures and be quickly implemented? Or will start-up time be complicated and costly? Many

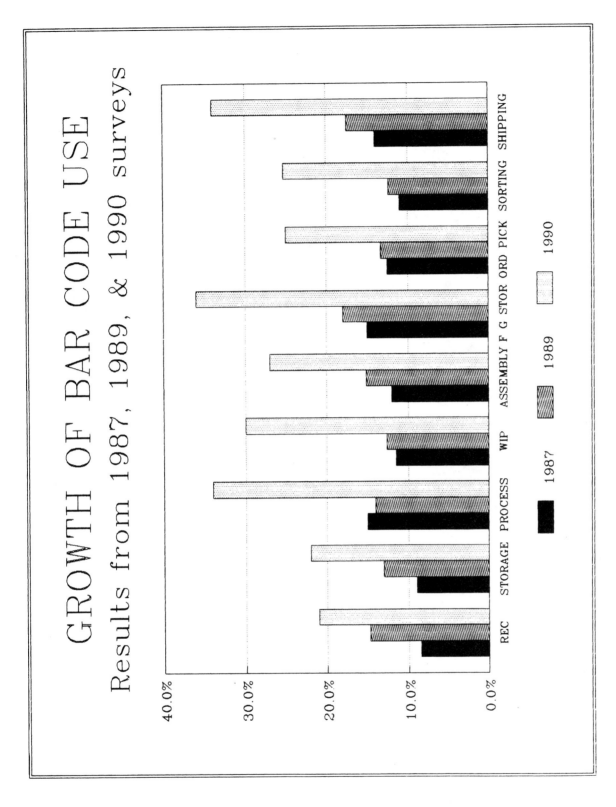

1-1 GROWTH OF BAR CODE USE

3

times a company will purchase an excellent system but one that is far too sophisticated for their needs, leading to unnecessary problems. These systems can take years before all the "bugs" are out and proper adaptation takes place. Unless there is a problem in your operation, or the operation is to be reorganized, the system should adapt to the operation—not the operation to the system.

Economic justification (see Figure 1-2) is usually the deciding factor in determining the purchase of a system. This is where you must convince upper management that the purchase of expensive technology is well worth the investment. Because the initial outlay is extremely expensive, an attractive return on investment (ROI) is vital.

The calculation factors used to determine savings vary according to the method used. It is important to include not only tangible savings, such as reductions in time and labor, but also the intangibles. Intangible savings are much harder to calculate. Will the new system improve operations, which in turn will affect customer service? Will this result in higher sales? Will improved production scheduling increase production, which in turn will improve market fulfillment? There are many questions that management must address to determine the results of intangible savings.

PERSONNEL

As warehousing changed from a necessary evil to a vital part in the material flow process, warehouse and distribution management became more complicated and required a greater degree of professionalism. This also holds true of warehouse personnel. In times past, common thinking was that "anyone" could load and unload a shipment. This was a terrible misconception, and many companies eventually paid the price for this thinking.

Now, as warehouses have become largely automated, it is even more important to realize that quality people are needed to receive, pick, pack, inventory, and perform all other warehouse functions. Management will be responsible for hand picking personnel and providing comprehensive training for them. A receiving clerk, for example, must now not only know his or her normal job function but must also be computer literate and able to process data.

A comprehensive training problem should be established to provide personnel with a thorough knowledge of operation procedures, including safety and health requirements. Employees who are well trained from the beginning, and have clearly defined guidelines, will perform at a greater rate of proficiency than those who do not. Because your responsibilities are increased due to the added complexity of the operation, the ability to delegate authority to quality people is essential.

COMMUNICATION

Clear, concise, and complete communications are always a vital tool for warehousing and distribution. As operations within a warehouse become more integrated, the need for effective communications become even more important. To be a successful manager, you must communicate with upper management, sales, customer service, supervisors, personnel, and other departments within your area of responsibility. Because of the

COST JUSTIFICATION WORKSHEET

SYSTEM/EQUIPMENT TO BE PURCHASE:_____

MANUFACTURER:_____

TOTAL PURCHASE PRICE:_____

LIFE EXPECTANCY OF PRODUCT:_____

DEPARTMENT(S) TO BE IMPLEMENTED:_____

(A) POTENTIAL ANNUAL SAVINGS = $_____

(B) CAPITAL INVESTMENT = $_____

(C) DEPRECIATON PERIOD = _____

(D) ANNUAL DEPRECIATION B DIVIDED BY C = $_____

(E) ANNUAL PAYBACK A – D = $_____

(F) TOTAL SAVINGS E x C = $_____

SUMMARY OF ANALYSIS:_____

_____

_____

_____

_____

_____

_____

COMPLETED BY _____   DATE _____

1-2 COST JUSTIFICATION WORKSHEET

wide scope of activities involved, you must not only communicate verbally, but you must have excellent written communication skills as well.

Also, gathering information and communicating that information in a timely manner is vital to the overall operation process. You must be familiar with a large variety of forms and reports that you encounter daily. You will be constantly receiving information from them, relaying information to others, or providing information. These forms and reports play an integral part in the everyday activities of a warehouse or distribution manager. The following chapters are an invaluable resource of forms and reports for all warehouse and distribution professionals. The accumulated information of these forms and reports gives you the complete knowledge to obtain and distribute all the necessary information to run your operation at peak proficiency.

Chapter Two

RECEIVING

The receiving department is responsible for receipt of all incoming material. Its primary functions are unloading carriers, processing receipts, maintaining accurate records, and informing appropriate departments.

Three main areas of concern are wrong merchandise received, damages, and incorrect piece count. Each shipment must be matched up with a corresponding purchase order, and all item numbers must be checked. Receivers must inspect cartons for holes and crush marks, especially on corners, where the majority of damages occur. Also, they must check to see if cartons have been retaped by carrier. If there is retaping, this should alert the receiver that the carton was handled roughly, or even had merchandise taken out. All piece counts should be double-checked and verified. All exceptions, whether damages, shortages, and so on, must be noted on carrier's freight bill. Finally, this information must be accurately and quickly relayed to materials management, inventory control, purchasing, and accounts payable. With all this to do, it is easy to understand why forms, reports, and recordkeeping are an integral part of the receiving department.

This chapter details the forms, reports, and recordkeeping that are vital in maintaining an efficient and well-run operation.

FREIGHT BILLS

A freight bill is a legal document between the inbound carrier and the receiver, verifying that the shipment was delivered and that merchandise was received in good condition.

Any discrepancy must be noted on the freight bill at time of delivery. The three forms shown are excellent examples for the modes of delivery discussed.

2-1. FREIGHT BILL—COMMON CARRIER

Each common carrier will have its own personalized bill, but all will be similar in format and information.

Key Information

- Pro Number or Freight Bill Number (This number is needed in all correspondence with the freight carrier.)
- Shipper's Name and Address
- Number of Pieces
- Description of Merchandise Shipped
- Rate (This is the charge per 100 pounds of merchandise.)
- Total Charges
- Freight Shipped Prepaid or Collect
- Received in Good Condition Except as Noted (If shipment is short or pieces came in damaged, mark freight bill appropriately here.)

2-2. FREIGHT BILL—AIRFREIGHT

The form shown is used by an airfreight carrier and includes customs information. Special attention should be given to the carrier's liability statement, which declares that liability is limited to $50.00 per shipment. To cover a shipment of greater value, additional insurance is required by shipper.

Key Information

- Carrier's Reference Number
- Name of Importing Carrier
- Bill of Lading or Airway Bill Number
- Liability Statement
- Customs Permit Attached/Customs (only on imported shipments)
- Carton(s) Held by U.S. Customs (Customs will hold one or several cartons for inspection. The main reason for inspection is to ensure each item imported is properly labeled showing country of import.)

RECEIVING DOCUMENTATION

2-3. RETURN GOODS AUTHORIZATION—BASIC

The receiving department should never accept return merchandise without prior authorization. The form shown is issued by the receiving company and gives permission to the shipper to return specified items.

Key Information

- Authorization Number (usually preprinted)
- Reason for Return
- Freight Responsibility (This declares who is responsible for the freight charges.)
- Return Authorized by (signature, usually by customer service department or sales rep)

2-4. RETURN GOODS AUTHORIZATION—DETAILED

The form shown is from a furniture manufacturer, detailing information such as packing instructions, carrier to ship by, and disposition of merchandise.

Key Information

- Authorization Number (R/A Number)
- Packing Instructions
- Statement That Merchandise Must Be Returned Within 30 Days
- Reason for Return (e.g., returned for inspection, damage)
- Disposition of Merchandise (e.g., merchandise returned to stock)

2-5. PACKING LIST—BASIC

A packing list gives a description of the shipment, including items shipped, quantity, and purchase order number. When a shipment does not correspond with the packing list, the shipper should be notified immediately. The form shown gives primary information concerning the shipment.

Key Information

- Customer Order Number
- Vendor's Order Number
- Stock Number
- Quantity Shipped

2-6. PACKING LIST—DETAILED

This is a more detailed form giving additional information, such as terms of sale.

Key Information

- Terms
- F.O.B. (free on board) (This means that the expenses up to the point specified are for the account of the seller.)
- Purchase Order Number
- Stock Number (by item)
- Quantity Shipped

2-7. PURCHASE ORDER

A purchase order acts as a contract between the buyer and seller, authorizing the purchase of merchandise. The receiving department should have a copy of the purchase order to match up with the packing list. This allows the receiver to ascertain the authorization of delivery, that merchandise corresponds in whole or in part to what was ordered, and that the piece count corresponds to the order. The form shown is a basic purchase order listing required information.

Key Information

- "Ship to" Address (This can differ from billing address.)
- Purchase Order Number
- Item Number
- Quantity Ordered
- Special Instructions

2-8. RECEIVING TALLY

This form is used when unloading large quantities of bulk items. It enables the receiver to maintain an accurate carton count and record any exceptions during unloading.

Key Information

- Item Number
- Quantity per Carton
- Cartons per Pallet
- Total Cartons
- Damage Cartons

2-9. RECEIVING RECORD—BASIC

For every shipment received, a receiving record should be made and matched up with the packing list and purchase order. The form shown lists all the basic, necessary information concerning a shipment.

Key Information

- Receiving Record Number
- Vendor
- Purchase Order Number
- Carrier
- Pro Number
- Collect/Prepaid

2-10. RECEIVING RECORD—DETAILED

This form gives a complete summary of the shipment involved and includes a breakdown of different items received.

Key Information

- Receiving Record Number
- Carrier Name
- Prepaid or Collect
- Item Number
- Quantity
- Purchase Order Number
- Whether Shipment Received Is Partial or Complete
- Number of Cartons Received OK or Damaged
- Total Number of Cartons

2-11. RECEIVING REPORT—PARTIAL DELIVERY

This form is used to record a shipment of a partial delivery. The form shown, used by a government agency, includes accounting and invoice data.

Key Information

- Purchase Order Number
- Vendor
- Agency Identification

- Description and Quantity of Items Delivered
- Accounting and Liquidation Information (completed by accounting department)
- Shipper Information
- Invoice Information

2-12. DAILY RECEIVING REPORT

This form gives a summary of shipments received on a daily basis. It is ideal for a receiving manager to monitor the workload.

Key Information

- Total Number of Shipments Received
- Total Number of Cartons
- Number of Receiving Staff

2-13. DAILY SUMMARY OF MATERIALS RECEIVED

The form shown is used by a manufacturing company to log materials received and to record which department they were delivered to.

Key Information

- Received from
- Purchase Order Number
- Whether Shipment Is Complete or Partial
- Carrier Name (received via)
- Department Delivered to

2-14. DAILY RECEIVING SCHEDULE

The form shown is used by a company that requires an appointment for all deliveries. This form enables the receiving manager to set up inbound shipments according to a time schedule and to determine the number of daily receiving personnel required.

Key Information

- Appointment Time
- Vendor
- Purchase Order Number
- Carrier
- Total Cartons

2-15. FREIGHT INSPECTION REPORT

This form is used in the event of loss or damage to part of a shipment. The form shown is used by the delivering carrier to determine cause, result, and disposition of damaged merchandise.

Key Information

- Shipping/Receiving Information (name and address)
- Information Concerning Loss
- Information Concerning Damage (e.g., apparent cause of damage, condition of container)
- Type of Container
- Disposition of Damaged Freight
- Detailed Description of Exceptions

2-16. MATERIAL INSPECTION REPORT

The form shown is used by quality control to report on the quality and acceptance of a shipment. The material usually stays in receiving's holding area until disposition of the material is decided.

Key Information

- Vendor
- Carrier
- Inspected on Dock/in Quality Control
- Quantity Accepted
- Quantity Rejected
- Reason for Rejection
- Disposition

2-17. MATERIAL REJECTION NOTICE

This letter notifies the supplier that all or part of a shipment has been rejected. It is issued by the purchasing department, with one copy sent to the receiving department.

Key Information

- Purchase Order Number
- Material Ordered
- Quantity Received
- Quantity Rejected

- Reason for Rejection
- Disposition

2-18. OVERAGE, SHORTAGE, AND DAMAGE REPORT

The form shown is used to give a complete description of the exception received. One copy should stay in receiving's file, one copy should be attached to the receiving record, and one copy should be sent to purchasing.

Key Information

- Purchase Order Number
- Vendor
- Indication of Overage, Shortage, or Damage
- Description of Loss or Damage
- Description of Items

2-19. LOCATOR CARD

The form shown is used by an electronics company to give a location to stock items. The receiving department fills in the item number, date, receiving number, and purchase order number, then delivers the merchandise to a holding area. The warehouse then fills in the rest as the item is assigned a location.

Key Information

- Item Number
- Receiving Number
- Location (e.g., aisle, position, and tier)

2-20. STOCK RECORD CARD

This form is used to keep a running inventory on stock items. A minimum/maximum number of units are determined and quantities are ordered accordingly.

Key Information

- Item
- Location (e.g., bin, shelf)
- Minimum and Maximum Number of Units
- Stock Number
- Receiving Information

- Depletion Information (i.e., items released from stock)
- Balance on Hand

2-21. STORES WITHDRAWAL FORM

When a company uses a stores department, a withdrawal form is needed to transfer material from receiving. Because the stores department is used to distribute material throughout the warehouse, receiving and stores must work closely together.

Key Information

- Requested and Approved by (signatures)
- Section
- Item Number
- Material Code
- Quantity
- Backorder Purchase Order Number
- Issued and Received by (signatures)

FLOWCHARTS

2-22. FLOWCHART—MATERIALS

A typical materials flow will take received merchandise to a holding area, with samples going to quality control. When materials are approved, they are then distributed to the warehouse (i.e., finished goods) or to manufacturing (i.e., unfinished goods). After materials are inventoried, they are available for shipments, going into a pick/pack operation and then on to distribution.

2-23. FLOWCHART—PAPERWORK

When a shipment comes in, the receiver should match the freight bill with the packing list and with a copy of the purchase order. After the shipment is received, a receiving record is created and attached. At this time any additional paperwork, such as an overage, shortage, and damage report, should also be attached. Copies should be forwarded to purchasing and materials management, with original paperwork going to accounts payable.

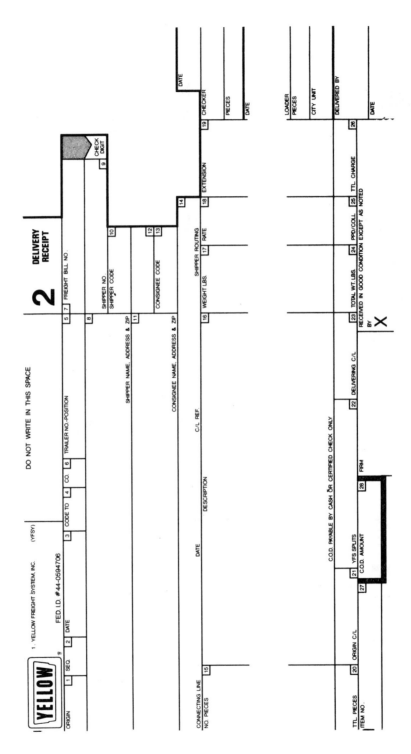

2-1 FREIGHT BILL—COMMON CARRIER

16

ENTRY NO.		

STEVENS AIRFREIGHT
11 JUNEAU BOULEVARD
WOODBURY, N.Y. 11797

(718) 656-5422   API 65422

DATE	OUR REF. NO.

IMPORTING CARRIER	LOCATION	FROM PORT OF / ORIGIN AIRPORT

B/L OR AWB NO.	ARRIVAL DATE	FREE TIME EXP.	LOCAL DELIVERY OR TRANSFER BY (DELIVERY ORDER ISSUED TO)

DELIVER TO ⬇

⬆ PICK-UP BY

THE CARRIER OR CARTMAN TO WHOM THIS ORDER IS ASSIGNED WILL BE HELD RESPONSIBLE FOR ANY STORAGE AND DEMURRAGE CHARGES RESULTING FROM NEGLIGENCE.

IMPORTANT: NOTIFY US AT ONCE IF DELIVERY CANNOT BE EFFECTED AS INSTRUCTED.

MARKS & NOS.	DESCRIPTION & WT.

DELIVERY ORDER: The liability of STEVENS AIRFREIGHT is limited to fifty dollars ($50.00) per shipment unless a greater valuation is declared to STEVENS AIRFREIGHT and charges for such greater value paid, at the rate of ten cents ($.10) per each one hundred dollars ($100.00) of declared value. Such value must be declared in writing and accepted by STEVENS AIRFREIGHT.

CUSTOMS PERMIT	PKG. NOS. HELD BY U.S. CUSTOMS – TO FOLLOW	GO #
☐ ATTACHED ☐ LODGED WITH U.S. CUSTOMS		

RECEIVED IN GOOD ORDER

PER   DATE

2-2 FREIGHT BILL—AIRFREIGHT

```
                                                                   4301
                    RETURN GOODS AUTHORIZATION


  SHIP TO:_____        FROM:_____

          _____              _____

          _____              _____


    ┌──────────┬──────────────────┬──────────┬──────────────┐
    │ QUANTITY │   DESCRIPTION    │  P.O. #  │    AMOUNT     │
    ├──────────┼──────────────────┼──────────┼──────────────┤
    │          │                  │          │              │
    ├──────────┼──────────────────┼──────────┼──────────────┤
    │          │                  │          │              │
    ├──────────┼──────────────────┼──────────┼──────────────┤
    │          │                  │          │              │
    ├──────────┼──────────────────┼──────────┼──────────────┤
    │          │                  │          │              │
    ├──────────┼──────────────────┼──────────┼──────────────┤
    │          │                  │          │              │
    └──────────┴──────────────────┴──────────┴──────────────┘


  REASON FOR RETURN:_____

  _____


  FREIGHT RESPONSIBILITY     [] CUSTOMER      [] ABC MFG

  SHIP VIA_____

  CUSTOMER  SIGNATURE_____DATE_____


  RETURN AUTHORIZED BY_____DATE_____


                        PACKING SLIP
```

2-3 RETURN GOODS AUTHORIZATION—BASIC

BEVIS
CUSTOM FURNITURE, INC.®

P.O. BOX 2280
FLORENCE, AL 35630

(205) 766-6497
1-800-551-3325
1-800-821-6360 (ALABAMA)
1-800-635-7247 (FAX)

AUTHORIZATION TO
RETURN MERCHANDISE

R / A NUMBER

CUSTOMER NO.

AUTHORIZED BY _____

CUSTOMER		S H I P T O	BEVIS CUSTOM FURNITURE, INC ROUTE 4, BOX 34B FLORENCE, AL 35630

ATTN: **TAG**

IT IS VERY IMPORTANT THAT THE MERCHANDISE LISTED BELOW BE RETURNED AS SOON AS POSSIBLE. WHENEVER POSSIBLE, PLEASE USE THE ORIGINAL CARTONS AND PACKING. IF THIS IS NOT POSSIBLE, USE OTHER PACKING TO ADEQUATELY PROTECT THE PRODUCT.

IF THE MERCHANDISE IS NOT RETURNED WITHIN 30 DAYS, YOU WILL BE INVOICED FOR THE PRODUCT.

FREIGHT

☐ Prepaid

☐ Collect

☐ Deadhead

R / A DATE	CUSTOMER P.O. NUMBER	BEVIS REFERENCE NO.	BEVIS INVOICE NO.	NO CHARGE #	MUST SHIP BY (CARRIER)

QUAN.	MODEL NUMBER	DESCRIPTION	UNIT PRICE	AMOUNT

(BELOW FOR BEVIS USE ONLY)

☐ 30% RESTOCKING FEE   ☐ FREIGHT UP   ☐ FREIGHT BACK

☐ RETURNED FOR INSPECTION   ☐ DAMAGE   ☐ DEFECT   ☐ REFUSED

☐ SENT REPLACEMENT   ☐ BEVIS TO FILE CLAIM

☐ ISSUE CREDIT UPON RETURN

COMMENTS

INSPECTED BY:	
RECEIVED BY:	
DATE RETURNED:	
CARRIER:	
PRO #:	

☐ MERCHANDISE RETURNED TO STOCK

☐ MERCHANDISE UNUSABLE

☐ ISSUED CALL TAGS   Date _____

AMOUNT   DATE   INITIALS

☐ ISSUED CREDIT $ _____ _____ _____

2-4 RETURN GOODS AUTHORIZATION—DETAILED

PACKING SLIP NO. _____

CUSTOMER NO. _____
DATE SHIPPED _____

SOLD TO	SHIP TO

YOUR ORDER NO.	OUR ORDER NO.	ORDER DATE	SHIPPED VIA	FOB	TOTALS ➤	NO. OF CTNS.	TOTAL WEIGHT

QUANTITY	STOCK NUMBER	DESCRIPTION	QUANTITY SHIPPED	NUMBER OF CARTONS	TOTAL WEIGHT

PACKED BY	DATE	CHECKED BY	DATE	PLEASE NOTIFY US IMMEDIATELY IF ANY ERROR IS FOUND IN THIS SHIPMENT — PLEASE SEND A COPY OF THIS FORM WITH ANY CORRESPONDENCE — THANK YOU.

2-5 PACKING LIST—BASIC

PACKING LIST

SOLD TO

SHIP TO

CUSTOMER NO. _____

TERMS _____

SALES _____

APP. SHIP WEEK _____

DATE SHIPPED _____

FOB _____

ROUTING _____

INTEREST WILL BE CHARGED AT _____ % PER MONTH
THIS EQUALS AN _____ % ANNUAL RATE.

YOUR ORDER NO.	ORDER DATE	OUR ORDER NO.

ITEM	QUANTITY ORDERED	DESCRIPTION

QUANTITY SHIPPED	NO. OF CARTONS	TOTAL WEIGHT	PACKED BY (Initials)

THANK YOU FOR YOUR ORDER

THIS ORDER WAS SHIPPED FROM OUR PLANT IN
GOOD CONDITION – IF IT ARRIVES DAMAGED
FILE CLAIM WITH CARRIER IMMEDIATELY!

TOTALS	QUANTITY	CARTONS	TOTAL WEIGHT
PACKED BY			DATE
CHECKED BY			DATE

2-6 PACKING LIST—DETAILED

PURCHASE ORDER

SOLD TO:

PURCHASE ORDER	
NUMBER:	
ORDER DATE:	
REQUIRED DATE:	

PURCHASE ORDER NUMBER
MUST APPEAR ON ALL
INVOICES, PACKING
SLIPS & PACKAGES

SHIP TO:

*** NO SUBSTITUTIONS ALLOWED

TERMS:	FOB:	[ ] ORIGINAL
SHIP VIA:		[ ] CONFIRMING COPY

ITEM	DESCRIPTION	QUANTITY	UNIT	PRICE	AMOUNT

GROSS AMOUNT	%DISCOUNT	TAX	SHIP.CHRG	TOTAL
	−	+	+	=

AUTHORIZED SIGNATURE:

2-7 PURCHASE ORDER

RECEIVING TALLY

ITEM NUMBER_____DESCRIPTION_____

QUANTITY PER CARTON_____

CARTONS PER PALLET TIER_____

TIERS PER PALLET_____CARTONS PER PALLET_____

PALLET NUMBER	REC'D	PALLET NUMBER	REC'D	PALLET NUMBER	REC'D
1		11		21	
2		12		22	
3		13		23	
4		14		24	
5		15		25	
6		16		26	
7		17		27	
8		18		28	
9		19		29	
10		20		30	

TOTAL FULL PALLETS_____ = _____CARTONS

PARTIAL PALLET(S)_____ = _____CARTONS

TOTAL = _____CARTONS

DAMAGED CARTONS_____

UNLOADED BY:_____CHECKED BY:_____

2-8 RECEIVING TALLY

```
: ┌──────────────────────────────┐
: │ RECEIVING                     │
: │ RECORD NO. 11085              │
: │                              └──────────────────────────────────────┐
: │                                                                      │
: │  VENDOR_____  P.O. NUMBER_____  DATE_____   │
: │                                                                      │
: │  CARRIER_____  PRO NUMBER_____  TOTAL CARTONS____  │
: │                                                                      │
: │  [] COLLECT  [] PREPAID   RECEIVER'S SIGNATURE_____    │
: └──────────────────────────────────────────────────────────────────────┘
```

2-9 RECEIVING RECORD—BASIC

RECEIVING REPORT   No. _____

Received From _____ On (Date) _____
Address _____ Ship. Date _____
_____ Ship. Number _____

Via ☐ Truck _____   ☐ UPS   ☐ PP   ☐ Picked Up
    ☐ Other_____

No. Pkgs.	No. Cases	No. Ctns.	Skids			(Check One)		If Collect Amount
						Prepaid	Collect	

Quantity	Part #	Description	Weight	Receipt Posted By (Initial)

Our P.O. No._____ Complete Shipment _____ Partial Shipment _____
Our Job No. _____
    ☐ Good Condition   Received By _____
    ☐ Damaged (Explain)   Checked By_____
    _____   Refused By _____
    ☐ Other _____   Reason_____
Delivered To _____ Date _____
                    (Department)

2-10 RECEIVING RECORD—DETAILED

RECEIVING REPORT - PARTIAL DELIVERY

PARTIAL DELIVERY NO.	REQUISITION NO.	PURCHASE OR FIELD ORDER NO.

INSTRUCTIONS

1. USE THIS FORM TO REPORT PARTIAL DELIVERIES ON A PURCHASE OR FIELD ORDER.
2. FOR EACH ITEM ALSO REPORT THE QUANTITIES RECEIVED TO DATE.
3. USE THE RECEIVING REPORT COPY OF THE ORIGINAL ORDER TO REPORT THE FINAL DELIVERY.
4. IF POSSIBLE COMPLETE THIS FORM BY TYPEWRITER.

VENDOR'S NAME AND ADDRESS	AGENCY

REQ. ITEM NO.	DESCRIPTION	THIS DELIVERY QUANTITY	UNIT	TO DATE QUANTITY	

ACCOUNT CODE						AMOUNT		BUS	AUTO FR.	P. P.	EX.	RAIL
FUND	APPROP.	PROGRAM	OBJECT			LIQUIDATION	NET INVOICE					
								CARRIER				
								SHIPPING DOC. NO.		COL.	PPD.	NO. OF PIECES
								CENTRAL RECEIVING BY				
								DIVISION OR UNIT RECEIVED FOR				
								DIVISION OR UNIT RECEIVED BY				
								DATE OF RECEIPT			FRT. CHARGE	

CHECKED AND APPROVED FOR PAYMENT BY:	DATE	NUMBER	AMOUNT	DISCOUNT	VOUCHER NO.	WARRANT NO.

— INVOICE —

2-11 RECEIVING REPORT—PARTIAL DELIVERY

DAILY RECEIVING REPORT

DATE:_____   PAGE_____OF_____PAGES

# OF CTNS.	VENDOR	INBOUND CARRIER	UNLOADED BY

TOTAL NUMBER OF SHIPMENTS RECEIVED ———

TOTAL NUMBER OF CARTONS———

NUMBER OF RECEIVING STAFF ON THIS SHIFT_____

SUPERVISOR(S) ON THIS SHIFT

_____
SIGNATURE OF RECEIVING MANAGER

2-12 DAILY RECEIVING REPORT

DAILY SUMMARY OF MATERIAL RECEIVED

Receiving Clerk _____   Date _____

Received From	P.O. No. or Req. No.	Shipment (Check One) Complete	Shipment (Check One) Partial	Quantity	Weight	Description	Received Via	Charges Paid	Delivered To

Comments:

2-13 DAILY SUMMARY OF MATERIALS RECEIVED

DAILY RECEIVING SCHEDULE

DATE:_____

TIME	CARRIER	VENDOR/PO#	NUMBER OF PIECES
8:00 A.M.			
8:30			
9:00			
9:30			
10:00			
10:30			
11:00			
11:30			
12:00 P.M.			
12:30			
1:00			
1:30			
2:00			
2:30			
3:00			
3:30			
4:00			
		TOTAL PCS REC'D_____	

2-14 DAILY RECEIVING SCHEDULE

_____ COMPANY

FREIGHT INSPECTION REPORT

STATION			DATE OF INSPECTION
INSPECTED AT			ADDRESS
INBOUND MANIFEST	DATE		CAR OR TRAILER
SHIPPER			ADDRESS
CONSIGNEE			ADDRESS
INBOUND SEALS		NAME OF DELIVERING DRAYMAN	
DATE DELIVERED	DATE UNPACKED	DATE EXCEPTIONS REPORTED	

DID CONSIGNEE GIVE CLEAR RECEIPT?
☐ YES   ☐ NO

LOSS

EVIDENCE OF PILFERAGE OR ROBBERY?

ITEMS PACKED IN EACH CONTAINER	DID COMPARISON CHECK WITH INVOICE OR WEIGHT OF PACKAGE VERIFY LOSS?

IN YOUR OPINION, IS CONDITION OF THE CONTENTS A RESULT OF THE ACTION CAUSING DAMAGE TO THE CONTAINER   ☐ YES   ☐ NO

DESCRIBE INTERIOR PACKING

NUMBER OF ITEMS PACKED IN EACH CONTAINER

VALUE OF MERCHANDISE IN GOOD CONDITION	HOW DETERMINED?

DAMAGE

APPARENT CAUSE OF DAMAGE	COND. OF CONTAINER
CONCEALED	WET
PRIOR TO LOADING OR AFTER UNLOADING	CREASED
INADEQUATE PACKING	DENTED
IMPROPER CONTAINER	BROKEN
OVERHEAD WEIGHT	CRUSHED
DIRTY TRAILER	TORN
LEAKY TRAILER	LEAKINGS
INHERENT NATURE OF COMM	PUNCTURES
	RE-COOPERED

TYPE OF CONTAINER

CRATE	BUNDLES
BOX	BAGS
CORRUGATED BOX	
STEEL DRUMS	NEW
BARRELS	SECOND HAND
PAILS	TEST WEIGHT

DISPOSITION OF DAMAGED FREIGHT

HAS DAMAGED MERCHANDISE ANY SALVAGE VALUE?
☐ YES   ☐ NO   ☐ REPAIR   ☐ ALLOWANCE

CAN DAMAGED PARTS BE REPLACED OR REPAIRED?

TO BE PICKED UP	DUMPED
RETURNED TO SHIPPER	
WEIGHT OF DAMAGED ITEMS	WHERE PHOTOGRAPHS TAKEN?

STATE FULLY DETAILED DESCRIPTION OF EXCEPTIONS, SHOWING STOCK AND SERIAL NUMBERS AND ANY ADDITIONAL INFORMATION THAT MAY ASSIST IN DETERMINING LIABILITY.

_____

_____

_____

_____

_____

_____

_____

MAKE RECOMMENDATIONS FOR PREVENTING SIMILAR DAMAGE ON REVERSE SIDE.

NOTE:

_____ INSPECTOR

THIS REPORT IS MERELY A STATEMENT OF FACTS AND NOT AN ACKNOWLEDGMENT OF CARRIER'S LIABILITY; NOR IS IT TO BE CONSIDERED AS A FORMAL CLAIM WITHIN THE MEANING OF SEC. 2(B) OF THE BILL OF LADING CONTRACT.

_____ CONSIGNEE

2-15 FREIGHT INSPECTION REPORT

MATERIAL INSPECTION AND RECEIVING REPORT	1. PROC. INSTRUMENT IDEN(CONTRACT)		(ORDER) NO	6. INVOICE NO. DATE	7. PAGE OF 8. ACCEPTANCE POINT
2. SHIPMENT NO.	3. DATE SHIPPED	4. B/L TCN		5. DISCOUNT TERMS	

9. PRIME CONTRACTOR	CODE		10. ADMINISTERED BY	CODE
11. SHIPPED FROM (If other than 9)	CODE	FOB:	12. PAYMENT WILL BE MADE BY	CODE
13. SHIPPED TO	CODE		14. MARKED FOR	CODE

15. ITEM NO.	16. STOCK/PART NO. DESCRIPTION (Indicate number of shipping containers - type of container - container number.)	17. QUANTITY SHIP/REC'D •	18. UNIT	19. UNIT PRICE	20. AMOUNT

21. PROCUREMENT QUALITY ASSURANCE

A. ORIGIN

☐ PQA ☐ ACCEPTANCE of listed items has been made by me or under my supervision and they conform to contract, except as noted herein or on supporting documents.

B. DESTINATION

☐ PQA ☐ ACCEPTANCE of listed items has been made by me or under my supervision and they conform to contract, except as noted herein or on supporting documents.

DATE	SIGNATURE OF AUTH GOVT REP	DATE	SIGNATURE OF AUTH GOVT REP
TYPED NAME AND OFFICE		TYPED NAME AND TITLE	

22. RECEIVER'S USE

Quantities shown in column 17 were received in apparent good condition except as noted.

DATE RECEIVED ___ SIGNATURE OF AUTH GOVT REP

TYPED NAME AND OFFICE

• If quantity received by the Government is the same as quantity shipped, indicate by (✔) mark, if different, enter actual quantity received below quantity shipped and encircle.

23. CONTRACTOR USE ONLY

2-16 MATERIAL INSPECTION REPORT

```
                              Date:


                    Subject:  P.O. #
                              Your #




        .
        .
        .
        .


  Gentlemen:

  We have rejected material on subject purchase order.

  Amount Rejected:

  Material Ordered:

  Reason for Rejection:


  ☐ Please pick up above in our Receiving Department on our
    Purchasing Shipping Order No. _____.

  ☐ Above will be returned to you on our Purchasing Shipping
    Order No. _____.

  ☐ Please furnish shipping instructions for return of above
    material.

  ☐ Please send replacement on Purchase Order No. _____
    enclosed.

  ☐ Please issue credit.

                              Very truly yours,



                              Purchasing Department
```

2-17 MATERIAL REJECTION NOTICE

```
                    O S & D   REPORT

    DATE_____              P.O. NUMBER_____

   ┌───┬──────────────┐          CARRIER_____
   │ V │              │
   │ E │              │          PRO NUMBER_____
   │ N │              │
   │ D │              │          B/L TOTAL COUNT_____
   │ O │              │
   │ R │              │          RECEIVED_____
   └───┴──────────────┘


    SHIPMENT RECEIVED HAS  [] OVERAGE   OF _____CTN(S)

                           [] SHORTAGE OF _____CTN(S)

                           [] DAMAGE   OF _____CTN(S)


    IF SHIPMENT WAS SHORT, IS THERE EVIDENCE OF PILFERAGE
    BEFORE DELIVERY? DESCRIBE:_____

    _____


    IF SHIPMENT HAD DAMAGE, DESCRIBE CONDITION OF CARTONS
    AND INDICATE LOSS OR DAMAGE WHICH OCCURRED.

    _____

    _____
```

ITEM NUMBER	DESCRIPTION	NUMBER OF CARTONS
_____	_____	_____
_____	_____	_____
_____	_____	_____

```
                          _____
                          SIGNATURE OF RECEIVING MANAGER
```

2-18 OVERAGE, SHORTAGE, AND DAMAGE REPORT

LOCATOR CARD

ITEM NO._____

DATE
REC'D_____

RECEIVING
NUMBER _____

P.O.
NUMBER_____

AISLE	POSITION	TIER

RECEIVED BY_____

2-19 LOCATOR CARD

STOCK RECORD CARD

ITEM						SIZE		BIN		MINIMUM		STOCK NO.	
						UNIT		SHELF		MAXIMUM			

RECEIVED			RELEASED			BALANCE	RECEIVED			RELEASED			BALANCE
DATE	ORDER	QUANTITY	DATE	ORDER	QUANTITY	ON HAND	DATE	ORDER	QUANTITY	DATE	ORDER	QUANTITY	ON HAND

2-20 STOCK RECORD CARD

STORES WITHDRAWAL FORM

Requested By:_____/_____/_____
                    Originator   Date   Section

Approved By:_____/_____
                    Supervisor   Date

Item #	Material Code	Description	Qty Req'd	Backorder Req/PO#

Issued By:_____Date_____

Received By:_____Date_____

2-21 STORES WITHDRAWAL FORM

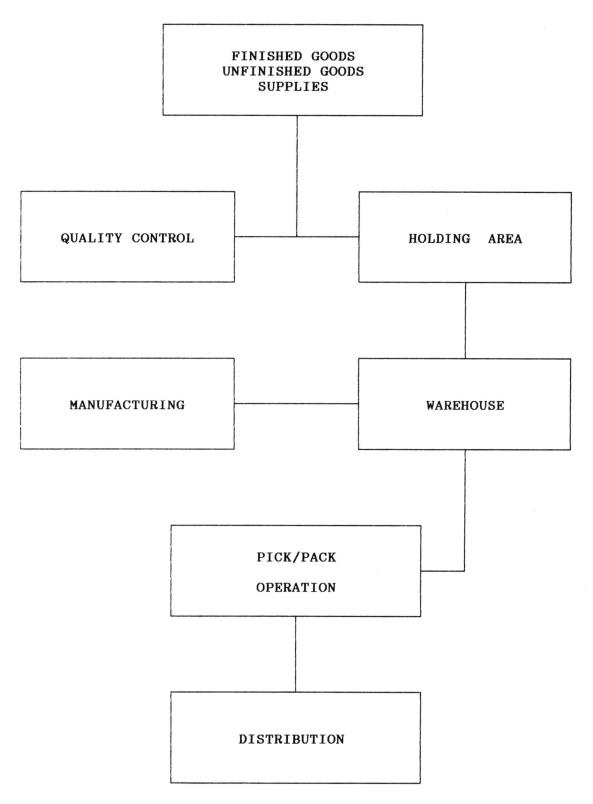

2-22 MATERIALS

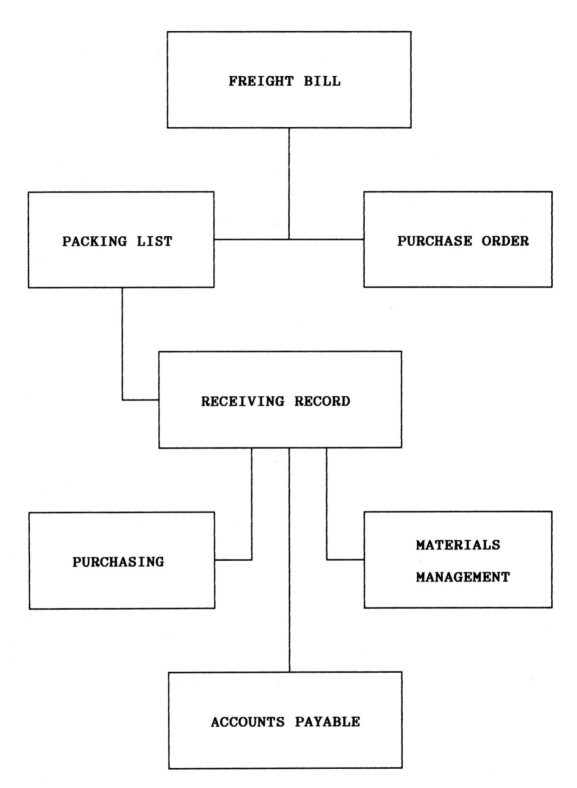

2-23 PAPERWORK

Chapter Three

SHIPPING

During the past ten years the shipping department has changed dramatically. Deregulation has allowed shippers to have more control and more options, while the economy forced companies to realize the high cost of shipping. These two factors combined to bring about a sophistication in methods used unparalleled in prior years.

Deregulation provides shippers a leverage to negotiate not only lower prices, but better service. Both are major concerns of companies competing for their share of the business market. Managers should weigh all their options when choosing their carrier and then sit down with that carrier's representative to arrive at the best possible working relationship.

Due to the many options and modes of transportation, and the complexity of international shipments, the shipping department is overloaded with paperwork. This chapter covers the forms and reports needed to ensure shipments are made efficiently and economically and that all information is communicated in a timely manner.

BILLS OF LADING

A bill of lading is a contract between shipper and carrier that provides proof that the merchandise was transferred from shipper to carrier and that the carrier has assumed responsibility for the cargo until it can prove it was delivered. The forms shown are the conventional format used by shippers and carriers.

3-1. BILL OF LADING—SHIPPER

The form shown is used by a furniture company and also acts as a packing list. Cartons shipped are listed according to classification.

Key Information

- Shipment Identification Number
- Consignee
- Billing Information
- Quantity Shipped
- Description
- Purchase Order Number
- Number of Cartons
- Description of Articles and Class
- C.O.D. Information (if any)
- Whether Freight Charges Are Prepaid or Collect

3-2. BILL OF LADING—COMMON CARRIER

This form is provided to the shipper by the delivering carrier. Upon pickup of goods, carrier will assign his pro number in the upper right-hand corner of the bill.

Key Information

- Customer's Purchase Order Number
- Shipper's Number
- Consignee
- C.O.D. Information (if any)
- Number of Shipping Units
- Description and Weight
- Whether Freight Charges Are Prepaid or Collect

3-3. BILL OF LADING—AIRFREIGHT

The form shown is a bill of lading used by an airfreight company. Since many airfreight shipments are international, the bottom left-hand corner marks whether customs papers or other necessary documents are attached.

Key Information

- Entry Number
- Reference Number
- Importing Carrier
- Location
- Bill of Lading or Airway Bill Number

- Consignee
- Marks and Numbers
- Whether the Customs Permit Is Attached or Lodged with U.S. Customs
- What Documents Are Attached
- Package Number Held by U.S. Customs

3-4. BILL OF LADING—FEDERAL EXPRESS

The form shown is used to ship packages via Federal Express within the continental United States, Alaska, and Hawaii.

Key Information

- Airbill Number
- Shipper's Information
- Consignee's Information
- Billing Reference
- Choice of Service (e.g., priority 1, overnight)
- Signature Release (i.e., authorization)
- Pickup Address If Desired
- Declared Value of Shipment

EXPORT DOCUMENTATION

3-5. COMMERCIAL INVOICE

Customs regulations require five copies of a commercial invoice or other document, such as a pro forma invoice, if a commercial invoice is not applicable. To ensure prompt customs clearance and proper rating of duty and tax, the invoice must contain all necessary information.

Key Information

- Name and Address of Shipper
- Name and Address of Consignee
- Invoice Number and Date
- Item Number
- Complete Description of Each Item
- Unit Value and Total Value of Each Item
- Total Value of the Shipment, Indicating Currency of Settlement (For articles of no commercial value, write "No Commercial Value.")

- Country of Origin (where manufactured), Terms of Sale, Total Carton Count, and Weight Should Be Typed In on Invoice

3-6. SHIPPER'S EXPORT DECLARATION

Shipper's export declarations are required to be filed for virtually all shipments, including hand-carried merchandise, from the United States to all foreign countries. They are also required to be filed for shipments between the United States and Puerto Rico and from the United States or Puerto Rico to the U.S. Virgin Islands.

Key Information

- Exporter's Information
- Exporter's Identification Number
- Bill of Lading/Airway Bill Number
- Ultimate Consignee
- Exporting Carrier
- Commodity Description
- Value in U.S. Dollars
- Export License Number or Symbol
- Bill of Lading or Airway Bill Number
- Signature of Exporter or Authorized Agent Certifying the Truth and Accuracy of the Information on the Shipper's Export Declaration

3-7. CANADA CUSTOMS INVOICE

This form is required for shipments going through Canada Customs.

Key Information

- Vendor's Name and Address
- Consignee's Name and Address
- Purchase Order Number
- Material Information and Selling Price
- Exporter's Name and Address (if different from vendor)
- Additional Charges

3-8. CONTINUATION SHEET

This form contains the balance of information on commodities being shipped that could not fit on page one of the Canada Customs Invoice.

Key Information

- Vendor's Name Only
- Consignee's Name Only
- Other References (including purchase order number)
- Purchaser (if Other than Consignee)
- Material Information and Selling Price

U.S. POSTAL SERVICE

3-9. EXPRESS MAIL LABEL

This label is used on all packages requiring next-day delivery. Packages cannot exceed 70 pounds in weight and 108 inches in combined length and girth.

3-10. PRIORITY MAIL LABEL

This label is used on all packages needing to be delivered within two business days.

3-11. REGISTERED MAIL RECEIPT

When shipping any package of value, it should be sent registered mail with additional insurance to cover the value of the item(s) shipped.

3-12. CERTIFIED MAIL RECEIPT

Certified mail is used when shipper requires a signature that the package was received.

3-13. INSURED MAIL RECEIPT

This receipt is shipper's proof that package was insured for the amount stated.

3-14. RETURN RECEIPT—DOMESTIC

For packages shipped within the United States requiring proof of delivery.

3-15. RETURN RECEIPT—FOREIGN

For packages shipped overseas requiring proof of delivery.

OTHER SHIPPING FORMS

3-16. DAILY SHIPPING REPORT—BASIC

This form is a basic shipping report, providing the shipper with a daily summary of shipments for that day. It is used to monitor work loads and labor time.

Key Information

- Total Number of Shipments
- Total Number of Cartons Shipped
- Number of Staff on That Shift

3-17. DAILY SHIPPING REPORT—DETAILED

This report provides more detailed information concerning each shipment. Included in this report is the complete name and address of consignee, time shipment was loaded, and total weight.

3-18. WEEKLY SHIPPING REPORT

This report allows the shipper to view the daily totals for that week, including the method of transportation used. A manager can review totals to determine labor needs and also to be aware of changes in shipping volume.

Key Information

- Number of Bills of Lading
- United Parcel Shipments
- Parcel Post Shipments
- Total Labor Hours

3-19. SHIPPING SUMMARY BY PRODUCT

This form is used to account for the daily shipment of a standard line of products. This example accounts not only for number of units sold, but also number of returns.

Key Information

- Name and Address of Warehouse
- Shipment Information
- Returns Information
- Net Shipments Totals
- Charges

3-20. SHIPPING SUMMARY BY RAIL CAR OR TRUCK

The form shown is used by a paper manufacturer to account for materials shipped by rail or truck.

Key Information

- Name and Address of Consignee
- Car or Truck Number
- Car Seal or Van Number
- Roll Number and Weight
- Bill of Lading Number

3-21. SHIPPING MANIFEST

This form is for shippers using a private fleet to ship to more than one distribution point on the same truck.

Key Information

- Intermediate Stops
- Seal Number
- Has Seal Been Tampered With
- Total Cartons Delivered
- Notation on Damages or Shortages

3-22. SHIPPING ORDER

This form is used to expedite a shipment and can also be used as a packing list.

Key Information

- "Sold to" Address
- "Ship to" Address
- Customer Order Number
- Material Information
- Shipment Summary

3-23. SHIPPING AUTHORIZATION—BASIC

The form shown provides authorization of shipment and gives all the basic information required.

Key Information

- "Sold to" Address
- "Ship to" Address

- Ship via Information
- Material Information

3-24. SHIPPING AUTHORIZATION—DETAILED

This shipping authorization provides more detailed information concerning the shipment. Included in this form is mode of transportation, special instructions, and shipment type.

Key Information

- Purchase Order Number
- "Ship to" Address
- Mode of Shipment
- Declared Value
- Special Instructions
- Shipment Type
- Material Information
- Shipment Summary

3-25. SHIPPING REQUEST

The form shown is for off-the-shelf shipments of a parts and components manufacturer. A shipping request is primarily used to ship items missed in order filling or items added to an order after shipment.

Key Information

- "Ship to" Address
- Accounting Data
- Description of Items
- Special Instructions
- Approval and Authorization (signatures)

3-26. SHIPPING POLICY

This chart shows the effect that the terms of sale have on ownership, responsibility for shipping charges, and filing of claims.

Key Information

- Terms of Sale
- Buyer Responsibility
- Seller Responsibility

GRAPHS

3-27. MONTHLY SHIPPING TOTALS

This bar graph shows the monthly shipping totals for one year. It is ideal for presentations and meetings because it is easy to comprehend and allows the reader to see important information quickly. At one glance a manager can review the past year's shipping volume and find the highs and lows. This graph shows the volume in cartons and can easily be made to show the volume in dollars.

3-28. THREE-MONTH YEARLY SHIPPING COMPARISON

This graph compares the shipping totals for the quarter with that of the prior year. This allows management to get an early look at projected goals and expectations.

3-29. TWO-YEAR COMPARISON BY MONTH

This graph provides the shipping volume for a two-year period and clearly shows a yearly comparison. It is ideal to use in order to justify change in operation procedure or to show the need for additional warehouse space for the shipping department.

RECEIVED, subject to the classifications and tariffs in effect on the date of the issue of this Bill of Lading,

NO. 152277

Freight Bill No.
CARRIER USE

Shipment Identification No.

CONSIGNEE (TO)

SOLD TO:

FOR PAYMENT, SEND BILL TO:

SHIPPER'S INTERNAL DATA

SID No.

QTY. ORDERED	QTY. SHP.	QTY. B/O	MODEL NUMBER	DESCRIPTION	COLOR	PURCHASE ORDER NUMBER	NUMBER OF CARTONS			
							TOPS	Wt.	BASES	Wt.

SUB TOTAL →

CARRIER: _____ CARRIERS NO: _____

FROM: _____ AT: _____

RECEIVED, subject to the classifications and tariffs in effect on the date of the issue of this Original Bill of Lading. the property described below in apparent good order except as noted (contents and condition of contents of packages unknown), marked, consigned and destined as indicated below which said carrier (the word carrier being understood throughout this contract as meaning any person or corporation in possession of the property under the contract) agrees to carry to its usual place of delivery at said destination, if on its route, otherwise to deliver to another carrier on the route to said destination. It is mutually agreed, as to each carrier of all or any said property over all or any portion of said route to destination, and as to each party at any time interested in all or any of said property, that every service to be performed hereunder shall be subject to all the terms and conditions of the Uniform Domestic Straight Bill of Lading set forth (1) in Uniform Freight Classification in effect on the date hereof if this is a rail or railwater shipment, or (2) in the applicable motor carrier Classifications or tariff if this is a motor carrier shipment.
Shipper hereby certifies that he is familiar with all the terms and conditions of the said bill of lading, including those on the back thereof, set forth in the classification of tariff which governs the transportation of this shipment and the said terms and conditions are hereby agreed to by the shipper and accepted for himself and his assigns.

Subject to Section 7 of conditions, of applicable bill of lading. If this shipment is to be delivered to the consignee without recourse on the consignor, the consignor shall sign the following statement.
The carrier shall not make delivery of this shipment without payment of freight and all other lawful charges.

Per _____
(Signature of consignor)

ROUTE			DELIVERY CARRIER		CAR OR VEHICLE NUMBER	
	No. Shipping Units	Description Of Articles, Special Marks And Exceptions	Weight (Subject To Corr.)	Class Or Rate	Charges	
		CARTONED TABLE TOPS (KD CLS 70)	1.			
		CARTONED TABLE LEGS (KD CLS 70)	2.			
		CARTONED CHAIRS (SU CLS 125) 80590 Sub-7	3.			
		CARTONED CHAIRS (SU CLS 150) 80590 Sub-2	4.			
		CARTONED SCREEN PANELS (KD CL 70) 82500	5.			
		CARTONED FOLDING TABLES (KD CL 70)	6.			
		CARTONED CHAIRS (KD CLS 85) 80590 SUB 10	7.			

Rec'd $ _____
to apply in prepayment of the charges on the property described hereon.

Agent or Cashier

Per _____
(The signature here acknowledges only the amount prepaid.)

C.O.D. SHIPMENT

C.O.D. Amt. _____

Collection Fee _____

Total Charges _____

FREIGHT CHARGES ARE

† The fibre boxes used for this shipment conform to the specifications set forth in the boxmaker's certificate thereon, and all other requirements of Rule 41, of the Consolidated Freight Classification.
† This is to certify that the above-named articles are properly classified, described, packaged, marked, and labeled, and are in proper condition for transportation according to the applicable regulations of the Department of Transportation.
* If the shipment moves between two ports by a carrier by water, the law requires that the bill of lading shall state whether it is "carrier's or shipper's weight."
† Shipper's imprints in lieu of stamp, not a part of Bill of Lading approved by the Interstate Commerce Commission.
NOTE—Where the rate is dependent on value, shippers are required to state specifically in writing the agreed or declared value of the property.
The agreed or declared value of the property is hereby specifically stated by the shipper to be not exceeding

SHIPPER	BEVIS CUSTOM FURNITURE, INC.-Rt. 4, Box 34B, Florence, AL 35630	CARRIER		
PER		PER		DATE

ORIGINAL

3-1 BILL OF LADING—SHIPPER

STRAIGHT BILL OF LADING - SHORT FORM - Original-Not Negotiable
RECEIVED, subject to the classifications and tariffs in effect on the date of issue of this Original Bill of lading.

NOT to be used for ORDER NOTIFY SHIPMENTS.   DATE

YELLOW FREIGHT SYSTEM, INC. YFSY ®

(NAME OF CARRIER)   (SCAC)   NOTE: DRIVER   AFFIX   PRO   NUMBER   LABEL   HERE.

CUSTOMER P.O. NO.	ROUTE		SHIPPER'S NUMBER

TO: CONSIGNEE

On COD Shipments the letters "COD" must appear before consignee's name.

FROM: SHIPPER

STREET   STREET

(DESTINATION) CITY, STATE, ZIP   (ORIGIN) CITY, STATE, ZIP

C.O.D.   AMT $ FEE PPD ☐   COL ☐

IS CUSTOMER'S CHECK ACCEPTABLE FOR C.O.D.?   YES ☐   NO ☐

NO. SHIPPING UNITS	(X) HM	KIND OF PACKAGING, DESCRIPTION OF ARTICLES, SPECIAL MARKS AND EXCEPTIONS (LIST HAZARDOUS MATERIALS FIRST)	WEIGHT LBS. (SUBJECT TO CORRECTION)
▼ TOTAL			TOTAL ▶

NOTE - Where the rate is dependent on value, shippers are required to state specifically in writing the agreed or declared value of the property. The agreed or declared value of the property is hereby specifically stated by the shipper to be not exceeding

$ _____
per _____

(Signature of Consignor)

Subject to Section 7 of the conditions, if this shipment is to be delivered to the consignee without recourse on the consignor, the consignor shall sign the following statement:

The carrier shall not make delivery of this shipment without payment of freight and all other lawful charges.

FREIGHT CHARGES

PREPAID ☐   COLLECT ☐

FREIGHT PREPAID EXCEPT WHEN COLLECT BOX ABOVE IS CHECKED.

RECEIVED, subject to the classifications and tariffs in effect on the date of the issue of this Bill of Lading, the property described above in apparent good order, except as noted (contents and condition of contents of packages unknown), marked, consigned, and destined as indicated above which said carrier (the word carrier being understood throughout this contract as meaning any person or corporation in possession of the property under the contract) agrees to carry to its usual place of delivery at said destination, if on its route, otherwise to deliver to another carrier on the route to said destination. It is mutually agreed as to each carrier of all or any of, said property over all or any portion of said route to destination and as to each party at any time interested in all or any said property, that every service to be performed hereunder shall be subject to all the bill of lading terms and conditions in the governing classification on the date of shipment. Shipper hereby certifies that he is familiar with all the bill of lading terms and conditions in the governing classification and the said terms and conditions are hereby agreed to by the shipper and accepted for himself and his assigns.

This is to certify that the above-named materials are properly classified, described, packaged, marked and labeled, and are in proper condition for transportation according to the applicable regulations of the Department of Transportation.

SHIPPER:

PER:

YELLOW FREIGHT SYSTEM, INC.

DRIVER   TRAILER

PIECES   DATE

MARK "X" IN "HM" COLUMN FOR HAZARDOUS MATERIALS

3-2 BILL OF LADING—COMMON CARRIER

ENTRY NO.		

STEVENS AIRFREIGHT
11 JUNEAU BOULEVARD
WOODBURY, N.Y. 11797
(718) 656-5422   API 65422

DATE	OUR REF. NO.

IMPORTING CARRIER	LOCATION	FROM PORT OF / ORIGIN AIRPORT

B/L OR AWB NO.	ARRIVAL DATE	FREE TIME EXP.	LOCAL DELIVERY OR TRANSFER BY (DELIVERY ORDER ISSUED TO)

DELIVER TO

PICK-UP BY

THE CARRIER OR CARTMAN TO WHOM THIS ORDER IS ASSIGNED WILL BE HELD RESPONSIBLE FOR ANY STORAGE AND DEMURRAGE CHARGES RESULTING FROM NEGLIGENCE.

IMPORTANT: NOTIFY US AT ONCE IF DELIVERY CANNOT BE EFFECTED AS INSTRUCTED.

MARKS & NOS.	DESCRIPTION & WT.

DELIVERY ORDER: The liability of STEVENS AIRFREIGHT is limited to fifty dollars ($50.00) per shipment unless a greater valuation is declared to STEVENS AIRFREIGHT and charges for such greater value paid. at the rate of ten cents ($.10) per each one hundred dollars ($100.00) of declared value. Such value must be declared in writing and accepted by STEVENS AIRFREIGHT.

CUSTOMS PERMIT	PKG. NOS. HELD BY U.S. CUSTOMS – TO FOLLOW	GO #
☐ ATTACHED ☐ LODGED WITH U.S. CUSTOMS		

DOCUMENTS ATTACHED	DELIVERY CHGS.	
☐ DEL. ORDER, ☐ B/L, ☐ DOCK REC. ☐		
		PER

3-3 BILL OF LADING—AIRFREIGHT

FEDERAL EXPRESS®

USE THIS AIRBILL FOR DOMESTIC SHIPMENTS WITHIN THE CONTINENTAL U.S.A., ALASKA AND HAWAII.
COMPLETE PURPLE AREAS. SEE BACK OF AIRBILL FOR MORE INSTRUCTIONS.
(QUESTIONS? CALL 800-238-5355 TOLL FREE.

AIRBILL NUMBER
4784095621

4 7 8 4 0 9 5 6 2 1

DATE

1 Sender's Federal Express Account Number

AIRBILL NUMBER
4784095621

From (Your Name)   Your Phone Number (Very Important)
( )

Company   Department/Floor No.

Street Address

City   State   ZIP Required For Correct Invoicing

2 To (Recipient's Name)   Recipient's Phone Number (Very Important)
( )

Company   Department/Floor No.

Exact Street Address (Use of P.O. Boxes or P.O. ● Zip Codes Will Delay Delivery And Result In Extra Charge.)

City   State   ZIP Street Address Zip Required

H HOLD FOR PICK-UP AT THIS FEDERAL EXPRESS LOCATION:
Street Address (See Service Guide or Call 800-238-5355)

City   State

ZIP ● Zip Code of Street Address Required

3 YOUR BILLING REFERENCE INFORMATION (FIRST 24 CHARACTERS WILL APPEAR ON INVOICE.)

PAYMENT ☐ Bill Sender   ☐ Bill Recipient's FedEx Acct. No.   ☐ Bill 3rd Party FedEx Acct. No.   ☐ Bill Credit Card
☐ Cash   Fill in Account Number below   Fill in Account Number below   Fill in Credit Card Number below

4 SERVICES
CHECK ONLY ONE BOX

PRIORITY 1
1 ☐ Overnight Delivery   6 ☐ OVERNIGHT LETTER ★
Using Your Packaging   (Our Packaging)
9¾"x12¼"

OVERNIGHT DELIVERY
USING OUR PACKAGING

2 ☐ Courier-Pak Overnight Envelope★
12"x15½"

3 ☐ Overnight Box   A
12¼"x 17¾"x 3"

4 ☐ Overnight Tube   B
38"x 6"x 6"x 6"
★Declared Value Limit $100.

STANDARD AIR
5 ☐ Delivery not later than
second business day

SERVICE COMMITMENT

PRIORITY 1 - Delivery is scheduled early next business morning in most locations. It may take two or more business days if the destination is outside our primary service areas.

STANDARD AIR - Delivery by second business day or not later than second business day. It may take three or more business days if the destination is outside our primary service areas.

DELIVERY AND SPECIAL HANDLING
CHECK SERVICES REQUIRED

1 ☐ HOLD FOR PICK-UP
(Fill in Section H at right)

2 ☐ DELIVER WEEKDAY

3 ☐ DELIVER SATURDAY (Extra charge)

4 ☐ DANGEROUS GOODS
(P-1 and Standard Air Packages only. Extra charge)

5 ☐ CONSTANT SURVEILLANCE SERVICE (CSS)
(Extra charge) (Do Not Complete Section 5)

6 ☐ DRY ICE   ___ Lbs.

7 ☐ OTHER SPECIAL SERVICE ___

8 ☐

9 ☐ SATURDAY PICK-UP
(Extra charge)

10 ☐

PACKAGES	WEIGHT	YOUR DECLARED VALUE (See right)	OVER SIZE
	LBS		
	LBS		
	LBS		
	LBS		
Total	Total	Total	

Received At
1 ☐ Regular Stop   2 ☐ On-Call Stop   5 ☐ Station
3 ☐ Drop Box   4 ☐ B.S.C.

Federal Express Corp. Employee No.

Date/Time For Federal Express Use

5 Sender authorizes Federal Express to deliver this shipment without obtaining a delivery signature and shall indemnify and hold harmless Federal Express from any claims resulting therefrom.

Release
Signature:

Federal Express Use

Base Charges

Declared Value Charge

Origin Agent Charge

Other

Total Charges

YOUR DECLARED VALUE

DAMAGE OR LOSS
We are liable for no more than $100 per package in the event of physical loss or damage, unless you fill in a higher Declared Value to the left and document higher actual loss in the event of a claim. We charge 30¢ for each additional $100 of declared value up to the maximum shown in our Service Guide. Declared value restrictions are shown on the back of the Sender's Copy of this airbill. We make no expressed or implied warranties.

DELAY
There is always a risk of late delivery or non-delivery. In the event of a late delivery Federal Express will, at your request and with some limitations, refund all transportation charges paid. See back of Sender's Copy of this airbill for further information.

CONSEQUENTIAL DAMAGES
We will not be responsible or liable for any loss or damage resulting from delay, non-delivery or damage to a package, except as noted above. This includes loss of sales, income, interest, profits, attorney fees and other costs, but is not limited to these items. Such damages are called "consequential damages."

DO NOT SHIP CASH OR CURRENCY

PART
#2041738900
FEC-S-750-25
REVISION DATE
10/86
PRINTED U.S.A. WCSE

3-4 BILL OF LADING—FEDERAL EXPRESS

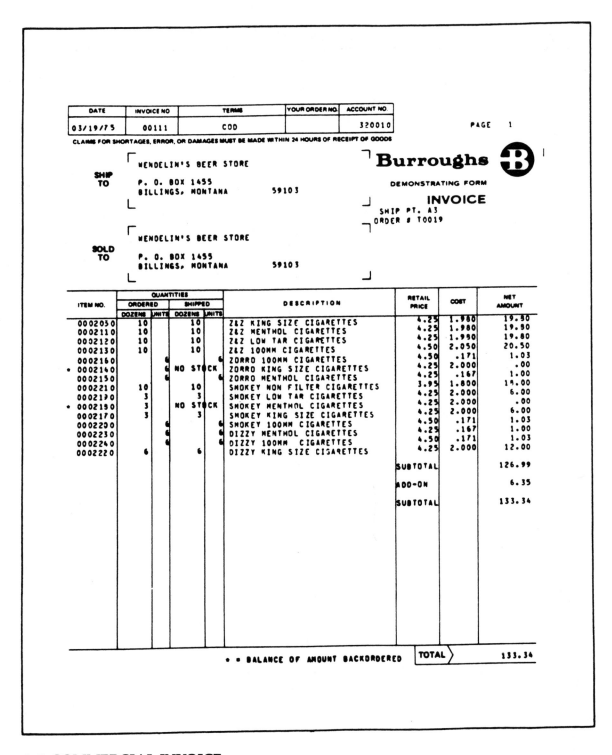

	QUANTITIES							
ITEM NO.	ORDERED		SHIPPED		DESCRIPTION	RETAIL PRICE	COST	NET AMOUNT
	DOZENS	UNITS	DOZENS	UNITS				
0002030	10		10		Z&Z KING SIZE CIGARETTES	4.25	1.980	19.50
0002110	10		10		Z&Z MENTHOL CIGARETTES	4.25	1.980	19.50
0002120	10		10		Z&Z LOW TAR CIGARETTES	4.25	1.950	19.80
0002130	10		10		Z&Z 100MM CIGARETTES	4.50	2.050	20.50
0002160		6		6	ZORRO 100MM CIGARETTES	4.50	.171	1.03
• 0002140		6	NO STOCK		ZORRO KING SIZE CIGARETTES	4.25	2.000	.00
0002150		6		6	ZORRO MENTHOL CIGARETTES	4.25	.167	1.00
0002210	10		10		SMOKEY NON FILTER CIGARETTES	3.95	1.800	14.00
0002130	3		3		SMOKEY LOW TAR CIGARETTES	4.25	2.000	6.00
• 0002190	3		NO STOCK		SMOKEY MENTHOL CIGARETTES	4.25	2.000	.00
0002170	3		3		SMOKEY KING SIZE CIGARETTES	4.25	2.000	6.00
0002290		6		6	SMOKEY 100MM CIGARETTES	4.50	.171	1.03
0002230		6		6	DIZZY MENTHOL CIGARETTES	4.25	.167	1.00
0002240		6		6	DIZZY 100MM CIGARETTES	4.50	.171	1.03
0002220	6		6		DIZZY KING SIZE CIGARETTES	4.25	2.000	12.00
					SUBTOTAL			126.99
					ADD-ON			6.35
					SUBTOTAL			133.34

• • BALANCE OF AMOUNT BACKORDERED   TOTAL ⟩   133.34

3-5 COMMERCIAL INVOICE

FORM **7525-V** (1-1-88)   **SHIPPER'S EXPORT DECLARATION**   OMB No. 0607-0018

1a. EXPORTER *(Name and address including ZIP code)*

| | ZIP CODE | 2. DATE OF EXPORTATION | 3. BILL OF LADING/AIR WAYBILL NO. |

b. EXPORTER'S EIN (IRS) NO.   **c.** PARTIES TO TRANSACTION
☐ Related   ☐ Non-related

4a. ULTIMATE CONSIGNEE

b. INTERMEDIATE CONSIGNEE

5. FORWARDING AGENT

6. POINT (STATE) OF ORIGIN OR FTZ NO.   **7.** COUNTRY OF ULTIMATE DESTINATION

8. LOADING PIER *(Vessel only)*   **9.** MODE OF TRANSPORT *(Specify)*

10. EXPORTING CARRIER   **11.** PORT OF EXPORT

12. PORT OF UNLOADING *(Vessel and air only)*   **13.** CONTAINERIZED *(Vessel only)*
☐ Yes   ☐ No

14. SCHEDULE B DESCRIPTION OF COMMODITIES,   *(Use columns 17—19)*
15. MARKS, NOS., AND KINDS OF PACKAGES

VALUE (U.S. dollars, omit cents)
(Selling price or cost if not sold)
(20)

D/F (16)	SCHEDULE B NUMBER (17)	CHECK DIGIT	QUANTITY — SCHEDULE B UNIT(S) (18)	SHIPPING WEIGHT (Kilos) (19)

21. VALIDATED LICENSE NO./GENERAL LICENSE SYMBOL   **22.** ECCN *(When required)*

23. Duly authorized officer or employee   The exporter authorizes the forwarder named above to act as forwarding agent for export control and customs purposes.

24. I certify that all statements made and all information contained herein are true and correct and that I have read and understand the instructions for preparation of this document, set forth in the "**Correct Way to Fill Out the Shipper's Export Declaration.**" I understand that civil and criminal penalties, including forfeiture and sale, may be imposed for making false or fraudulent statements herein, failing to provide the requested information or for violation of U.S. laws on exportation (13 U.S.C. Sec. 305; 22 U.S.C. Sec. 401; 18 U.S.C. Sec. 1001; 50 U.S.C. App. 2410).

Signature

Confidential - For use solely for official purposes authorized by the Secretary of Commerce (13 U.S.C. 301 (g)).

Title

Export shipments are subject to inspection by U.S. Customs Service and/or Office of Export Enforcement.

Date

25. AUTHENTICATION *(When required)*

3-6 SHIPPER'S EXPORT DECLARATION

CANADA CUSTOMS INVOICE

Revenue Canada Customs and Excise

| Page | of |

| 1. Vendor (Name and Address) | 2. Date of Direct Shipment to Canada |
| | 3. Other References (Include Purchaser's Order No.) |

4. Consignee (Name and Address)	5. Purchaser's Name and Address (if other than Consignee)
	6. Country of Transhipment
	7. Country of Origin of Goods / If Shipment Includes Goods of Different Origins, Enter Origins Against Items in 12.

| 8. Transportation: Give Mode and Place of Direct Shipment to Canada | 9. Conditions of Sale and Terms of Payment (i.e. Sale, Consignment Shipment, Leased Goods, etc.) |
| | 10. Currency of Settlement |

| 11. No. of Pkgs. | 12. Specification of Commodities (Kind of Packages, Marks and Numbers, General Description and Characteristics, i.e. Grade, Quality) | 13. Quantity (State Unit) | Selling Price | |
| | | | 14. Unit Price | 15. Total |

18. If any of fields 1 to 17 are included on an attached commercial invoice, check this box ☐

Commercial Invoice No. _____

| 16. Total Weight | | 17. Invoice Total |
| Net | Gross | |

| 19. Exporter's Name and Address (if other than Vendor) | 20. Originator (Name and Address) |

| 21. Departmental Ruling (if applicable) | 22. If fields 23 to 25 are not applicable, check this box ☐ |

23. If included in field 17 indicate amount:	24. If not included in field 17 indicate amount:	25. Check (if applicable):
(i) Transportation charges, expenses and insurance from the place of direct shipment to Canada $_____	(i) Transportation charges, expenses and insurance to the place of direct shipment to Canada $_____	(i) Royalty payments or subsequent proceeds are paid or payable by the purchaser ☐
(ii) Costs for construction, erection and assembly incurred after importation into Canada $_____	(ii) Amounts for commissions other than buying commissions $_____	(ii) The purchaser has supplied goods or services for use in the production of these goods ☐
(iii) Export packing $_____	(iii) Export packing $_____	

3-7 CANADA CUSTOMS INVOICE

52

Revenue Canada   Revenu Canada
Customs and Excise   Douanes et Accise

Page	of
	de

1 Vendor (Name only)/Vendeur (Nom seulement)	2 Other References (Include Purchaser's Order No.) Autres références (Inclure le n° de commande de l'acheteur)

3 Consignee (Name only)/Destinataire (Nom seulement)

4 Purchaser if other than Consignee and/or Importer (Name only)
Acheteur, s'il diffère du destinataire et (ou) de l'importateur (Nom seulement)

5 No of Pkgs Nbre de colis	6. Specification of Commodities (Kind of Packages, Marks and Numbers, General Description and Characteristics, i.e. Grade, Quality) Désignation des articles (Nature des colis, marques et numéros, description générale et caractéristiques, p. ex. classe, qualité)	7 Quantity (State Unit) Quantité (Préciser l'unité)	8. Unit Price Prix unitaire	Selling Price/Prix de vente 9 Total

3-8 CONTINUATION SHEET

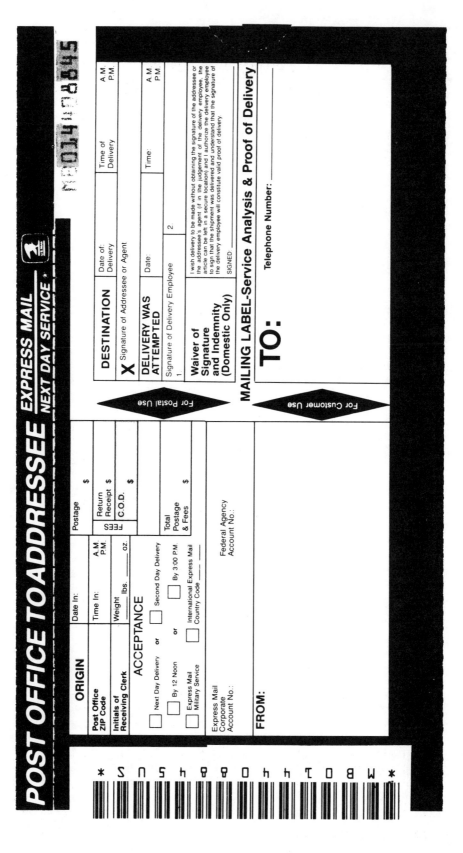

3-9 EXPRESS MAIL LABEL

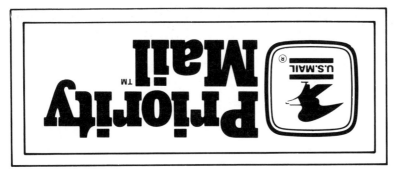

3-10 PRIORITY MAIL LABEL

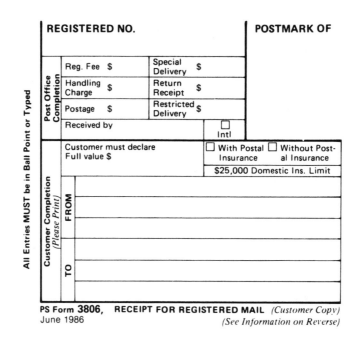

All Entries MUST be in Ball Point or Typed

REGISTERED NO.

POSTMARK OF

Post Office Completion

Reg. Fee $	Special Delivery $
Handling Charge $	Return Receipt $
Postage $	Restricted Delivery $
Received by	☐ Intl

Customer must declare Full value $ ☐ With Postal Insurance   ☐ Without Postal Insurance

$25,000 Domestic Ins. Limit

Customer Completion *(Please Print)*

FROM

TO

PS Form **3806**, **RECEIPT FOR REGISTERED MAIL** *(Customer Copy)*
June 1986   *(See Information on Reverse)*

3-11 REGISTERED MAIL RECEIPT

P 138 729 401

RECEIPT FOR CERTIFIED MAIL
NO INSURANCE COVERAGE PROVIDED
NOT FOR INTERNATIONAL MAIL
(See Reverse)

Sent to	
Street and No.	
P.O., State and ZIP Code	
Postage	$
Certified Fee	
Special Delivery Fee	
Restricted Delivery Fee	
Return Receipt showing to whom and Date Delivered	
Return Receipt showing to whom, Date, and Address of Delivery	
TOTAL Postage and Fees	$
Postmark or Date	

PS Form 3800, June 1985

Fold at line over top of envelope to the right of the return address.

CERTIFIED

P 138 729 401

MAIL

3-12 CERTIFIED MAIL RECEIPT

V-332 809 259

RECEIPT FOR INSURED MAIL
DOMESTIC—INTERNATIONAL

SAVE THIS RECEIPT UNTIL PACKAGE IS ACCOUNTED FOR

ADDRESSED FOR DELIVERY AT
(Post Office, State and County)

POSTAGE	AIR	$
INSURANCE COVERAGE		FEE
$		$
SPECIAL HANDLING		¢
DOMES-TIC ONLY ▶ Special Delivery		$
▶ Restricted Delivery		¢
RETURN RECEIPT *(Except to Canada)*		¢
Fragile ☐ Liquid ☐ Perishable ☐		TOTAL $
(Postmark)		Customer Over ▶
		Postmaster By

U.S. MAIL INSURED

V-332 809 259

NOTE: To file damage claim you must present
the article, container and packaging.

3-13 INSURED MAIL RECEIPT

UNITED STATES POSTAL SERVICE

OFFICIAL BUSINESS

SENDER INSTRUCTIONS

Print your name, address and ZIP Code in the space below.
- Complete items 1, 2, 3, and 4 on the reverse.
- Attach to front of article if space permits, otherwise affix to back of article.
- Endorse article "Return Receipt Requested" adjacent to number.

PENALTY FOR PRIVATE
USE, $300

RETURN TO ➡

Print Sender's name, address, and ZIP Code in the space below.

_____

_____

_____

3-14 RETURN RECEIPT—DOMESTIC

● **SENDER:** Complete items 1 and 2 when additional services are desired, and complete items 3 and 4.

Put your address in the "RETURN TO" Space on the reverse side. Failure to do this will prevent this card from being returned to you. The return receipt fee will provide you the name of the person delivered to and the date of delivery. For additional fees the following services are available. Consult postmaster for fees and check box(es) for additional service(s) requested.

1. ☐ Show to whom delivered, date, and addressee's address.   2. ☐ Restricted Delivery
   (Extra charge)   *(Extra charge)*

3. Article Addressed to:	4. Article Number
	Type of Service: ☐ Registered ☐ Insured ☐ Certified ☐ COD ☐ Express Mail ☐ Return Receipt for Merchandise
	Always obtain signature of addressee or agent and <u>DATE DELIVERED</u>.
5. Signature — Address **X**	8. Addressee's Address *(ONLY if requested and fee paid)*
6. Signature — Agent **X**	
7. Date of Delivery	

3-14 (Continued)

POSTAL SERVICE OF THE UNITED STATES OF AMERICA
Administration des Postes des Etats-Unis d'Amérique

C5
Postmark of the office
returning the receipt
*Timbre du bureau
renvoyant l'avis*

PAR AVION

POSTAL SERVICE
Service des postes

To be returned by the
quickest route (air or
surface mail), á
découvert and postage
free.

*A renvoyer par la
voie la plus rapide
(aérienne ou de
surface), à découvert et
en franchise de port.*

PS Form 2865
Mar. 1985

RETURN RECEIPT
Avis de réception

To be filled out by the sender, who will indicate his address for the return of this receipt.
A remplir par l'expediteur, qui indiquera son adresse pour le renvoi du présent avis.

Name or firm	Nom ou raison sociale
Street and No.	Rue et no.
City, State and ZIP Code	Lieu et Pays
UNITED STATES OF AMERICA	*Etats-Unis d'Amérique*

3-15 RETURN RECEIPT—FOREIGN

To be filled out by the office of origin.
A remplir par le bureau d'origine.

Registered article / Envoi recommandé	☐ Letter / Lettre	☐ Printed Matter / Imprimé	☐ Other / Autre	☐ Express Mail International
☐ Insured parcel / Colis avec valeur déclarée	Insured Value Valeur déclarée		Article No.	

Office of mailing Bureau de depot	Date of posting Date de depot

Addressee (Name or firm)   Nom ou raison sociale du destinataire

Street and No.   Rue et No.

Place and country   Lieu et Pays

To be completed at destination.
A compléter à destination.

This receipt must be signed by the addressee or by a person authorized to do so by virtue of the regulations of the country of destination, or, if those regulations so provide, by the employee of the office of destination, and returned by the first mail directly to the sender.

Cet avis doit etre signé par le destinataire ou par une personne y autorisée en vertu des reglements du pays de destination, ou, si ces reglements le comportent, par l'agent du bureau de destination, et renvoye par le premier courrier directement à l'expediteur.

Postmark of the office
of destination
*Timbre du bureau
de destination*

The article mentioned above was duly delivered. *L'envoi mentionné ci-dessus a été dûment livré.*	Date
Signature of the addressee *Signature du destinataire*	Signature of the employee of the office of destination. *Signature de l'agent du bureau de destination.*

3-15 (Continued)

DAILY SHIPPING REPORT

DATE:_____   PAGE_____OF_____PAGES

# OF CTNS.	DESTINATION	SHIPPED VIA	LOADED BY

TOTAL NUMBER OF SHIPMENTS_____ OF CARTONS_____

NUMBER OF SHIPPING STAFF ON THIS SHIFT_____

SUPERVISOR THIS SHIFT

_____
SIGNATURE OF SHIPPING MANAGER

3-16 DAILY SHIPPING REPORT—BASIC

DAILY SHIPPING REPORT

REPORTING PERIOD: FROM _____ AM/PM TO _____ AM/PM

DATE _____ SHIFT _____ PAGE _____ OF _____ PAGES

TIME AM/PM	SHIPPED TO	DESCRIPTION OF CONTENTS	SHIPPED VIA	DESTINATION		# OF CTNS.	WEIGHT	SHIPMENT LOADED OUT BY
				CITY/STATE/ZIP	ZONE #			

COMPLETE THE INFORMATION BELOW ON THE LAST SHEET OF REPORT

SHIPPING STAFF ON THIS SHIFT

ASSISTANT SUPERVISOR THIS SHIFT

SUPERVISOR THIS SHIFT

☐ _____
☐ _____
☐ _____
☐ _____
☐ _____

FOR OFFICE USE ONLY

REVIEWED BY

AUDIT/APPROVAL BY

CLERK _____ CLERK _____

TITLE _____ TITLE _____

DATE _____ DATE _____

3-17 DAILY SHIPPING REPORT—DETAILED

WEEKLY SHIPPING REPORT

BILLS OF LADING [ ]   WEEK OF [ ]

UNITED PARCEL [ ]   NO. OF CTNS. [ ]

PARCEL POST [ ]

TOTAL ————[ ]

DAY	B/L	UPS	USPS	NUMBER OF CTNS.
MONDAY				
TUESDAY				
WEDNESDAY				
THURSDAY				
FRIDAY				
SATURDAY				
SUNDAY				
TOTALS				

TOTAL MAN HOURS FIRST SHIFT ————[ ]   TOTAL MAN HOURS SECOND SHIFT ————[ ]

FOR OFFICE USE ONLY	
REVIEWED BY	AUDIT/APPROVAL BY
CLERK	CLERK
TITLE DATE	TITLE DATE

3-18 WEEKLY SHIPPING REPORT

SHIPPING SUMMARY

WAREHOUSE_____   DATE_____

_____

_____   CONTRACT NUMBER_____

PRODUCT	SHIPMENTS	RETURNS	NET SHIPMENTS	
	CTN/PCS	CTN/PCS	CARTONS	PIECES
TOTALS				

TOTALS = | | |

TOTAL NET CARTONS _____ @ $_____ = $_____

TOTAL NET PIECES _____ @ $_____ = $_____

LOADING CHARGES $_____

MATERIALS (SEE ATTACHED) $_____

TOTAL DUE DISTRIBUTOR $_____

REASON FOR RETURNS:_____

_____

_____

SIGNATURE OF DISTRIBUTOR'S AGENT_____

3-19 SHIPPING SUMMARY BY PRODUCT

SHIPPING TALLY

SHIP TO:

_____

_____

_____

DATE SHIPPED_____

TOTAL WEIGHT_____

RAIL CAR OR TRUCK NO._____

CAR SEALS/VAN NOS._____

ROLL NO.	GROSS WEIGHT	ROLL NO.	GROSS WEIGHT

BILL OF LADING NO.	FREIGHT [ ] PREPAID [ ] COLLECT		
TOTAL ROLLS	TOTAL WEIGHT	LOADED BY	

CARRIER SIGNATURE_____

3-20 SHIPPING SUMMARY BY RAIL CAR OR TRUCK

NO. 5712

DATE:	TIME OF DEPARTURE:
FROM:	TO:
INTERMEDIATE STOPS:	SIGNATURE OF DRIVER

SEAL NUMBER	TIME OF ARRIVAL	TIME OF DEPARTURE

TIME OF ARRIVAL AT FINAL DESTINATION_____

HAS SEAL BEEN TAMPERED WITH?_____

DEPT.	NO. OF CARTONS	SIGNATURE OF RECEIVER

TOTAL CARTONS DELIVERED_____

ANY DAMAGES OR SHORTAGES?_____ IF YES, EXPLAIN:

_____
_____
_____

| _____ | _____ |
| DATE COMPLETED | SIGNATURE OF MANAGER |

3-21 SHIPPING MANIFEST

SOLD TO

SHIPPING ORDER

Customer No. _____

Terms _____

Sales _____

App. Ship Week _____

Date Shipped _____

FOB _____

Routing _____

SHIP TO

INTEREST WILL BE CHARGED AT   % PER MONTH
THIS EQUALS AN   % ANNUAL RATE.

YOUR ORDER NO.	ORDER DATE	OUR ORDER NO.

ITEM	QUANTITY ORDERED	DESCRIPTION		QUANTITY SHIPPED	NO. OF CARTONS	TOTAL WEIGHT	PACKED BY (Initials)

INSTRUCTIONS

1) PACK AND SHIP THE ABOVE PRODUCTS TO THE CUSTOMER'S SHIP TO ADDRESS PROVIDED ABOVE.
2) PLACE PACKING LIST IN WITH SHIPMENT.
3) RETURN ONE COPY OF THIS FORM TO OFFICE ON THE DAY OF SHIPMENT.

TOTALS	QUANTITY	CARTONS	TOTAL WEIGHT
PACKED BY			DATE
CHECKED BY			DATE

3-22 SHIPPING ORDER

| SHIPPING AUTHORIZATION | P.O. NO. |
| | DATE |

| SOLD TO: | SHIP TO: |
| | |

| SHIP VIA | [ ] PREPAID   [ ] COLLECT |
| REQUESTED BY | FOB |

QUANTITY	ITEM NO.	DESCRIPTION

TOTAL CTNS.	GROSS WT.	B/L NO.

SHIPPING CLERK	DATE
DRIVER	DATE
RECEIVER	DATE
APPROVED BY	**DATE**

3-23 SHIPPING AUTHORIZATION—BASIC

NO. 002175

SHIPPING AUTHORIZATION

PURCHASE ORDER NO._____   JOB NO._____

REQUESTED BY	SIGNATURE	DATE	
APPROVED BY	SIGNATURE	DATE	

MODE OF SHIPMENT:

[ ] UPS   [ ] BLUE LABEL

[ ] PARCEL POST   [ ] AIR PARCEL POST

[ ] AIR FREIGHT   [ ] AIR PRIORITY

[ ] SURFACE FREIGHT
                           SHIP TO:
[ ] OTHER_____

DECLARED VALUE $_____._____   _____

SPECIAL INSTRUCTIONS: _____

_____   _____

_____   _____

_____   ATTENTION:_____

_____   TELEPHONE:_____

ITEM	QUANTITY	PART NUMBER	DESCRIPTION

RECEIVED BY_____   SHIPPED BY_____
DATE_____   DATE_____

3-24 SHIPPING AUTHORIZATION—DETAILED

SHIPPING REQUEST

PURCHASE ORDER ☐ No. ___   SHIPPING REQUEST ☐ No. ___

SHIP TO

SHIP FROM ADDRESS

SHIPPED FROM

NO   NAME

FREIGHT PREPAID UNLESS INDICATED BELOW

COLLECT ☐

DATE SHIPPED

NO OF CARTONS

FREIGHT ACCOUNT

FREIGHT CHARGE

NO OF BOXES

SHIPPED VIA

BILL OF LADING NO

TOTAL WEIGHT

DEPT NO - LOG NO

PACKED BY

ACCOUNT CHARGE NO.	ACCOUNT CREDIT NO.											
ITEM NO	DESCRIPTION	SPECIAL INSTRUCTIONS (INDICATE CONTRACT NO IF APPLICABLE)	PART NUMBER-SUFFIX	INVEN. STATUS	QTY. ORDERED	QTY. SHIPPED	QTY B/O	UNIT COST	TOTAL COST	QUANTITY RECEIVED		

ORIGINATED BY

DATE   TEL. EXT.

APPROVED BY

DATE   DEPT NO

RECEIVED BY

DATE   DEPT NO

RETURN TO

DEPT NO

SHIPMENT SIGNED OUT BY

DATE

3-25 SHIPPING REQUEST

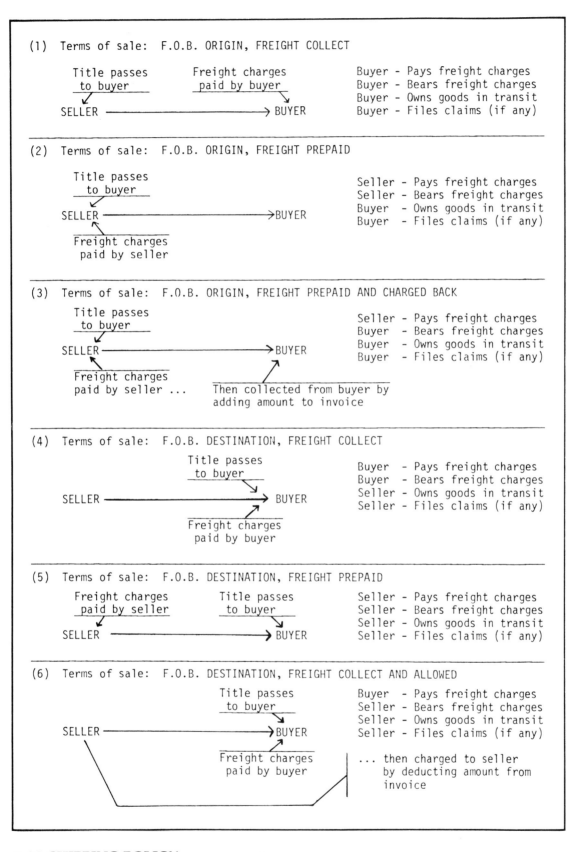

(1) Terms of sale: F.O.B. ORIGIN, FREIGHT COLLECT

Title passes to buyer — Freight charges paid by buyer

SELLER ──────────────→ BUYER

Buyer - Pays freight charges
Buyer - Bears freight charges
Buyer - Owns goods in transit
Buyer - Files claims (if any)

(2) Terms of sale: F.O.B. ORIGIN, FREIGHT PREPAID

Title passes to buyer

SELLER ──────────────→ BUYER

Freight charges paid by seller

Seller - Pays freight charges
Seller - Bears freight charges
Buyer - Owns goods in transit
Buyer - Files claims (if any)

(3) Terms of sale: F.O.B. ORIGIN, FREIGHT PREPAID AND CHARGED BACK

Title passes to buyer

SELLER ──────────────→ BUYER

Freight charges paid by seller ...

Then collected from buyer by adding amount to invoice

Seller - Pays freight charges
Buyer - Bears freight charges
Buyer - Owns goods in transit
Buyer - Files claims (if any)

(4) Terms of sale: F.O.B. DESTINATION, FREIGHT COLLECT

Title passes to buyer

SELLER ──────────────→ BUYER

Freight charges paid by buyer

Buyer - Pays freight charges
Buyer - Bears freight charges
Seller - Owns goods in transit
Seller - Files claims (if any)

(5) Terms of sale: F.O.B. DESTINATION, FREIGHT PREPAID

Freight charges paid by seller — Title passes to buyer

SELLER ──────────────→ BUYER

Seller - Pays freight charges
Seller - Bears freight charges
Seller - Owns goods in transit
Seller - Files claims (if any)

(6) Terms of sale: F.O.B. DESTINATION, FREIGHT COLLECT AND ALLOWED

Title passes to buyer

SELLER ──────────────→ BUYER

Freight charges paid by buyer

Buyer - Pays freight charges
Seller - Bears freight charges
Seller - Owns goods in transit
Seller - Files claims (if any)

... then charged to seller by deducting amount from invoice

3-26 SHIPPING POLICY

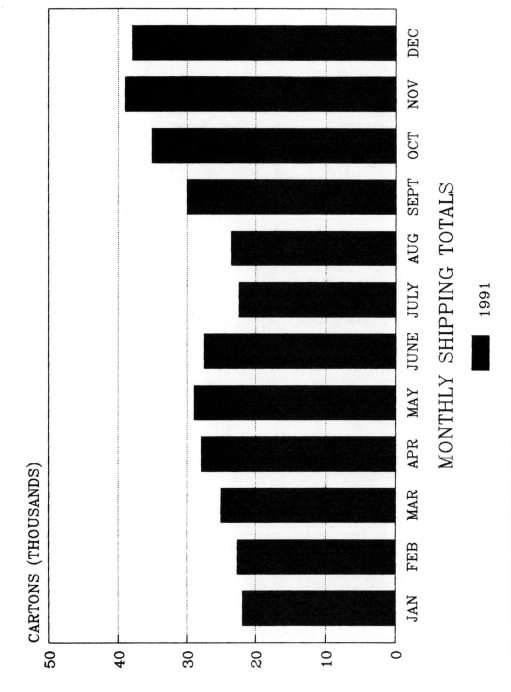

3-27 MONTHLY SHIPPING TOTALS

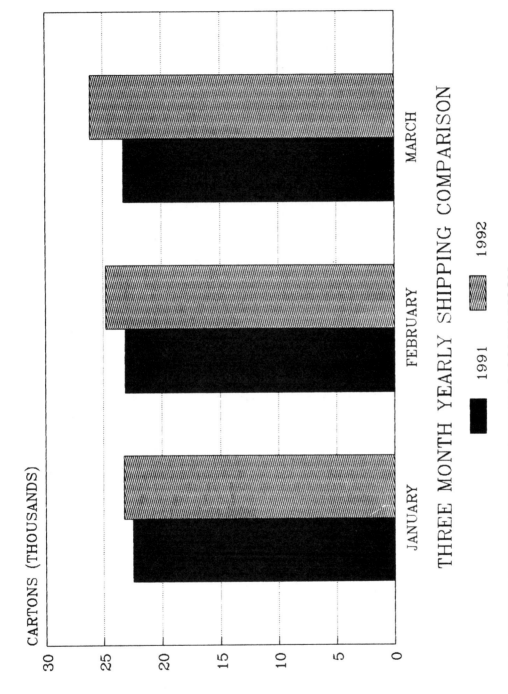

3-28 THREE-MONTH YEARLY SHIPPING COMPARISON

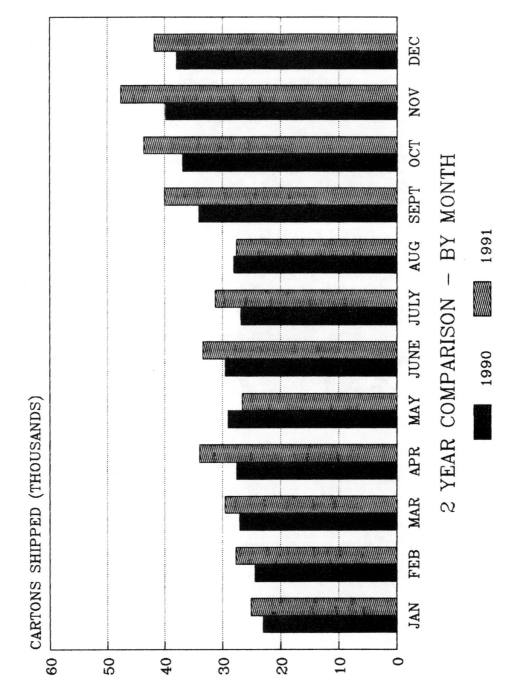

CARTONS SHIPPED (THOUSANDS)

2 YEAR COMPARISON – BY MONTH

■ 1990 ▨ 1991

3-29 TWO-YEAR COMPARISON BY MONTH

72

Chapter Four

ORDERPICKING

Within the next decade the orderpicking process, which has already evolved tremendously, will continue to advance dramatically. Targeted as a top priority by warehousing professionals, orderpicking productivity and accuracy will be affected by new technology and by corporate dedication to customer service.

Many consulting companies predict logistics costs to rise steadily this decade; therefore, corporations are looking to eliminate second and third shifts. Without a slowdown in volume, this can only be achieved by an increase in hourly production.

The elements for greater orderpicking productivity are reducing the time for traveling, extracting, and searching. Basically, this is achieved by automation and maximizing the orderpicking system. Also, to minimize search times and errors, picking documents and displays must be organized and easy to read.

This chapter covers orderpicking documentation from the original purchase order to the final packing slip to achieve maximum order integrity.

4-1. PURCHASE ORDER

The form shown is used to order merchandise, and it specifically states that no substitution of items will be allowed. Suppliers will order a particular item from various manufacturers; although basically the same item, it can have different variations. If the stock number ordered is unavailable, suppliers will substitute a comparable item, unless otherwise specified.

Key Information

- Purchase Order Number
- "Ship to" Address
- Item Number
- Quantity Ordered
- "No Substitutions" Statement

4-2. PICKING TICKET—BASIC

A pick ticket should be easy to read and understand. The form shown is basic, but it includes all the necessary information.

Key Information

- Location
- Item Number/Description
- Quantity Ordered
- Unit of Measure
- Quantity Shipped
- Quantity Backordered

4-3. PICKING TICKET—DETAILED

This form gives additional information, such as shipping instructions, terms, and whether substitutions are allowed.

Key Information

- Item(s) Ordered
- Substitution Allowed
- Location
- Quantity Shipped

4-4. PICKING TICKET WITH LABELS

The form shown is a detailed picking ticket that has shipping labels attached.

Key Information

- Pricing
- Standard Item Numbers and Description

- Key Code (for substitutions, back orders, etc.)
- Shipping Information

4-5. SALES ORDER PICK LIST

This form gives complete information concerning a sale by an account. On this form, remarks or special instructions are displayed under the pick list to inform the customer of policy, changes, and so on.

Key Information

- Pick List Number
- Sales Order Number
- Shipping Information
- Item Number/Description
- Location
- Quantity Ordered/Quantity Shipped
- Remarks

4-6. DAILY MATERIAL ORDER PICKING LIST

This form is a computer printout of all items being picked that day. This enables management to get a total picture of what is being sold, what is needed for orders, and what to prepare for stock movement.

Key Information

- Location
- Stock Number
- Quantity Ordered

4-7. DAILY BACKORDER LOG

This computer printout reports all backordered items for that day. Listed are the amount on backorder, quantity on order, and the purchase order number on which the item was ordered.

Key Information

- Stock Number
- Quantity on Backorder
- Quantity Ordered

4-8. BACKORDER STATUS REPORT

This report enables management to know whether the item will be received shortly or if it is not due in for some time. With this information, a decision can be made to ship the order complete, backorder the item, substitute an item, or possibly order from another supplier. Also, customer service can notify the end user with this information.

Key Information

- Stock Number
- Quantity on Order
- Estimated Date of Delivery (EDD)

4-9. PACKING LIST

When an order is completed, a packing list must accompany the shipment to ensure proper receipt by the consignee. Many companies use a four-part picking ticket, with the last part serving as a packing list; alternatively, a separate packing list can be created. Either way, it is essential that the buyer's purchase order number is shown. This allows the receiver to match the shipment quickly and properly with the order.

Key Information

- Purchase Order Number
- Items Shipped
- Total Number of Cartons

4-10. INVOICE

An invoice is the last process of orderpicking. From the information on the picking ticket, an invoice is create for billing. The form shown lists terms, shipping information, and complete pricing. Backordered items can be shown on invoice as being priced at $0.00. This alerts accounts payable that the order wasn't shipped complete, but the customer was not invoiced for backordered items.

Key Information

- Invoice Number
- Terms
- Items Invoiced
- Price/Extension

PURCHASE ORDER

SOLD TO:

NUMBER:	
ORDER DATE:	
REQUIRED DATE:	

PURCHASE ORDER NUMBER
MUST APPEAR ON ALL
INVOICES, PACKING
SLIPS & PACKAGES

SHIP TO:

*** NO SUBSTITUTIONS ALLOWED

TERMS:

FOB:

[ ] ORIGINAL

SHIP VIA:

[ ] CONFIRMING COPY

ITEM	DESCRIPTION	QUANTITY	UNIT	PRICE	AMOUNT

GROSS AMOUNT	%DISCOUNT	TAX	SHIP.CHRG	TOTAL
	−	+	+	=

AUTHORIZED SIGNATURE:

4-1 PURCHASE ORDER

```
            PICKING LIST                         DATE    01/04/92


SHIP TO ADDRESS                    DUPLICATE - 1

. . . . . . . . . . . . . . . . . . .    CUSTOMER   247900    SCHEDULE DATE   12/10/91

. . . . . . . . . . . . . . . . . . .    COMPANY    1         REQUEST DATE    12/10/91

. . . . . . . . . . . . . . . . . .


*** ACCEPTS BACKORDERS            ORDER NO.    REFERENCE    ORDER DATE
*** ACCEPTS PARTIAL SHIP          CO32698      5088         11/26/91

SHIP INSTRUCTIONS - UPS

     ORDER COMMENTS:  ALL FREIGHT MUST BE SHIPPED PREPAID
```

PACK CODE	LOCATION	ITEM NUMBER	QUANTITY ORDERED	U/M	QUANTITY ORDERED	QUANTITY BACKORD'D
6/CS	A2355	L4K	1	EA	_____	_____
1/CS	DD6743	55KE10	1	EA	_____	_____
1/CS	DD6755	551KE15	12	EA	_____	_____
12/CS	R1556	10-82	12	EA	_____	_____
1/CS	T1998	L168-BK	3	EA	_____	_____
1/CS	T1999	L168-BL	3	EA	_____	_____
1/CS	T2000	L168-PK	3	EA	_____	_____

4-2 PICKING TICKET—BASIC

PICKING TICKET

CRAFT COMMUNICATIONS
P.O. BOX 48
CENTEREACH, NEW YORK   11720

DECEMBER 30,1991   8:02:22

SALES ORDER: 36072   ORDER DATE: 12/28/91   PAGE: 1

CUSTOMER: SHIP TO:
THE WAREHOUSE EXECUTIVE   THE WAREHOUSE EXECUTIVE
1500 ROUTE 25   1500 ROUTE 25
CENTEREACH   NY   11720   CENTEREACH   NY   11720
ATT: ACCOUNTS PAYABLE

CUSTOMER PO#   S/O #   CUSTOMER #
101633   36072   190122

SHIP VIA   TERMS   SALESMAN   ROUTE
UPS   NET 30   HOUSE

LINE	QTY ORD'D	U/M	LOCATION	ITEM #/DESCRIPTION	SHIP'D	B/O
1	5,000	EA	A2455	JANUARY 92 ISSUE	_____	_____
2	5,000	EA	T1112	EQUIPMENT INSERT	_____	_____

ORDER TAKER: JL   ORDER ENTERER: JB   SUBSTITUTION: Y

PICKER_____   CHECKER_____   PACKER_____   NUMBER OF CARTONS_____

4-3 PICKING TICKET—DETAILED

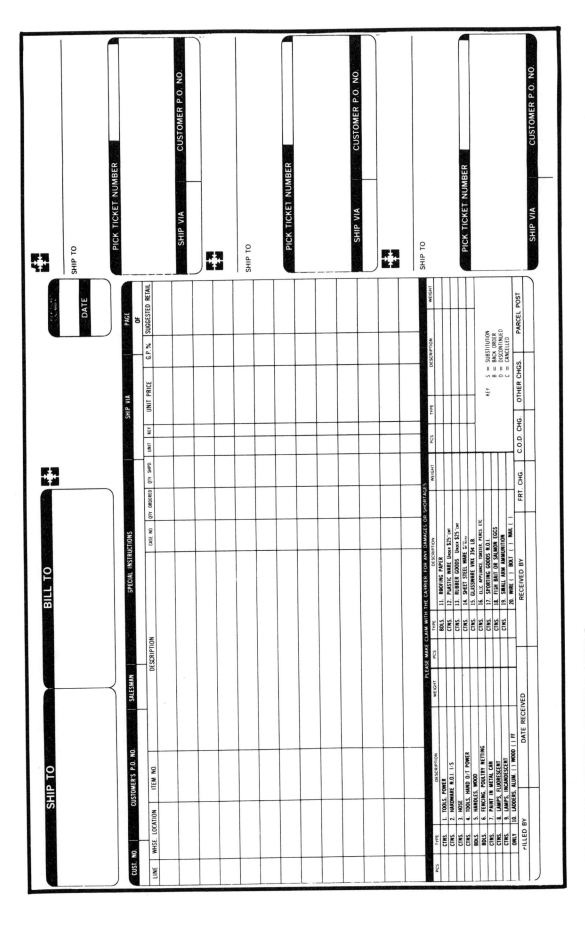

4-4 PICKING TICKET WITH LABELS

SALES ORDER PICK LIST

25-AUG-91

PICK LIST NO.: 17870	SHIP TO: CRAFT COMMUNICATIONS 4 CAMELOT DRIVE CENTEREACH NY 11720	SHIP DATE: 10-SEPT-91
SALES ORDER NO.: S141355		B/L NO. : ....
DATE ALLOCATED: 28-AUG-91		CARRIER : ....

WEIGHT: 6.432
CARTONS: 53
FREIGHT: ....
SHIP VIA : BEST WAY   INSURANCE: ....
FOB CODE : NYC

DEPT	PART # / DESCRIPTION	STORE	LOCATION	LOT	QUANTITY ORDERED	QUANTITY SHIPPED
001	1204 CABINET	0011	NYC	1505	6	6
001	1277 HUTCH	0011	NYC	2134	3	3
001	2148 FILE	0011	NYC	M118	36	36
001	2158 FILE	0011	NYC	M213	8	8

REMARKS: ALL FREIGHT CHARGES TO BE BILLED

REMARKS: **ATTENTION PRICE INCREASE EFFECTIVE 4/1/91

ITEMS ON BACKORDER: THIS ORDER IS SHIPPED COMPLETE

4-5 SALES ORDER PICK LIST

81

MATERIAL ORDER PICKING LIST FOR 06/12/91				PAGE 1
LOCATION	STOCK NUMBER	DESCRIPTION OF ITEM	QTY ORD'D	U/M
A2433	GSM11	PENS	264	DZ
A2987	PA33311	PENS	288	DZ
B1125	29067	MARKERS	144	DZ
C1087	654YEL	POST-IT	10	CS
C1092	655BLU	POST-IT	10	CS
C2132	6003412	MASKING TAPE	36	RLS
D1011	51266	TYPEWRITER	12	EA
D1222	51279	TYPEWRITER	4	EA
E2134	SC23044	WORD PROCESSOR	6	EA
E2135	SC23046	WORD PROCESSOR	1	EA

4-6 DAILY MATERIAL ORDER PICK LIST

```
                    ITEMS ON BACKORDER FOR 06/21/91                    PAGE 1

                                                BACKORDERED    QUANTITY    P.O.
STOCK NUMBER    DESCRIPTION         U/M         QUANTITY       ORDERED     NO.

22468675        CALCULATOR          EA              16            36       3407
24558769        CALCULATOR          EA              12            36       3407
2911234         BATTERY             EA               4            24       3419
7712349         MARKERS             DZ              48           144       3461
7712355         MARKERS             DZ              21           144       3461
8655431         DESK PAD            EA              11            48       3517
AA22134         TRAYS               EA               6            36       3588
B147983         PADS                CS              12            80       3651
B147988         PADS                CS               8            80       3651
```

4-7 **DAILY BACKORDER LOG**

BACKORDER STATUS REPORT

17-SEPT-91

ITEM NUMBER	DESCRIPTION	QUANTITY ON BO	QUANTITY ORDERED	E.D.D.
A7401	TRANSFORMER	47	144	10-17-91
A2287	TIMER	121	200	09-21-91
B45432	TQ ROD	11	48	10-20-91
C38461	WELD KIT	187	288	09/21/91
172349	CANVAS	17	100	11-17-91
21216	CANVAS	19	100	11-17-91

4-8 BACKORDER STATUS REPORT

	CRAFT COMMUNICATIONS	
	P.O. BOX 48	
	CENTEREACH, NY 11720	

SHIP VIA	CUSTOMER P.O. NO.	DATE ORDERED

SOLD TO :   SHIP TO:

CATALOG NUMBER	DESCRIPTION	UNITS	SHIPPED	B.O.

TOTAL CARTONS   CARRIER'S COPY

_____   **PACKING LIST**

4-9 PACKING LIST

SOLD TO:

NUMBER:

INVOICE
DATE:

ORDER
DATE:

INVOICE NUMBER
MUST APPEAR ON ALL
P.O., PACKING
SLIPS & PACKAGES

SHIP TO:

CUSTOMER NO:

SALESPERSON:

TERMS: FOB: DATE SHIPPED:

SHIP VIA: OTHER:

ITEM	DESCRIPTION	QUANTITY	UNIT	PRICE	AMOUNT

THANK YOU FOR YOUR ORDER.

SALES TAX:

FREIGHT:

TOTAL DUE: ••••••

4-10 INVOICE

Chapter Five

RETURNED MERCHANDISE

There are three vital parts of an effective returns department: receiving credit for defective merchandise, issuing credit to customers, and salvaging merchandise for return to inventory. Returned merchandise can be new items in original packaging being sent back because of overordering or items that were shipped or ordered incorrectly. Returning new items in the original packaging makes it easy to receive the merchandise back into inventory. However, when merchandise is returned as damaged or defective, and especially when it is not in the original packaging, the processing of returns can become time consuming and costly.

This chapter provides the necessary forms and procedures for sorting stock, getting return authorizations from vendors, issuing credit to customers, and returning good merchandise back into inventory.

RECEIVING CREDIT

All businesses deal with returned merchandise—from manufacturers returning defective parts to retailers returning an overshipment back to a supplier. Reasons for returns can vary, such as the order was canceled, the wrong item was ordered, the wrong item was shipped, the item was damaged, and so on.

Two issues that need to be determined immediately are the reason for return and who is at fault. Most suppliers charge a 10% to 30% restocking fee when they are not at fault for the return. Also, the buyer is responsible for all additional shipping charges.

It is important to be aware of the supplier's return policy. There is usually a 30-day limit after the actual receiving date, even if the buyer is not at fault. Also, a return authorization is required for all merchandise to be sent back, or the shipment will be refused.

An example of a vendor's return policy is as follows:

- The merchandise specified on return authorization must be returned within 30 days of the date of this authorization.
- Do not include or return any item not listed on this return authorization form.
- All returns must be shipped prepaid. In the case of our error, transportation credit will be allowed provided the return is made via the most economical means.
- Returns must be made to our distribution point shown on the authorization.
- We will not accept returned merchandise on a C.O.D. basis under any condition.
- All returns should be in the original packaging. If this is not possible, use other packing to protect the product adequately.
- All returned merchandise is subject to inspection to determine its disposition.
- Merchandise not in a resalable condition will be accepted for return at a salvage value only.
- All claims for goods lost or damaged in transit must be filed by the consignee with the carrier.
- Additional shipping labels to accommodate all the items on this return authorization are your responsibility. Please include the return authorization number which is on the upper right-hand corner of this document on any labels you so create.

5-1. RETURN AUTHORIZATION—BASIC

The form shown gives authorization to return indicated goods.

Key Information

- Return Authorization Number
- Items Being Returned
- Reason for Return
- Freight Responsibility
- Return Authorized by

5-2. RETURN AUTHORIZATION—DETAILED

The form shown is used by a furniture company to authorize return of merchandise. Included in this form is a section for the supplier to make disposition of return.

Key Information

- Customer Number
- Return Authorization Number
- Freight Prepaid/Collect
- Must Ship by Carrier (Whoever is responsible for freight charges decides on carrier.)
- Items Being Returned
- Reason for Return
- Restocking Fee/Credit
- Disposition of Merchandise

5-3. RETURNED GOODS NOTICE

This form is issued by the company returning merchandise to the supplier. As long as there is a return authorization number, an order can be returned on this notice. This form is prepared in triplicate: one copy for the office, one for shipping, and one sent with the returned merchandise.

Key Information

- Order Number
- Shipping Information ("returned to" address)
- Reason for Return
- Replacement to Be Made. Yes or No
- Merchandise Information (quantity, part numbers, description of merchandise)
- Authorized by (signature)
- Return Authorization Number

5-4. DEBIT MEMORANDUM

The form shown is used by the accounts payable department to deduct returned merchandise from billing. The information needed is supplied by the returns department.

Key Information

- Debit Memorandum Number
- Purchase Order Number
- Vendor's Invoice Number
- Return Authorization Number
- Debit Memorandum Disposition

- Shipping Information
- Returned Merchandise Information
- Reason for Return and Authorized by (signature)
- Total Debit Amount

5-5. RETURN AUTHORIZATION LABEL

To ensure that merchandise is received properly by the vendor and that credit is issued promptly, a return authorization label should be used.

Key Information

- Authorization Number
- Reference Number (such as an invoice or purchase order number)

5-6. F.A.K. CLASS 70 LABEL

When shipping returns, carriers should be alerted that the shipment should be billed at the lower class rate. F.A.K. (freight all kinds) Class 70 must be on the bill of lading, with labels on all cartons.

ISSUING CREDIT

5-7. RETURN TO VENDOR

The form shown is used to return merchandise to supplier. When a vendor makes a pickup using a house carrier, it can also substitute as a bill of lading.

Key Information

- Return to Vendor Number
- Invoice and Purchase Order Number
- Merchandise Information (e.g., item number and description)
- Price/Extension
- Reason for Return
- Action Requested
- Authorized by (signature)

5-8. RETURNED GOODS NOTIFICATION

This form is used to notify the traffic and receiving departments that authorization has been given for a customer to return specified items. This allows receiving to prepare for the return and to recognize the return as authorized.

Key Information

- Reference Number
- Whether the Notice is for Customer Return or Customer Pickup
- Purchase Order and Invoice Numbers
- Return Authorization Number
- Items Being Returned
- Reason for Return
- Request/Authorized by (signatures)

5-9. RECEIVING RECORD

All returns must be handled as regular receiving, and a receiving record must be issued. The receiving department matches up the freight bill with a copy of the return authorization or returned goods notification and logs in the freight. However, depending on the operation, instead of being processed through regular channels, the paperwork and return go through the returns department, which determines the disposition of the returned goods.

Key Information

- Receiving Record Number
- Vendor (shipper)
- Purchase Order Number (Return Authorization Number can be substituted)
- Carrier Name

5-10. CUSTOMER RETURN REPORT

This form is used to complete all information concerning the returned merchandise, including sales information and disposition of returned goods.

Key Information

- Report Number
- Date Return Received
- Merchandise Information
- Sales Recapitulation Information
- Disposition of Returned Items

5-11. DISPOSITION OF MERCHANDISE REPORT

The form shown is used to give a disposition breakdown of returned merchandise on a daily basis. The information is then transferred to a monthly summary report.

Key Information

- Returned Merchandise Information
- Reason for Return
- Disposition (i.e., whether the merchandise has been returned to inventory or vendor)
- Total Pieces Returned

5-12. MONTHLY RETURNED MERCHANDISE REPORT

This form is an accumulation of the daily disposition-of-merchandise reports. It allows management to track problems, such as a high percentage of defective goods or wrong items shipped.

Key Information

- Total Pieces Shipped and Total Pieces Returned
- Percentage of Returns
- Reasons for Returns
- Percentage per Reason
- Identification of Any Specific Item Frequently Returned, with the Reason

5-13. CREDIT MEMORANDUM

This form is used to issue credit for returned merchandise.

Key Information

- Credit Memorandum Number
- P.O. and Invoice Numbers
- Item Information
- Price/Extension/Total
- Reason for Credit
- Authorized by (signature)

5-14. RETURNS MANIFEST

This form is used by a company to pick up returns at various locations and return them to the company's main warehouse and distribution facility. The driver records the information and attaches the dealer's paperwork.

Key Information

- Name of Dealer
- Return Authorization Number
- Number of Cartons
- Dealer's Signature

5-15. RETURNED FREIGHT REPORT

The form shown is used to report a shipment that was unable to be delivered for various reasons. If the shipment reenters the warehouse, and an immediate disposition is not certain, a new receiving record must be made. The record is held until disposition is determined. If the shipment is redelivered, the record is marked void. If the order is canceled, it is then handled as "returned merchandise."

Key Information

- Consignee Name and Address
- Bill of Lading and Pro Numbers
- Reason(s) for Return
- Dock Location

5-16. SERVICE ORDER

This form is used to record information when servicing defective or damaged merchandise at an outside location. If the merchandise must be returned to the warehouse for repair, the service order acts as a "temporary" return to vendor.

Key Information

- Item Information
- Description of Problem
- Action Taken
- Final Disposition

5-17. REPAIR TAG

This tag is used to record the condition of merchandise and acts as an identifying label.

Key Information

- Date Received, Date Promised, and Date Delivered
- Item Identification

- Problem Reported
- Action Taken

5-18. MATERIAL RETURNED TO INVENTORY

The form shown is used to log good merchandise back into inventory. This form can be used for returned goods, interdepartmental transfers, returns from trade shows, release from quality control, and so on.

Key Information

- Quantity of Pieces
- Item Number and Description
- Return to Vendor Number
- Location of Inventory

4301

RETURN GOODS AUTHORIZATION

SHIP TO:_____   FROM:_____

_____   _____

_____   _____

QUANTITY	DESCRIPTION	P.O. #	AMOUNT

REASON FOR RETURN:_____

_____

FREIGHT RESPONSIBILITY   [] CUSTOMER   [] ABC MFG

SHIP VIA_____

CUSTOMER SIGNATURE_____DATE_____

RETURN AUTHORIZED BY_____DATE_____

PACKING SLIP

5-1 RETURN AUTHORIZATION—BASIC

BEVIS
CUSTOM FURNITURE, INC.®

P.O. BOX 2280
FLORENCE, AL 35630

(205) 766-6497
1-800-551-3325
1-800-821-6360 (ALABAMA)
1-800-635-7247 (FAX)

AUTHORIZATION TO RETURN MERCHANDISE

R / A NUMBER

CUSTOMER NO.

AUTHORIZED BY _____

CUSTOMER		S H I P T O	BEVIS CUSTOM FURNITURE, INC ROUTE 4, BOX 34B FLORENCE, AL 35630

ATTN: TAG

IT IS VERY IMPORTANT THAT THE MERCHANDISE LISTED BELOW BE RETURNED AS SOON AS POSSIBLE. WHENEVER POSSIBLE, PLEASE USE THE ORIGINAL CARTONS AND PACKING. IF THIS IS NOT POSSIBLE, USE OTHER PACKING TO ADEQUATELY PROTECT THE PRODUCT.

IF THE MERCHANDISE IS NOT RETURNED WITHIN 30 DAYS, YOU WILL BE INVOICED FOR THE PRODUCT.

FREIGHT
☐ Prepaid
☐ Collect
☐ Deadhead

R / A DATE	CUSTOMER P.O. NUMBER	BEVIS REFERENCE NO.	BEVIS INVOICE NO.	NO CHARGE #	MUST SHIP BY (CARRIER)

QUAN.	MODEL NUMBER	DESCRIPTION	UNIT PRICE	AMOUNT

(BELOW FOR BEVIS USE ONLY)

☐ 30% RESTOCKING FEE   ☐ FREIGHT UP   ☐ FREIGHT BACK

☐ RETURNED FOR INSPECTION   ☐ DAMAGE   ☐ DEFECT   ☐ REFUSED

☐ SENT REPLACEMENT   ☐ BEVIS TO FILE CLAIM

☐ ISSUE CREDIT UPON RETURN

COMMENTS

INSPECTED BY:	
RECEIVED BY:	
DATE RETURNED:	
CARRIER:	
PRO #	

☐ MERCHANDISE RETURNED TO STOCK

☐ MERCHANDISE UNUSABLE

☐ ISSUED CALL TAGS   Date _____
      AMOUNT   DATE   INITIALS

☐ ISSUED CREDIT $ _____

USE THIS COPY AS PACKING LIST

5-2 RETURN AUTHORIZATION—DETAILED

RETURNED GOODS NOTICE

Our Order No. _____

Date _____

Returned to _____

Via _____

☐ Prepaid $
☐ Collect

Address _____

Returned because _____

_____

Replacement to be made ☐ Yes ☐ No

Quantity	Part or Cat. No.	Description	Price		Total	

Return O.K'd by _____

(Supplier's Representative)

Returned by _____

Address _____

Return Authorization No. _____

Instructions: Prepare in triplicate, one for Office, one for Shipping, one to be mailed with returned merchandise.

5-3 RETURNED GOODS NOTICE

DEBIT MEMORANDUM

BILL TO:

SHIP TO:

DM NUMBER:	
DEBIT MEMO DATE:	
OUR P.O. NUMBER:	
VENDOR INVOICE:	
VENDOR RMA NUMBER:	
RMA AUTHORIZED BY:	

DEBIT MEMORANDUM DISPOSITION:
☐ REPLACEMENT EXPECTED   ☐ CREDIT ONLY
☐ CHECK TO BE ISSUED   ☐ OTHER:

INSURE:	COLLECT: ☐ YES ☐ NO	DATE SHIPPED:
SHIP VIA:		SHIPPED BY:

ITEM	DESCRIPTION	QUANTITY	UNIT	PRICE	AMOUNT

REASON FOR RETURN:

SUBTOTAL	
LESS RESTOCK CHRG	
FREIGHT	

AUTHORIZED SIGNATURE:

TOTAL DEBIT AMNT	

5-4 DEBIT MEMORANDUM

```
┌─────────────────────────────────────────────┐
│ F │                                         │
│ R │                                         │
│ O │                                         │
│ M │                                         │
├───┴─────────────────────────────────────────┤
│           AUTHORIZED RETURN                 │
├─────────────────────────────────────────────┤
│ Authorization              Reference        │
│ Number _____       Number _____ │
├───┬─────────────────────────────────────────┤
│ T │                                         │
│ O │                                         │
│   │                                         │
│   │                                         │
└───┴─────────────────────────────────────────┘
```

5-5 RETURN AUTHORIZATION LABEL

```
┌───────────────────────────────────────┐
│ ┌───────────────────────────────────┐ │
│ │ RETURNED FINISHED GOODS           │ │
│ │                                   │ │
│ │ F.A.K. Class 70                   │ │
│ │ CARRIER _____    R/A # _____  │ │
│ ├───────────────────────────────────┤ │
│ │ Ship To:                          │ │
│ │ Bevis Custom Furniture, Inc.      │ │
│ │ Rt. 4, Box 34B                    │ │
│ │ Florence, AL 35630       85-A-046 │ │
│ └───────────────────────────────────┘ │
└───────────────────────────────────────┘
```

5-6 F.A.K. CLASS 70 LABEL

CRAFT COMMUNICATIONS
P.O. BOX 48
CENTEREACH, NY 11720

RETURN TO VENDOR   **NO. 3282**

_____

_____

_____

| DATE ISSUED: |
| INVOICE NO.: |
| PURCHASE ORDER NO.: |

QTY	ITEM NO.	ITEM DESCRIPTION	PRICE	AMOUNT
		TOTAL		

REASON FOR RETURN

[ ] DEFECTIVE
[ ] ORDERED WRONG
[ ] WRONG ITEM SENT
[ ] DUPLICATE ORDER
[ ] OTHER_____

ACTION REQUESTED

[ ] ISSUE FULL CREDIT
[ ] ISSUE REPLACEMENT
[ ] REPAIR AND RETURN
[ ] OTHER_____
_____

_____   _____
AUTHORIZED SIGNATURE   DATE

5-7 RETURN TO VENDOR

RETURNED GOODS NOTIFICATION

Warehouse/Traffic _____   From:

Warehouse/Receiving _____   Date_____

                                   Reference No._____

Notice of Customer Return _____ Instructions_____

Notice of Customer Pick Up _____ _____

Customer_____

Address_____City_____State_____Zip_____

Purchase Order No._____   Invoice No._____

Return Authorization No._____

Items Being Returned:

Quantity	U/M	Item No.	Description
_____	_____	_____	_____
_____	_____	_____	_____
_____	_____	_____	_____
_____	_____	_____	_____

Reason For Return_____

_____

_____

Name of Person Requesting Return_____

Department_____

Authorized By_____

5-8 RETURNED GOODS NOTIFICATION

RECEIVING
RECORD NO. 11085

VENDOR_____   P.O. NUMBER_____   DATE_____

CARRIER_____   PRO NUMBER_____   TOTAL CARTONS_____

[ ] COLLECT [ ] PREPAID   RECEIVER'S SIGNATURE_____

5-9 RECEIVING RECORD

CUSTOMER RETURN REPORT

FROM

_____

_____

_____

_____

_____

REPORT DATE _____

REPORT # _____

DATE RTN. RECEIVED _____

TIME OF DAY REC. _____

REPORT FILED BY:

_____

ITEM	QUANTITY	DESCRIPTION OF ITEMS RECEIVED	UNIT PRICE	AMOUNT

OFFICE ADMINISTRATION SECTION - TO BE COMPLETED FOR DISPOSITION OF RETURNED GOODS

SALES ORDER RECAP:

DATE SHIPPED _____

CUSTOMER ORD. # _____

OUR ORDER # _____

SALES _____

COMMISSION PAID _____

COMMISSIONS CHG. BK. _____

CREDIT ISSUE DATE _____

CREDIT TO ISSUE TO CUSTOMER

YES ☐ NO ☐ EXPLAIN BELOW _____

NOTES ON DISPOSITION OF RETURNED ITEMS & CREDIT

_____

_____

_____

_____

_____

5-10 CUSTOMER RETURN REPORT

DISPOSITION OF MERCHANDISE REPORT

DATE: <u>JULY 11, 1992</u>

QUANTITY	ITEM #	DESCRIPTION	REASON FOR RET	DISPOSITION
1	2807	CHAIR	WRONG COLOR	RET TO STOCK
1	11401	DESK	CRACKED PANEL	RET TO VENDOR
1	PP354	COMPUTER	DEFECTIVE	REPAIR & RET
1	88117	CHAIR	DEFECTIVE BASE	REPAIR & RET
2	2806	CHAIR	DUPLICATE ORDER	RET TO STOCK
2	11911	DESK	DUPLICATE ORDER	RET TO STOCK
1	SS432	LATERIAL	DAMAGED	RET TO VENDOR
1	BC557	COMPUTER	ORDER CANCELLED	RET TO STOCK

5-11 DISPOSITION OF MERCHANDISE REPORT

MONTHLY RETURNED MERCHANDISE REPORT

MONTH OF_____1992

TOTAL PIECES SHIPPPED_____   TOTAL PIECES RETURNED_____

PERCENTAGE OF RETURNS_____

LIST TOTAL PIECES RETURNED PER CORRESPONDING REASON:

DEFECTIVE/DAMAGED	CUSTOMER ERROR	COMPANY ERROR

PERCENTAGE OF DEFECTIVE/DAMAGED MERCHANDISE_____

PERCENTAGE CAUSED BY CUSTOMER ERROR_____

PERCENTAGE CAUSED BY COMPANY ERROR_____

DID ANY ONE ITEM HAVE A HIGH PERCENTAGE OF RETURN [ ] YES [ ] NO
IF YES, LIST ITEM NUMBER AND REASON_____

_____

_____

WAS THERE ANY SPECIFIC REASON FOR HIGH DEFECTIVE/DAMAGED/
CUSTOMER ERROR/COMPANY ERROR [ ] YES   [ ] NO
IF YES, EXPLAIN_____

_____

COMMENTS/SUGGESTIONS_____

_____

_____

_____
SIGNATURE

5-12 MONTHLY RETURNED MERCHANDISE REPORT

CREDIT MEMORANDUM

FROM_____   NO. 1308

_____   DATE_____

TO		YOUR P.O. NO.
		OUR INVOICE NO.
		SALESMAN

YOUR ACCOUNT HAS BEEN CREDITED AS FOLLOWS

QUANTITY	U/M	DESCRIPTION	PRICE	AMOUNT
		TOTAL		

REASON FOR CREDIT	AUTHORIZED BY

5-13 CREDIT MEMORANDUM

RETURNS MANIFEST

DATE: _____   FACILITY: _____   ROUTE: _____

DEALER	RA #	# CARTONS	CUSTOMER SIGNATURE

5-14 RETURNS MANIFEST

```
+-------------------------------------------------------------+
|                  RETURNED FREIGHT REPORT                    |
|                                                             |
|                                     DATE:_____          |
|                                                             |
|  CONSIGNEE_____   B/L #_____    |
|                                                             |
|           _____   PRO #_____    |
|                                                             |
|           _____                          |
|                                                             |
|  REASON FOR RETURN (CIRCLE ALL THAT APPLY)                  |
|                                                             |
|      1. DAMAGED                  8. REFUSAL TO PAY F/C       |
|      2. SHIPMENT NOT COMPLETE    9. INSIDE DELIVERY          |
|      3. ORDER CANCELLED         10. MISLOADED               |
|      4. RECONSIGNMENT           11. RECEIVING CLOSED        |
|      5. APPOINTMENT REQUIRED    12. CANNOT LOCATE           |
|      6. UNAUTHORIZED RETURN     13. ON STRIKE              |
|      7. REFUSAL TO PAY COD      14. OTHER_____      |
|                                                             |
|  DOCK LOCATION_____ |
|                                                             |
|  DRIVER'S SIGNATURE_____ |
|                                                             |
+-------------------------------------------------------------+
```

5-15 RETURNED FREIGHT REPORT

```
                    SERVICE ORDER                    NO. 2809

                                        DATE:_____

    COMPANY:_____      CONTACT:_____

    ADDRESS:_____      DEPARTMENT:_____

            _____      TELEPHONE:_____

  O
  F   ITEM NUMBER AND DESCRIPTION:_____
  F
  I   PROBLEM:_____
  C
  E   _____

      ACTION TAKEN:_____
  S
  E   _____
  R
  V   _____
  I
  V   [] REPAIRED
  E   [] RETURNED TO WAREHOUSE FOR REPAIR
  M   [] RETURNED TO MANUFACTURER
  A   [] ITEM TO BE REPLACED
  N   [] REPLACEMENT PARTS ORDERED
      [] RETURNED FOR CREDIT


      APPROVED BY:_____      SERVICEMAN:_____

  W
  A   [] REPAIRED AND REPLACED        [] PARTS ORDERED
  R   [] REPLACEMENT ISSUED           [] RETURNED TO INVENTORY
  E   [] RETURNED TO VENDOR
  H
  O
  U   SERVICE/WAREHOUSE MANAGER:_____
  S
  E
```

5-16 SERVICE ORDER

```
REPAIR TAG                    CC 18081

CUSTOMER_____

ADDRESS_____

       _____
```

Date Received	Date Promised	Date Delivered

```
Item Identification_____

Trouble Reported_____

Action Taken_____

       _____
```

CRAFT COMMUNICATIONS
P.O. BOX 48
CENTEREACH, NY 11720

5-17 REPAIR TAG

MATERIAL RETURNED TO INVENTORY				
DATE:				#2137
QUANTITY	ITEM #	DESCRIPTION	RTV #	LOCATION
___	___	___	___	___
___	___	___	___	___
___	___	___	___	___
___	___	___	___	___
___	___	___	___	___
___	___	___	___	___
___	___	___	___	___
___	___	___	___	___
___	___	___	___	___
___	___	___	___	___
___	___	___	___	___

SIGNED_____

DEPARTMENT_____

5-18 MATERIAL RETURNED TO INVENTORY

Chapter Six

INVENTORY CONTROL

During the last few years, due to economic factors, companies have sought to run their businesses on the least amount of inventory possible. Although this is good business sense, it also brings with it many problems.

For example, fulfilling customer orders as quickly as possible becomes much more challenging. By maintaining a low inventory, companies cannot always fill unexpected large orders, therefore creating a high percentage of back orders. Also, ordering a product leaves a company at the mercy of its supplier, which can be a harrowing experience. Using just-in-time (JIT) delivery effectively is the best way to combat low inventory. But with many companies and products, JIT is not always feasible. This is why inventory management has become more of a strategic part of business than ever before; the inventory manager must maintain enough stock on hand to satisfy customer orders, and at the same time not tie up cash flow, the vital objective of most companies.

Inventory control begins with the receipt of an item. Depending on which system the company uses, goods are inventoried either manually or via a computer terminal, and the stock-keeping unit (SKU) starts the warehouse cycle. During this journey, the opportunity to lose track of an SKU or an entire lot becomes very possible. This chapter covers the forms and reports needed to maintain and follow the SKU throughout the warehouse cycle. It includes forms for taking inventory, locating stock, and making material transfers.

6-1. SOURCE OF SUPPLY SELECTOR

The information on this form is used to select the best supplier for a particular item, while maintaining a record of alternate suppliers.

Key Information

- Item
- Specifications
- Quantity Needed
- Source
- Pricing
- Quality

6-2. REQUEST FOR PURCHASE ORDER

The form shown is used to initiate a purchase order for needed merchandise.

Key Information

- Vendor
- Date Wanted
- Quantity
- Description
- Charge to
- Requested by

6-3. PURCHASE ORDER

A purchase order is used to order inventory from a vendor, and it becomes a binding contract when accepted. All terms and conditions must be clearly defined.

Key Information

- Purchase Order Number
- Shipping Information
- Terms
- Item/Description/Quantity
- Pricing
- Authorized Signature

6-4. INVENTORY RECORD—BASIC

The form shown is a card used to record the inventory status of an item. Information on the ordered items is listed, and when an item is received, it is recorded on the card. Each time an item is sold it is deducted, and the new balance is shown.

Key Information

- Item Number
- Order Date, Number, and Quantity Ordered
- Date Received and Quantity
- Date Sold and Quantity
- Balance on Hand

6-5. INVENTORY RECORD—DETAILED

This form is more detailed than the basic inventory record: it gives additional ordering information, such as alternate suppliers, the minimum inventory level, and the reorder quantity.

Key Information

- Primary and Alternate Supplier(s)
- Item Number
- Delivery Time
- Minimum Order
- Minimum and Maximum Inventory Levels
- Reorder Point and Reorder Quantity

6-6. BAR CODE LABEL

Bar coding can be used for numerous inventory control applications, including identifying, counting, verifying, and recording. The label shown is used to assign a stock number to an item.

6-7. INVENTORY TAG

An inventory tag is used to identify raw materials, uncrated goods, returns, equipment, and so on. Primary information shows description, stock number, and location.

Key Information

- Date Received
- Description
- Stock Number
- Location

6-8. STOCK LOCATION RECORD

Depending on the type of location system used, a record of the item and quantity must be logged, showing location. The record shown is used in a random-location system, where stock location is determined by current availability of space.

Key Information

- Stock Number
- Location Number—Primary or Bulk
- Quantity Received
- Quantity Withdrawn
- Location Balance/Item Balance

6-9. STOCK STATUS REPORT

The report shown is used by management to review the daily status of items in inventory.

Key Information

- Item Number
- Quantity on Hand
- Quantity Committed
- Quantity on Order
- Year to Date Sales

6-10. MONTHLY STOCK STATUS REPORT

This report is used by management to determine the monthly movement of inventory, to look for changes, and to decide if any corrections to current inventory levels are necessary.

Key Information

- Stock Number
- Quantity in Inventory
- Quantity on Order
- Sales per Month

6-11. BACKORDER STATUS REPORT

This report is vital to managers for determining order fulfillment and inventory needs.

Key Information

- Stock Number
- Quantity on Back Order
- Quantity Ordered
- Estimated Delivery Date

6-12. OUT-OF-STOCK NOTICE

This form is used to notify management of an item being out of stock. When this happens, it is a good time to check and adjust inventory records, if needed.

Key Information

- Item Number
- Storage Location
- Comments (e.g., reason for out of stock, information regarding expected in-stock dates)
- Reported by/to

6-13. MATERIAL TRANSACTION REQUISITION

This form is used by a department to requisition material from within a warehouse, usually from stores. Accurate recordkeeping is essential to prevent inventory from being "lost" in-house.

Key Information

- Reference Number (e.g., invoice or P.O. number)
- Reason for Requisition ("planned manufacturing issue," "unplanned manufacturing issue," etc.)
- Item Number/Description
- Quantity

6-14. INTERDEPARTMENTAL TRANSFER

This form is used to transfer merchandise from one department to another.

Key Information

- Stock Number
- From/to

- Reason for Transfer
- Authorized by

6-15. MOVE TICKET

The form shown is used by a production department to transfer finished goods to the shipping department.

Key Information

- Ticket Number
- From Department/To Department
- Product/Model Number
- Quantity

6-16. MATERIAL RETURNED TO STOCK

This form is used by a department to return to stock surplus material or finished goods that are no longer needed.

Key Information

- Department
- Issue Date
- Item Number and Description
- Quantity
- Reason for Return

6-17. INVENTORY COUNT SHEET

This form is used to record physical inventory. To maintain inventory accuracy, one person should call out count, one person should enter the numbers, and a third person should double-check and verify.

Key Information

- Department Being Inventoried
- Location
- Called/Entered/Checked by
- Priced/Extended/Checked by
- Part Number/Description
- Quantity

- Unit of Measure
- Cost and Market Prices and Extensions, with Inventory Value

6-18. MANAGEMENT CONTROL REPORT

This report informs management of inventory activity year to date, including monthly average and current month usage.

Key Information

- Stock Number
- Opening Balance
- Average Usage
- Current Month Usage
- Quantity on Order

6-19. INVENTORY VERIFICATION CARD

This is used to verify inventory counts when a discrepancy is suspected. It can also be used to spot-check inventory counts.

Key Information

- Item Number
- Description
- Location
- Inventory Count
- Verified Count

SOURCE OF SUPPLY SELECTOR

INSTRUCTIONS FOR USE

1. Enter specifications.
2. Check either Price, Delivery, or Quality to indicate most important consideration at this time.
3. Estimate usage rate. Could a larger quantity be used? If so, would a larger quantity entitle purchaser to a better price?

ITEM:

SPECIFICATIONS:

Quantity Needed:

By
When?

Usage Rate:

Last
Price:

Last Source:

SOURCE	PRICE REQUESTED ON (DATE)	PRICES DUE IN (DATE)	☐ PRICE		☐ DELIVERY TIME FROM DATE OF ORDER	☐ QUALITY	PRICE BREAKS AT THESE QUANTITIES	SUITABLE SUBSTITUTE? IF SO, DESCRIBE
			TOTAL	UNIT				
1.								
			F.O.B.:					
2.								
			F.O.B.:					
3.								
			F.O.B.:					
4.								
			F.O.B.:					

ORDER AWARDED	BASIS FOR AWARD	REMARKS
TO:		
P.O. No.:		
DATE:		
TERMS:		

6-1 SOURCE OF SUPPLY SELECTOR

REQUEST FOR PURCHASE ORDER

Date _____ No. _____

VENDOR

TO BE SHIPPED TO

DATE WANTED | SHIP VIA | ☐ ORIGINAL ORDER | ☐ * VERBAL ORDER PLACED SEND CONFIRMATION

F.O.B. | TERMS

QTY.	DESCRIPTION	UNIT PRICE	TOTAL PRICE	OUR REFERENCE

CHARGE TO ORDER NUMBER _____ ACCOUNT NUMBER _____

THIS REQUISITION PREPARED BY _____ (SIGNATURE)

* MARK ORDER "CONFIRMATION OF VERBAL ORDER DO NOT DUPLICATE"

PURCHASE ORDER NO. _____

PURCHASE ORDER PREPARED BY _____ (SIGNATURE)

DISTRIBUTION OF THIS FORM ☐ PURCHASING AGENT ☐ FILES

DATE OF ORDER _____

6-2 REQUEST FOR PURCHASE ORDER

PURCHASE ORDER

SOLD TO:

| NUMBER: |
| ORDER DATE: |
| REQUIRED DATE: |

PURCHASE ORDER NUMBER MUST APPEAR ON ALL INVOICES, PACKING SLIPS & PACKAGES

SHIP TO:

*** NO SUBSTITUTIONS ALLOWED

| TERMS: | FOB: | [ ] ORIGINAL |
| SHIP VIA: | | [ ] CONFIRMING COPY |

ITEM	DESCRIPTION	QUANTITY	UNIT	PRICE	AMOUNT

TOTAL

| GROSS AMOUNT | %DISCOUNT | TAX | SHIP.CHRG |
| | − | + | + | = |

AUTHORIZED SIGNATURE:

6-3 PURCHASE ORDER

122

ORDERED		RECEIVED				SOLD								
DATE	ORD. NO.	QUAN.	DATE	ORD. NO.	QUAN.	BAL.	DATE	ORD. NO.	QUAN.	BAL.	DATE	ORD. NO.	QUAN.	BAL.

6-4 INVENTORY RECORD—BASIC

RUNNING INVENTORY

ITEM _____ No. _____

PRIMARY SUPPLIER		PHONE NUMBER		MINIMUM INVENTORY	
ADDRESS		CONTACT		MAXIMUM INVENTORY	
CATALOG NUMBER	UNIT COST	DELIVERY TIME	MINIMUM ORDER	RE-ORDER POINT	
ALTERNATE SUPPLIER(S)			PHONE(S)	RE-ORDER QUANTITY	

DATE	PURCHASE ORDER NUMBER	IN	OUT	BALANCE	DATE	PURCHASE ORDER NUMBER	IN	OUT	BALANCE

6-5 INVENTORY RECORD—DETAILED

ARNO

4522430031001 0   1

30-99-99-99   0807

ITEM NO: K2 31242   SLOT: 02

DTL QTY: 2 CN   CTN PK: 25 EA

LOC: _____   QTY: _____

6-6 BAR CODE LABEL

11062

_____INVENTORY DATE_____

QUANTITY

SIZE

DESCRIPTION

RAW - IN PROCESS - FINISHED

LOCATION

COUNTED BY	CHECKED BY	
UNIT PRICE	TOTAL VALUE	INDEX NUMBER

TAG Nº   11062

6-7 INVENTORY TAG

STOCK NUMBER	DESCRIPTION	LOCATION NUMBER		PRIMARY QUANTITY
		PRIMARY	BULK	BULK QUANTITY

DATE RECEIVED	QUANTITY RECEIVED	QUANTITY WITHDRAWN	ITEM BALANCE

6-8 STOCK LOCATION RECORD

STOCK STATUS REPORT

PROD CODE	ITEM NUMBER	ON HAND	UNIT MEAS	ON ORDER	QTY COMM	TM SALES	LM SALES	PRE MO SALES	YTD SALES
AA	005456	3009	EA	0	42	42	87	60	129
AA	006575	321	EA	1000	16	8	20	121	28
AA	012349	1123	EA	0	8	0	13	10	13
AA	012389	231	DZ	0	8	4	12	16	16
AA	035356	29	EA	144	13	13	25	9	38
AA	045578	87	GR	12	12	12	36	12	48
AA	067853	2431	EA	0	144	60	52	44	112
AA	098765	1111	EA	0	78	78	188	206	266
AA	103567	6544	DZ	0	1213	1000	2576	2500	3576
AA	107533	342	RL	0	71	71	112	123	183
AB	114356	12	EA	144	6	6	4	11	10
AB	116245	0	EA	5000	646	646	1954	1768	2600
AB	125643	187	EA	2409	100	34	96	60	130
AB	127654	125	GR	0	14	14	12	12	26
AB	127787	213	GR	0	4	4	2	1	6
BB	128896	43	DZ	0	9	9	24	16	33
BB	223643	113	EA	0	15	8	100	65	108
BB	226578	129	EA	0	12	12	60	46	72
BB	231457	32	EA	144	24	24	12	12	36
BB	247865	3219	EA	0	1244	244	546	426	790
BB	248598	544	EA	0	131	36	48	36	84
BB	254367	0	EA	616	96	96	144	96	240
BB	255643	121	DZ	0	24	24	41	65	65
BB	265784	11	DZ	0	1	1	5	7	6
BB	276542	0	DZ	100	10	0	10	12	10
BB	298653	5647	EA	0	1009	857	1000	823	1857
BB	305443	2091	EA	2000	676	600	2400	2877	3000
BB	309874	487	EA	0	4	4	144	96	148

6-9 STOCK STATUS REPORT

MONTHLY STOCK STATUS REPORT

STOCK NUMBER	ON HAND	ON ORDER	JAN SALES	FEB SALES	MAR SALES	APR SALES	MAY SALES	JUN SALES	JUL SALES	AUG SALES	SEP SALES	OCT SALES	NOV SALES	DEC SALES
005456	3009		87	82	71	166	143	124	96	79	188	196	211	
006575	321	200	20	18	24	56	60	43	21	36	96	144	135	
012349	1123		13	6	10	24	30	16	9	15	76	112	121	
012387	231	144	12	9	12	18	24	21	16	12	69	89	114	
034526	29	212	25	29	36	24	30	43	24	30	91	108	125	
035555	87		36	24	24	36	35	36	25	27	56	96	87	
065743	2431		52	96	112	144	116	96	78	87	144	100	124	
067958	1111		188	156	96	110	203	168	108	96	237	255	198	
095675	6544	144	2576	2400	2610	2400	2667	2145	1685	1859	2744	3122	3218	
106544	342	1000	112	144	160	188	217	108	96	144	208	188	208	
108976	12	409	4	12	16	24	88	60	48	49	155	244	266	
113858	0		1954	1250	1850	1250	2111	2400	1800	2134	2777	3214	3122	
125467	187		96	60	96	108	233	144	108	98	216	321	344	
127653	125		12	30	48	60	45	35	24	31	96	108	112	
221378	213		2	12	8	16	13	20	8	16	45	97	109	
223147	43		24	15	23	12	23	16	12	21	78	116	94	
234677	313		100	17	96	66	76	60	48	65	119	114	111	
236642	129	200	60	48	72	96	69	60	72	96	211	196	172	

6-10 MONTHLY STOCK STATUS REPORT

BACKORDER STATUS REPORT

17-SEPT-91

ITEM NUMBER	DESCRIPTION	QUANTITY ON BO	QUANTITY ORDERED	E.D.D.
A7401	TRANSFORMER	47	144	10-17-91
A2287	TIMER	121	200	09-21-91
B45432	TQ ROD	11	48	10-20-91
C38461	WELD KIT	187	288	09/21/91
172349	CANVAS	17	100	11-17-91
21216	CANVAS	19	100	11-17-91
27683	TQ KIT	40	144	10-28-91
31143	TQ ADAPTOR	116	300	10-01-91
31145	TQ ADAPTOR	22	300	10-01-91

6-11 BACKORDER STATUS REPORT

129

OUT OF STOCK NOTICE

ITEM NO.	DESCRIPTION	STOCK STORAGE LOCATION

COMMENTS

REPORTED		TITLE	DATE
BY			
TO			

6-12 OUT-OF-STOCK NOTICE

GFI MATERIAL TRANSACTION REQUISITION

REF # _____

DATE ___/___/___

Code		Description		Code		Description
05	IP -	Planned Mfg. Issue		14	RM -	Production Receipt To Stock
07	IU -	Unplanned Mfg. Issue		09	PB -	Pick Complete By Item
16	RS -	Component Return To Stock		10	PC -	Pick Complete By Order
19	SC -	Mfg. Component Scrap		11	RC -	Miscellaneous Receipt
20	SM -	Mfg. Order Scrap		06	IS -	Miscellaneous Issue
15	RP -	Purchase Order Receipt			-	

MACH #

MANUFACTURE ORDER #	ITEM #	DESCRIPTION	WHSE	QUANTITY	U/M	ORDER COMPLETE	COMMENTS

ISSUED BY: _____   RECEIVED BY: _____

DATA ENTRY

6-13 MATERIAL TRANSACTION REQUISITION

131

INTERDEPARTMENTAL TRANSFER

DATE: _____

FROM: _____
DEPARTMENT/LOCATION

TO: _____
DEPARTMENT/LOCATION

QUANTITY	ITEM #	DESCRIPTION

REASON FOR TRANSFER_____

_____

_____

_____
AUTHORIZED SIGNATURE

6-14 INTERDEPARTMENTAL TRANSFER

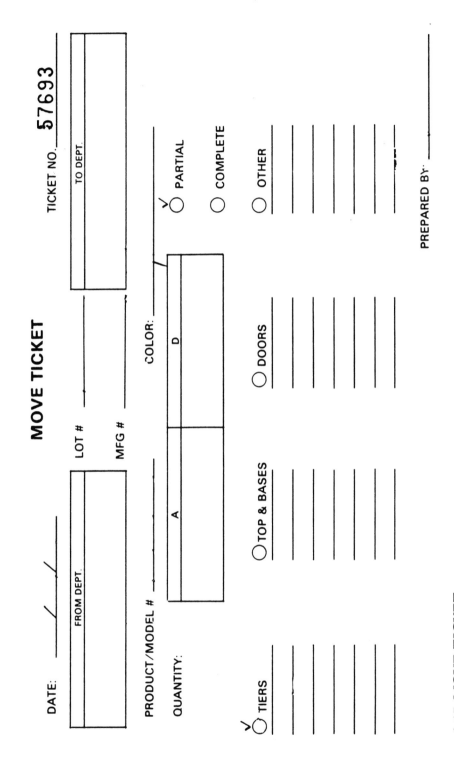

6-15 MOVE TICKET

MATERIAL RETURNED TO STOCK

DATE:_____

DEPARTMENT:_____   DEPARTMENT NO.:_____

ISSUE DATE	QUANTITY	ITEM NUMBER	DESCRIPTION

REASON FOR RETURN: _____

_____

_____

_____

_____   _____
DEPARTMENT HEAD   STORES MANAGER

6-16 MATERIAL RETURNED TO STOCK

INVENTORY

DATE _____
PAGE NO. _____

Department _____ Location _____

Called By _____ Entered By _____ Checked By _____

Priced By _____ Extended By _____ Checked By _____

✓	Part Number	Description	Quantity	Unit	COST		MARKET		Inventory Value	
					Price	Extension	Price	Extension		

☐ Total   ☐ Forward

6-17 INVENTORY COUNT SHEET

MANAGEMENT CONTROL

PROD CODE	STOCK NUMBER	STOCK DESCRIP	OPENING BALANCE	TO DATE RECEIPTS	CURRENT MONTHS USAGE	ON HAND QTY	ON ORDER QTY	AVE MONTHLY USAGE
AA	005456	TQ KIT	3009		42	2967		72
AA	006543	CANVAS	321	100	67	354		112
AA	017543	END CAP	1123		145	978		201
AA	018674	ADAPTCO	231	96	70	257	96	122
AA	032586	CIRCUIT	29	144	25	173		44
AA	035433	TQ BAG	87	12	11	99	12	54
AA	067443	CANVAS	2431		1155	1276	3000	1590
AA	068723	CHANN	1111		144	967		216
AB	092356	WIRE	234	5000	1233	4001	5000	2550
AB	102654	TQ ROD	6544		1876	4668	2000	1887
AB	106785	TQ ROD	2356	1000	780	2576		1109
AB	113226	BOARD	-9		356	-365	1500	471
AB	118764	BOARD	453	1500	411	1542		512
AC	125432	SUPPL	27	96	18	105		30
AC	134765	PROMA	0	235	57	178	265	81
AC	134899	PROMA	837	250	344	743		350
BB	221345	QC ROD	87	100	212	-25	900	275
BB	234111	QC ROD	111	1000	312	799		234
BB	254475	MANUA	3	500	86	417		79
BB	278543	WIRE	6544		2311	4233		1875
BB	329754	RULER	876		299	577	1200	433
BB	336668	MEASU	457		116	341		97
BB	412875	MARKE	271		34	237		31

6-18 MANAGEMENT CONTROL REPORT

| ITEM NUMBER_____ | | DESCRIPTION_____ | |
| LOCATION: BULK:_____ | | PRIMARY:_____ | |

INVENTORY COUNT	DATE	VERIFIED COUNT	DATE

CALLED BY:_____   ENTERED BY:_____   CHECKED BY:_____

6-19 INVENTORY VERIFICATION CARD

Chapter Seven

PRODUCTION

The production of goods is achieved through the combined efforts of two departments: production control, which is responsible for planning and scheduling, and the production department, which actually manufactures the goods. Because there are so many variables involved—such as material shortages, excessive employee absences, or machine breakdowns—communication between the two departments is vital. Production control must supply the production department with all order requirements and scheduling, and the production department must report any slowdowns to production control so planning and scheduling can be adjusted. Also, both departments must work closely with inventory control to coordinate order fulfillment.

Although the warehouse or distribution manager is not directly involved in the production process, a knowledge of the forms and procedures used is a valuable resource for you. Because production interfaces with inventory control, material storage, and shipment of the finished product, you should have a working knowledge of the entire material flow cycle. Each business is unique in its needs, and the forms and reports presented in this chapter give a varied sample of production records and communications.

7-1. DAILY PRODUCTION SCHEDULE

Production control is responsible for scheduling. Flexibility should be included in the daily schedule to allow for unforeseen problems, such as machine breakdown. The form shown lists each job with a time schedule and total piece count expected.

139

Key Information

- Shift
- Customer and Job Number
- Order Number
- Total Hours
- Total Pieces

7-2. MASTER PRODUCTION SCHEDULE

Scheduling for the year is extremely difficult but vital for planning production requirements. Long-range planning is required to adjust inventory, shift levels, and other factors during peak periods for production control. Although manufacturers with long lead times can schedule more easily than can those with short lead times, changes can occur that will hurt a rigid long-term schedule. Flexibility is a must when forecasting long-range schedules. The form shown lists customers' orders with corresponding schedule dates.

Key Information

- Customer and Job Number
- Scheduled Time Period of Production Run
- Order Number and Pieces Required

7-3. SIX MONTHS' PRODUCT REQUIREMENT SCHEDULE

This form is used when the sales forecast determines inventory and production requirements. It is used mainly in continuous and repetitive manufacturing businesses.

Key Information

- Period Covered
- Products
- Projected Inventory and Production Levels

7-4. ONE-YEAR PRODUCTION PLAN

The form shown combines sales forecast, inventories, and production requirements in a continuous manufacturing business. Inventory is subtracted from the sales forecast, and the difference is scheduled for production on a quarterly basis.

Key Information

- Projected Sales for Year (columns 2–4 on form)
- Inventory Forecast (column 5)

- Production Forecast (columns 11–15)
- Explanatory Notes

7-5. PRODUCTION ROUTING SHEET

A routing sheet is used by a manufacturer making a variety of components for many different products. The information recorded assists production control and provides an instruction plan to the production floor.

Key Information

- Part Number and Material Description
- Routing Specifications (e.g., operation code number, department, group)
- Production Data (e.g., pieces per hour, class, setup time)

7-6. RAW MATERIAL REQUISITION

The form shown is used to obtain additional raw material required for production.

Key Information

- Requested by (department)
- Job Number and Product Name
- Quantity
- Item Number and Description

7-7. PRODUCTION ORDER

This form is used to initiate production of an item(s), listing all required specifications and delivery time.

Key Information

- Customer (identified by job number)
- Item Quantity
- Specifications
- Expected Delivery Date

7-8. PRODUCTION ORDER BY PRODUCT

The form shown is used by a door manufacturer to give complete specifications for production of doors and frames.

Key Information

- Single-Door Data
- Frame Data

7-9. PRODUCTION ORDER CHANGE

In the event of a change in the original production order, either a new order or an order change should be issued. All involved departments should receive a copy of the change.

Key Information

- Customer Name and Order Number
- Job Number
- Item and Part Number
- Change from/Change to (description)
- Departments Notified
- Issued by

7-10. DAILY PRODUCTION REPORT

The form shown is used to report to production control the work completed for that day, including an explanation for any delays. Each shift is responsible for completing a report.

Key Information

- Shift
- Customer Order Number
- Item Number and Quantity Produced
- Total Hours
- Total Pieces
- Explanation of Delays/Work Stoppage

7-11. MONTHLY PRODUCTION REPORT

This form is used to report total production for the month. It helps management to compare actuals against projected figures and to adjust scheduling if needed.

Key Information

- Job Number
- Total Pieces Produced
- Total Hours
- Percentage of Defective and Scrap Pieces

7-12. PRODUCTION PERFORMANCE REPORT

The form shown is a report by product, detailing production and shipments. The change in inventory is the difference between total shipments and shipments against load.

Key Information

- Product Name
- Allotment
- Production Data (tonnage allotment, past due data)
- Shipping and Performance Data (e.g., current and total loads, total shipments)

7-13. MONTHLY PRODUCTION RELEASE

This form is used when production is done on a routine basis. It establishes the rate of production and alerts inventory control of the movement of material into each operation.

Key Information

- Identification Data (e.g., bar sizes)
- Production Calculation (lines 1–4)
- Production Requirements (e.g., net total bar requirements, acid requirements)

7-14. CHECKING WORK-IN-PROGRESS

This form allows management to check on production progress at any time during the process. It also "forces" the production department to commit to the status of an order and inform of any delays.

Key Information

- Project/Job Number
- Reason for Work Check
- Current Status
- Obstacles
- Recommendations

7-15. SURPLUS PRODUCTION LABEL

When production exceeds the quantity needed for a sales order, additional pieces are labeled as surplus. These pieces can either be put into inventory or the company can try to sell them to the ordering customer, sometimes at discounted prices.

Key Information

- Stock Number
- Description
- Lot Number and/or Job Number

7-16. RAW MATERIAL RETURN TO INVENTORY

The form shown is used to return excess material back into inventory.

Key Information

- Department Returning the Raw Material
- Issue Date
- Quantity
- Reason for Return

7-17. MATERIAL SCRAP REPORT

Companies dealing with a large quantity of scrap material should keep records of unusable or salable scrap for inventory control.

Key Information

- Identification Data (i.e., part number and description)
- Quantity of Material Returned
- Reason for Scrapping
- Unit Cost and Total Cost
- Approved by (signature)

7-18. YEARLY PRODUCTION TOTALS BY MONTH

The graph shown is used to enable management to interpret production totals for the past year. By breaking it up monthly, trends can be seen and low production months can be examined. For example, management can check a low month to determine if it was due to low sales or poor production performance.

Key Information

- Total Pieces Produced per Month

7-19. MONTHLY PRODUCTION TOTALS BY PRODUCT

The graph shown allows management to determine production proficiency according to product. Key factors are whether item production met sales and inventory quotas and what the determining factors were in declining production levels.

Key Information

- Month-by-Month Records
- Item Number
- Total Pieces Produced per Month

7-20. TWO-YEAR COMPARISON BY MONTH

This graph is used to examine the latest year's production total against the previous year's. Sales volume is compared with the totals to determine proficiency and accuracy in forecasting. The graph also helps develop the next year's sales forecasting and production scheduling.

Key Information

- Month-by-Month Records for Two Consecutive Years
- Total Pieces Produced per Month

PRODUCTION SCHEDULE

PAGE ____ OF ____

DATE: _____

SHIFT ____

CUSTOMER	JOB NUMBER	ORDER NUMBER	START	STOP	TOTAL HRS.	TOTAL PCS.

7-1 DAILY PRODUCTION SCHEDULE

MASTER PRODUCTION SCHEDULE

1992

CUSTOMER AND JOB NUMBER	JAN	FEB	MAR	APR	MAY	JUN	JUL	AUG	SEP	OCT	NOV	DEC
ALLTAC 284-112		ORDER NUMBER 36571/55,750										
ARTFLOW 284-175							ORDER NUMBER 2127/960					
BELTAIRE GARDENS 284-178		ORDER NUMBER 786443/25,000 SHIP IN QUANTITIES OF 5,000										
BOW402 285-120						ORDER NUMBER B3317/17,000						
CALTECH 285-121				ORDER NUMBER 11543/7,500								
CRESTLINE 285-132						ORDER NUMBER 3214/10,000						

7-2 MASTER PRODUCTION SCHEDULE

147

PRODUCTION AND INVENTORY PLAN

PERIOD: Feb. thru July, 19   DATE: _____

Product - HP Range	Feb.		March		April		May		June		July	
	Inv.	Prod.	Inv.	Prod.	Inv.	Prod.	Inv.	Prod.	Inv.	Prod.	Inv.	Prod.
Motors 1/10 thru 1/4:												
143-1104-1												
143-1108-1												
143-1130-1												
143-1141-2												
150-1410-1												
150-1420-2												
150-1422-2												
165-1801-1												
Motors 1/3 thru 1/2:												

7-3 SIX MONTHS' PRODUCT REQUIREMENT SCHEDULE

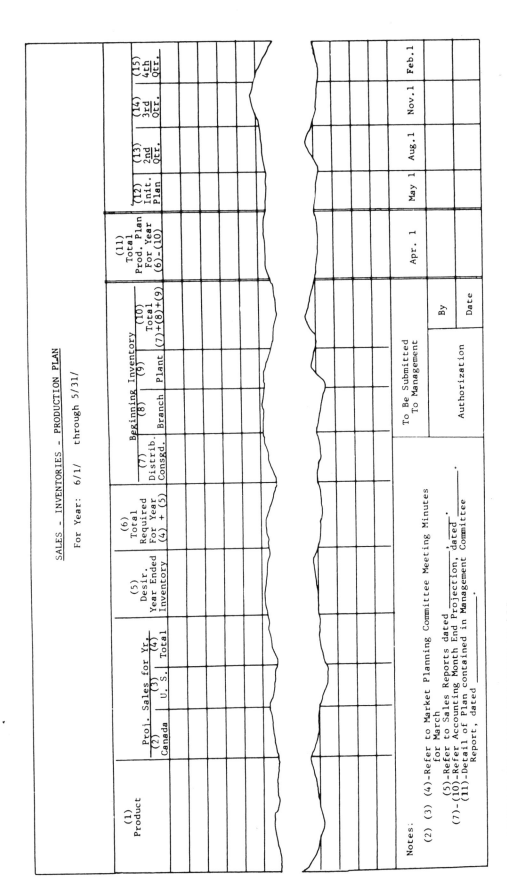

SALES - INVENTORIES - PRODUCTION PLAN

For Year: 6/1/   through 5/31/

(1) Product	Proj. Sales for Yr.		(5) Desir. Year Ended Inventory	(6) Total Required For Year (4) + (5)	Beginning Inventory		(10) Total (7)+(8)+(9)	(11) Total Prod. Plan For Year (6)-(10)	(12) Init. Plan	(13) 2nd Qtr.	(14) 3rd Qtr.	(15) 4th Qtr.
	(2) Canada	(3) U.S. (4) Total			(7) Distrib. Consgd.	(8) Branch (9) Plant						
									May 1	Aug.1	Nov.1	Feb.1
								Apr. 1				

Notes:

(2) (3) (4)-Refer to Market Planning Committee Meeting Minutes
for March
(5)-Refer to Sales Reports dated _____.
(7)-(10)-Refer to Accounting Month End Projection, dated _____.
(11)-Detail of Plan contained in Management Committee
Report, dated _____.

To Be Submitted
To Management

	By
Authorization	Date

7-4 ONE-YEAR PRODUCTION PLAN

149

SPECIFICATIONS AND ROUTING SHEET

PART NUMBER	PART NAME	SUB ASSEMBLY NO.	JOB ORDER NO.
WRITTEN BY	CHECKED BY	APPROVED BY	DATE	RELEASE APPROVAL
MATERIAL SPECIFICATION NO.	MATERIAL CODE NO.	MATERIAL DESCRIPTION	RELEASE DATE

OPERATION CODE NO.	OPERATION DESCRIPTION	DEPT.	GROUP	MACH-INE	EQUIPMENT DESCRIPTION	PIECES PER HOUR	LABOR		
							CLASS	SET UP TIME	MAN HOURS

7-5 PRODUCTION ROUTING SHEET

RAW MATERIAL REQUISITION

DATE:_____

REQUESTED BY:_____

DEPARTMENT

JOB NUMBER:_____   PRODUCT:_____

QUANTITY REQUESTED	ITEM NUMBER/DESCRIPTION	QUANTITY ISSUED

_____   _____
REQUESTED BY   FULLFILLED BY

7-6 RAW MATERIAL REQUISITION

PRODUCTION ORDER

JOB NUMBER: DATE:

ITEM NUMBER: DESCRIPTION:

QUANTITY: DIMENSIONS:

MATERIAL CODE NO.:   MATERIAL DESCRIPTION:

SPECIFICATIONS:

SPECIAL INSTRUCTIONS:

ESTIMATED DATE OF COMPLETION:

RELEASE DATE:

APPROVED BY:

7-7 PRODUCTION ORDER

S I N G L E D O O R S		F R A M E S	
Door Style:		Type of Wood:	
Size of Door:		Frame Thickness:	
Type of Wood:		Frame Width:	
Type of Door:		Door Stops:	
☐ Interior ☐ Exterior		☐ Fixed ☐ Applied	
Glass Thickness:		Size Door Stops:	
Door Thickness:		Type Weather Stripping:	
Door Width:			
Door Length:		Order By: Date:	
Panel Cutters:			

D O U B L E D O O R S			
Number of Hinges: ☐ 2 ☐ 3 ☐ 4 ☐ 5 ☐ 6 Other:			
"T" Astricals:			
Type of Deadbolts:		Which Door Active:	
Lockset:		☐ Right ☐ Left	

7-8 PRODUCTION ORDER BY PRODUCT

PRODUCTION ORDER CHANGE

CUSTOMER		ORDER NUMBER	DATE

JOB NUMBER	ITEM/PART NUMBER	CHANGE FROM	CHANGE TO

MAIN OFFICE [ ]
PLANT MANAGER [ ]
PRODUCTION CONTROL [ ]
PRODUCTION MANAGER [ ]
TRAFFIC [ ]

SCHEDULING [ ]
SALES [ ]
CREDIT [ ]
TRAFFIC [ ]
ORDER PROCESSING [ ]

ISSUED BY

7-9 PRODUCTION ORDER CHANGE

153

PRODUCTION REPORT

JOB NUMBER _____   SHIFT _____   DATE _____

CUSTOMER ORDER NO.	QUANTITY	ITEM NO. DESCRIPTION	START	STOP	TOTAL HOURS	TOTAL PIECES	SCRAP

EXPLANATION OF DELAYS/WORK STOPAGE

FROM	TO

PREPARED BY _____   APPROVED BY _____

7-10 DAILY PRODUCTION REPORT

154

PRODUCTION REPORT

PAGE OF
/ /

JOB NUMBER	ITEM NUMBER	QUANTITY ORDERED	QUANTITY PRODUCED	TOTAL HOURS
			TOTAL PIECES	TOTAL HOURS

% DEFECTIVE _____

% SCRAP _____

_____ PREPARED BY

_____ APPROVED BY

7-11 MONTHLY PRODUCTION REPORT

TONNAGE ALLOTMENT AND PRODUCTION PERFORMANCE

MONTH _____   WEEK ENDED _____

PRODUCTS	TONNAGE ALLOTMENT	PAST DUE	CURRENT LOAD	TOTAL LOAD	TOTAL SHIPMENTS	SHIPMENTS AGAINST LOAD	% PERFORM.
BLOOMS							
BILLETS							
TOTAL SEMI-FINISHED							
WIRE RODS							
LOW + MED. CARBON WIRE							
HIGH CARBON WIRE							
SPECIAL WIRE							
TOTAL ROD + MFGRS. WIRE							
FENCE							
NAILS							
BARB WIRE							
MERCHANT WIRE							
TOTAL MERCHANT PROD.							
WIRE FABRIC							
CONSTRUCTION PRODUCTS							
REJECTED BILLETS							
REJECTED RODS							
REJECTED WIRE PROD.							
GRAND TOT.-WIRE PROD.							
H.R. SHEETS							
C.R. SHEETS							
H.R. EXCESS PRIMES							
C.R. EXCESS PRIMES							
TOTAL PRIME SHEETS							
H.R. SECOND SHEETS							
C.R. SECOND SHEETS							
TOTAL PRIME + SECONDS							
CONVERSION SERVICE							
SPECIALTIES							
TOTAL PRODUCTS							

REMARKS

7-12 PRODUCTION PERFORMANCE REPORT

	MONTHLY PRODUCTION RELEASE BAR, POWDER AND ACID MONTH _____			
		BAR SIZES		
		10 KG.	3.5 KG.	2.2 KG.
1. FORECASTED SALES REQUIREMENTS				
2. PLUS OR (MINUS) DIFFERENCE BETWEEN ESTIMATED AND ACTUAL USAGE FOR PREVIOUS PERIOD				
3. PLUS OR (MINUS) DIFFERENCE BETWEEN SCHEDULED PRODUCTION AND ACTUAL PRODUCTION FOR PREVIOUS PERIOD				
4. PLUS OR (MINUS) SCHEDULED CHANGES IN PLANNED INVENTORY LEVELS				
5. NET TOTAL BAR REQUIREMENTS (SUM OF ITEMS 1 TO 4, INCLUSIVE)				
6. ACID YIELD FACTOR		1.672	1.624	1.624
7. ACID REQUIREMENTS (ITEM 5 X ITEM 6)	TOTAL			
8. POWDER YIELD FACTOR		0.7	0.7	0.7
9. POWDER REQUIREMENTS (ITEM 7 X ITEM 8)	TOTAL			

7-13 MONTHLY PRODUCTION RELEASE

```
┌─────────────────────────────────────────────────────────────────┐
│ ┌──────────────────────────────────────────┐  ┌──────────────┐  │
│ │  FORM:                    DATE:           │  │ Project:     │  │
│ │                                           │  │              │  │
│ │      TO:                                  │  │              │  │
│ │                                           │  │              │  │
│ │      Re:                                  │  │              │  │
│ │                                           │  │              │  │
│ │ Since we are rapidly approaching  ___/___/___,                 │
│ │ which is the completion date for this project,                 │
│ │ the following information                 └──────────────┘  │
│ │ is needed for:            ☐ milestone check                  │
│ │                           ☐ review                          │
│ │                           ☐ meeting                         │
│ │                           ☐ presentation                    │
│ │                           ☐ _____                    │
│ │                                                             │
│ │ I need to know:                                             │
│ │                                                             │
│ │     Current status:                                         │
│ │                                                             │
│ │         ☐ Ahead     ☐ On Time    ☐ Temp. Delay    ☐ Behind  │
│ │                                                             │
│ │     Probability of completion on schedule:                  │
│ │                                                             │
│ │         ☐ High      ☐ Good (*)  ☐ Poor (*)                  │
│ │                                                             │
│ │     Probability of coming in on budget:                     │
│ │                                                             │
│ │         ☐ High      ☐ Good (*)  ☐ Poor (*)                  │
│ │ Obstacles:                                                  │
│ │                                                             │
│ │                                                             │
│ │                                                             │
│ │                                                             │
│ │ Recommendations:                                            │
│ │                                                             │
│ │                                                             │
│ │                                                             │
│ │                                                             │
│ │                                                             │
│ │              * establish date for followup                  │
│ └─────────────────────────────────────────────────────────────┘
```

7-14 CHECKING WORK-IN-PROGRESS

```
_____     _____
            STOCK  NUMBER                        UNIT  PACK

_____
                         DESCRIPTION

_____          _____
        LOT  NUMBER                        JOB  NUMBER

_____          _____
         PACKED  BY                           DATE

                         SURPLUS
                        PRODUCTION
```

7-15 SURPLUS PRODUCTION LABEL

3807

MATERIAL RETURN TO INVENTORY

DEPARTMENT: _____   DATE: _____

ISSUE DATE	QUANTITY	ITEM NUMBER	DESCRIPTION

REASON FOR RETURN: _____

_____

_____

_____   _____
DEPARTMENT HEAD   INVENTORY MANAGER

7-16 RAW MATERIAL RETURN TO INVENTORY

MATERIAL SCRAP REPORT

DATE_____

PART NO./DESCRIPTION	QUANTITY	REASON FOR SCRAPPING

JOB NO.	LOT NO.	UNIT COST	TOTAL COST

INSPECTED BY	APPROVED BY

7-17 MATERIAL SCRAP REPORT

PRODUCTION TOTALS FOR 1992

PIECES (THOUSANDS)

7-18 YEARLY PRODUCTION TOTALS BY MONTH

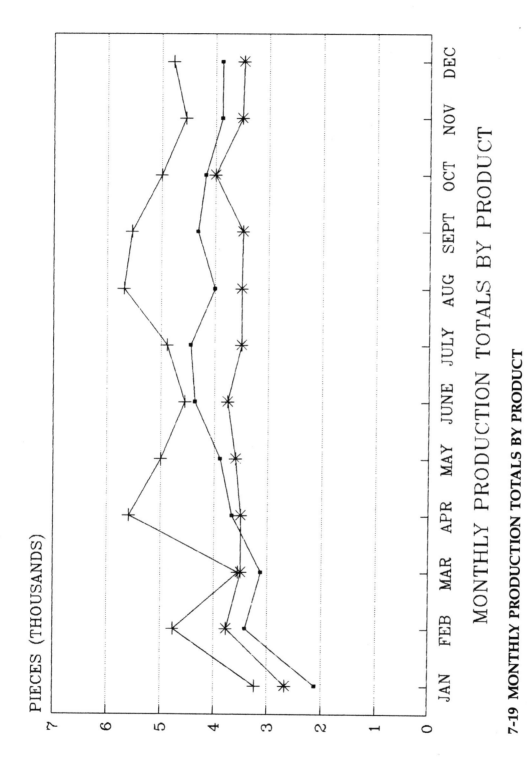

PIECES (THOUSANDS)

MONTHLY PRODUCTION TOTALS BY PRODUCT

7-19 MONTHLY PRODUCTION TOTALS BY PRODUCT

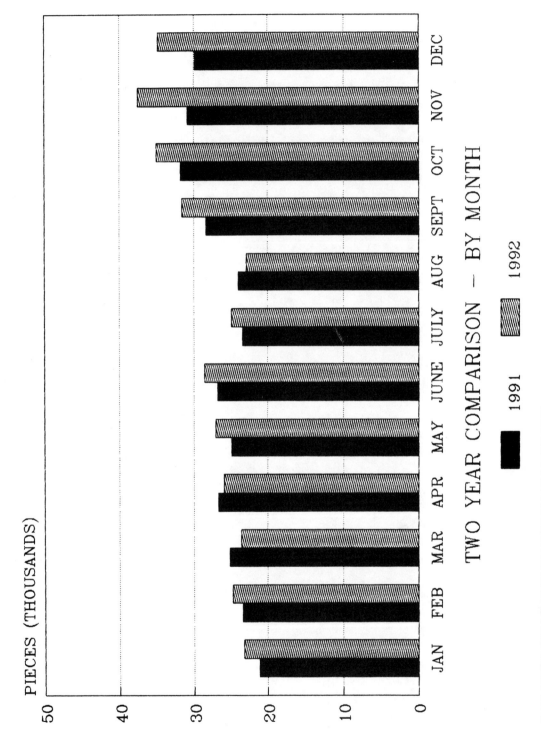

PIECES (THOUSANDS)

TWO YEAR COMPARISON – BY MONTH

1991   1992

7-20 TWO-YEAR COMPARISON BY MONTH

Chapter Eight

CLAIMS: LOSS AND DAMAGES

Transportation claims are never an easy process—mainly because there are at least three different parties involved: the shipper, the carrier, and the consignee. The process becomes even more difficult when a freight forwarder or multiple carriers are involved.

A properly filed claim begins while merchandise is being received. Receiving personnel must carefully examine all freight for exterior damage, especially on the corners, which is the most likely point of damage. When a carton is damaged, the goods should be inspected for interior damage. If damage is found or shipment has a shortage, it must be noted on the freight bill.

When an exception is made on a freight bill, it makes the claim easier to substantiate and therefore easier to process and collect. In the event that a shortage or damage is discovered after delivery, it becomes more difficult to ascertain the responsible party. Burden of proof is on the consignee to show that goods were received damaged or items missing from mixed pack. A concealed loss and damage claim must be filed. A standard claim form can also be used. This must be done immediately after discovery. As much information as possible should be supplied to allow the shipper and/or the carrier to ascertain the point in shipment where loss or damaged occurred.

This chapter covers all the forms and reports needed to file a claim and collect payment. Also included are forms to file a freight overcharge, trace shipments, obtain freight substantiation, and determine responsibility for filing claims.

8-1. STANDARD FREIGHT CLAIM—COMMON CARRIER

The form shown is used by the consignee to file a freight claim against the carrier for loss or damage. All information requested must be filled in completely or the processing of the claim will be delayed until such information is obtained. The claimant should assign a claim number, which will be used by the carrier and claimant as reference in all correspondence.

Key Information

- Claimant's Number
- Reason for Claim (loss or damage)
- Freight Bill Number and Date
- Shipper
- Consignee and Destination
- Detailed Statement Showing How Amount Claimed Is Determined
- Documents to Support Claim (All three documents should be submitted if possible. If claimant can not produce one or more of the documents, the reason must be explained under "Remarks.")

8-2. CLAIM FORM—U.S. POSTAL SERVICE

For filing claims with the U.S. Postal Service, PS Form 3812 is used. A claim can only be filed with the Postal Service if a parcel is insured and/or sent C.O.D. This form has two sections. One section is to be completed by the party filing the claim, the other section by the post office.

Key Information

- Claim Number
- Reason for Claim (e.g., complete loss, partial loss, complete damage)
- Mailer/Payee Name and Address
- Addressee/Payee Name and Address
- Description of Lost or Damaged Contents
- Postal Insurance Claim Payment Identification
- Post Office Section (i.e., information to be completed by Post Office)

8-3. FREIGHT INSPECTION REPORT

This form is used by a carrier to report all information concerning loss and/or damage to an inbound shipment. The main objective of this report is to determine the reason for loss or damage (including pilferage) and the disposition of the damaged freight.

Key Information

- Shipment Information
- Did Consignee Give Clear Receipt?

- Loss Inspection
- Apparent Cause of Damage
- Type of Container
- Disposition of Damaged Freight
- Description of Exceptions

8-4. INSPECTION REPORT OF LOSS OR DAMAGE DISCOVERED AFTER DELIVERY

The report shown is used to collect information concerning loss or damage to a shipment discovered after delivery. Because an exception wasn't noted on the freight bill at time of delivery, the burden of proof is on the consignee. As soon as loss or damage is discovered, all parties involved should be notified immediately. An inspection of the shipment can determine if the freight was packaged properly or if there was evidence of pilferage, and so on.

Key Information

- Shipping Information
- Shipment Inspection (e.g., regarding loss, damage, packaging, pilferage)
- Whether Shipment Had Prior Transportation? If So, Is Merchandise Still Packed in Original Container? (These questions are important because many loads are switched at different in-state terminals. The more a shipment is handled, the greater the possibility of damage. Also, though the probability of the merchandise being in different containers is unlikely, it is common for cartons to be retaped. A retaped carton usually demonstrates rough handling and also the possibility that merchandise was taken out of a carton containing more than one item.)
- Description of Loss or Damage
- Disposition of Damaged Freight

8-5. CONCEALED LOSS OR DAMAGE CLAIM—SHIPPER

This form is used when the shipper initiates the claim or supplies additional information. Questions are asked to determine point of damage or loss.

Key Information

- Shipper and Consignee Claim Numbers
- Point of Origin and Destination
- Packing Information (see questions 1 through 4 on sample form)
- Shipping Information (see questions 5 through 9 on sample form)

8-6. CONCEALED LOSS OR DAMAGE CLAIM—CONSIGNEE

The form shown is used by the consignee to gather additional information in support of a claim. This information should be obtained as soon as possible after discovery of loss or damage.

Key Information

- Shipper and Consignee Claim Numbers
- Point of Origin and Destination
- Questions Concerning Shipment

8-7. SUPPLEMENTAL WORKSHEET FOR LOSS AND DAMAGE CLAIMS

This form is prepared as a supplement to a concealed loss or damage claim. The form provides detailed information on packing and shipment handling.

Key Information

- Report Number
- Packing Information (i.e., dimensions and other specifications of cartons, crates, boxes, and other packing material used)
- Past Experience on Damage
- Receiving Facilities Questions Regarding Delivery of Shipment

8-8. OVERAGE, SHORTAGE, AND DAMAGE REPORT

This form can be used either by the carrier or consignee to report an overage, shortage, or damage of a shipment.

Key Information

- Over, Short, or Damage
- Carrier's Pro Number
- Carrier/Consignee/Shipper
- OS&D Information
- Remarks
- Action Taken

8-9. TRACER REQUEST

The form shown is used to initiate a tracer from either the carrier or shipper. This form could be used to check the location of an inbound shipment for estimated time of delivery or to check on items received short.

Key Information

- Shipper Name and Address
- Date of Shipment
- Purchase Order Number
- Carrier's Pro Number
- Item(s) Received Short

8-10. SHIPMENT TRACER

This form is used to initiate tracing a freight shipment that was shipped but not received in a reasonable amount of time.

Key Information

- Consignee Name and Address
- Shipper Name and Address
- Inbound Carrier Name and Address
- Message (e.g., what specifically is being traced, as in a partial shipment)
- Reply

8-11. TRACER—USPS

PS form 1510 is used to trace noninsured goods lost through the U.S. Postal Service.

Key Information

- Shipper and Consignee Information (see #4 and #5 in Part II-A)
- Type of Mail (see #8 in Part II-A)
- Special Services (see #9 in Part II-A)
- Description of Contents of Article (see #11 in Part II-A)
- Disposition of Article (see Part III)

8-12. FREIGHT BILL OVERCHARGE CLAIM

The form shown is used to submit an overcharge on a freight bill. This form can be used whether using carrier's standard rates or if the carrier and shipper have a contract rate agreement.

Key Information

- Claim Number
- Carrier's Pro Number (e.g., freight bill number)

- Shipper
- Date of Receipt
- Rate Charges Paid per Hundred Pounds
- Dollar Amount of What the Freight Charges Should Have Been
- Documents Submitted

8-13. SUBSTANTIATION REQUEST

The form shown is used when the invoice does not match the receiving record or other company documents and further proof of delivery is required.

Key Information

- Invoice Number(s) in Question
- Invoice Date and Amount
- Item(s) in Question

8-14. ASSIGNMENT OF CLAIM

This form can either be used by the original buyer or by the carrier to assign its interest in a damaged shipment to another party. This is usually done when multiple carriers are involved.

Key Information

- Assignment Statement
- Description of Shipment
- Shipper Identification
- Consignee Identification
- Freight Bill Number (e.g., waybill number)

8-15. BOND OF INDEMNITY

This form is used to ensure that the shipper or carrier will be reimbursed for payment made against a claim if and when any other party involved also makes payment.

Key Information

- Party to Whom Payment Is Made
- Claim Number
- Statement of Indemnity
- Authorized Signature

8-16. SHORTAGE CERTIFICATE

The form shown is used to certify that goods for which a claim has been paid will be returned if the goods are later received.

Key Information

- Claim Number
- Invoice Number
- Certification that Goods Will Be Returned or Paid For by the Consignee
- Signature of Consignee/Shipper

8-17. SAMPLE CLAIM PROCEDURE

This chart shows proper procedure for filing a claim, from the receiving process to the return to vendor.

Key Information

- Receiving Freight Procedure
- Reporting Shortage or Damage
- Claim Procedure

8-18. CLAIM RESPONSIBILITY CHART

This chart details who is responsible for filing a freight claim. The key to responsibility is terms of sale. Most shipments are F.O.B. (free on board) origin, which means that the buyer is responsible for filing. When the terms specify F.O.B. destination, the seller becomes responsible.

Key Information

- Terms of Sale
- Whether the Title Passes to the Buyer or the Seller
- Whether Freight Charges Are Paid by the Buyer or the Seller

8-19. CHECKLIST FOR FILING USPS CLAIMS

The checklist shown is used as a guideline in filing a claim with the U.S. Postal Service.

Key Information

- Which Form to Use for Each Type of Mail
- Time Limits for Filing Claims for Each Type of Mail
- What Additional Documents Must Be Submitted for Each Type of Mail

OD6 REV. 3/79
PRINTED IN THE U.S.A.

YELLOW FREIGHT SYSTEM, INC.

Standard Form for Presentation of Loss and Damage Claims

MAIL TO:	CLAIM PAYABLE TO:
YELLOW FREIGHT SYSTEM, INC. **P.O. Box 7903, 10990 Roe Avenue** **Overland Park, Kansas 66207**	FIRM NAME STREET & NO. OR P.O. BOX NO. CITY OR TOWN & STATE ZIP CODE

CLAIMANTS NUMBER   DATE PRESENTED

This Claim is made against the carrier for Loss ( ) Damage ( ) to the following described shipment:

FREIGHT BILL NO.   FREIGHT BILL DATE   ROUTED VIA

SHIPPER   ORIGIN

CONSIGNEE   DESTINATION

DESCRIPTION OF SHIPMENT   SALVAGE RETURNED TO CARRIER?

                                                                    YES   NO

DETAILED STATEMENT SHOWING HOW AMOUNT CLAIMED IS DETERMINED
(Number and description of articles, nature and extent of loss or damage, invoice price or articles, amount of claim, etc.)

	Total Amount Claimed

IN ADDITION TO THE INFORMATION GIVEN ABOVE, THE FOLLOWING DOCUMENTS ARE SUBMITTED IN SUPPORT OF THIS CLAIM*

(_____) 1. Original bill of lading, if not previously surrendered to carrier.
(_____) 2. Original paid freight ("expense") bill.
(_____) 3. Original invoice, or certified copy.
4. Other particulars obtainable in proof of loss or damage claimed:
REMARKS _____

_____

The foregoing statement of facts is hereby certified to as correct.

_____
(Signature of Claimant)

†Claimant should assign to each claim a number, inserting same in the space provided at the upper right hand corner of this form. Reference should be made thereto in all correspondence pertaining to this claim.
*Claimant will please check (✔) before such of the documents mentioned as have been attached, and explain under "Remarks" the absence of any of the documents called for in connection with this claim. When for any reason it is impossible for claimant to produce original bill of lading or paid freight bill, Claimant should indemnify carriers against duplicate claim supported by original documents.

8-1 STANDARD FREIGHT CLAIM—COMMON CARRIER

| Claim No. | | Forward To ☐ 5 ☐ 6 ☐ 11 ☐ 12 ☐ PDC | 20. Postmark of office accepting claim |

T O   B E   C O M P L E T E D   B Y   C U S T O M E R

➤ TO BE COMPLETED BY CUSTOMER ◄

1. ☐ Complete Loss ☐ Complete Loss of Contents ☐ Partial Loss ☐ Complete Damage ☐ Partial Damage ☐ No COD Rem't

2. ☐ Unnum-bered ☐ No. _____ ☐ COD AMT Due sender $ _____ 3. Special ☐ Delivery 4. Priority ☐ Mail

5. Post Office of Mailing *(City, State) (ZIP Code)*

Signature and phone number of employee accepting claim

6. Post Office of Address *(City, State) (ZIP Code)*

| 7. Date of Mailing Mon Day Yr / / | 8. Claim Date Mon Day Yr / / | 9. Postage | 10a. Ins. Fee | 10b. Other Fees |

11. Name and Address of Mailer-Payee ☐

21. Evidence of insurance *(or COD)* was: ☐ Mailing Receipt ☐ Wrapper

22. If claim is for damage, was wrapper, container & article presented to your office? ☐ YES ☐ NO *(If yes, describe condition of parcel & item upon receipt.)*

12. Name and Address of Addressee-Payee ☐ Show the exact name and address of the individual or company to whom or to which the article was sent.

13. Describe, using trade names if known, only those articles lost or damaged and specified value of each. Attach invoice if available or evidence of value.

14. Total Claimed *(Exclude Postage)*

Location of Damaged Article: ☐ Sender ☐ Addressee ☐ Disposed of as Waste ☐ Post Office at

Items 23 and 24 must be completed within 5 days of receipt from accepting Post Office.

23. If claim is for complete loss or COD, and there is a record of delivery, show to whom and when delivered. If COD, also show Money Order or check number, amount and date check was sent to mailer. If Money Order was not issued for COD, show "NONE ISSUED," and reason. If there is no record of delivery, so indicate.

15. To be completed by ADDRESSEE ONLY. Were items listed above received? ☐ YES ☐ NO Refused? ☐ YES ☐ NO

16. To be completed by ADDRESSEE ONLY. Did you pay COD Charges? ☐ YES ☐ NO If so, state to whom, where and date.

17. I declare under the penalties of perjury that this claim has been examined by me and to the best of my knowledge and belief, is true, correct and complete.

(Check No.)   *(Date check sent to mailer)*

| 18. Signature of Mailer | Date | Tel. No. *(Area Code)* ( ) |

(Money Order No.)   *(Amount)* $

| By | Title |

24. Postmark of Other Post Office

T O   B E   C O M P L E T E D   B Y   C U S T O M E R

| 19. Signature of Addressee | Date | Tel. No. *(Area Code)* ( ) |

| By | Title |

Postal Insurance Claim Payment Identification

Other Identification: Please show any information in this area that will help you match the payment check with your claim. *(e.g., Invoice No., Purchase Order, etc.)*

(Print or type name and current mailing address of payee.)

The collection of information on this form is authorized by 39 U.S.C. 403 & 404. Completion of this form is voluntary. This information will be used to adjudicate claims for loss or damage to insured mail and COD mail shipments, and may be disclosed to the appropriate agency, whether Federal, State or local, charged with the responsibility to investigate or prosecute a violation or potential violation of law, or charged with enforcing or implementing the statute, rule, regulation or order issued pursuant thereto. If this information is not provided, claims for loss or damage to insured and COD mail shipments will not be honored.

8-2 CLAIM FORM—U.S. POSTAL SERVICE

_____ **COMPANY**

FREIGHT INSPECTION REPORT

STATION		DATE OF INSPECTION	DAMAGE	
			APPARENT CAUSE OF DAMAGE	**COND. OF CONTAINER**
INSPECTED AT		ADDRESS	CONCEALED	WET
INBOUND MANIFEST	DATE	CAR OR TRAILER	PRIOR TO LOADING OR AFTER UNLOADING	CREASED
			INADEQUATE PACKING	DENTED
SHIPPER		ADDRESS	IMPROPER CONTAINER	BROKEN
			OVERHEAD WEIGHT	CRUSHED
CONSIGNEE		ADDRESS	DIRTY TRAILER	TORN
INBOUND SEALS	NAME OF DELIVERING DRAYMAN		LEAKY TRAILER	LEAKINGS
			INHERENT NATURE OF COMM	PUNCTURES
DATE DELIVERED	DATE UNPACKED	DATE EXCEPTIONS REPORTED		RE-COOPERED

DID CONSIGNEE GIVE CLEAR RECEIPT? ☐ YES ☐ NO	TYPE OF CONTAINER	
LOSS	CRATE	BUNDLES
EVIDENCE OF PILFERAGE OR ROBBERY?	BOX	BAGS
	CORRUGATED BOX	
	STEEL DRUMS	NEW
ITEMS PACKED IN EACH CONTAINER / DID COMPARISON CHECK WITH INVOICE OR WEIGHT OF PACKAGE VERIFY LOSS?	BARRELS	SECOND HAND
	PAILS	TEST WEIGHT

IN YOUR OPINION, IS CONDITION OF THE CONTENTS A RESULT OF THE ACTION CAUSING DAMAGE TO THE CONTAINER ☐ YES ☐ NO

DISPOSITION OF DAMAGED FREIGHT

DESCRIBE INTERIOR PACKING

HAS DAMAGED MERCHANDISE ANY SALVAGE VALUE? ☐ YES ☐ NO ☐ REPAIR ☐ ALLOWANCE	
CAN DAMAGED PARTS BE REPLACED OR REPAIRED?	
TO BE PICKED UP	DUMPED
NUMBER OF ITEMS PACKED IN EACH CONTAINER / RETURNED TO SHIPPER	
VALUE OF MERCHANDISE IN GOOD CONDITION / HOW DETERMINED? — WEIGHT OF DAMAGED ITEMS	WHERE PHOTOGRAPHS TAKEN?

STATE FULLY DETAILED DESCRIPTION OF EXCEPTIONS, SHOWING STOCK AND SERIAL NUMBERS AND ANY ADDITIONAL INFORMATION THAT MAY ASSIST IN DETERMINING LIABILITY.

_____

_____

_____

_____

_____

_____

_____

MAKE RECOMMENDATIONS FOR PREVENTING SIMILAR DAMAGE ON REVERSE SIDE.

NOTE: _____ INSPECTOR

THIS REPORT IS MERELY A STATEMENT OF FACTS AND NOT AN ACKNOWLEDGMENT OF CARRIER'S LIABILITY; NOR IS IT TO BE CONSIDERED AS A FORMAL CLAIM WITHIN THE MEANING OF SEC. 2(B) OF THE BILL OF LADING CONTRACT.

_____ CONSIGNEE

8-3 FREIGHT INSPECTION REPORT

INSPECTION REPORT OF LOSS OR DAMAGE DISCOVERED AFTER DELIVERY

TERMINAL _____ Date _____ , 19_____ Report Number _____

Shipper _____ Origin _____

Consignee _____ Destination _____

F/B No._____ Prepaid ☐ Collect ☐ _____ Date Consignee requested inspection _____

Date of Billing _____ 19_____ Date Delivered _____ 19_____ Loss or Damage _____ Could loss or damage have been noticed at time of delivery? _____

Date Un-Packed _____ 19_____ Date of Call _____ 19_____ Were goods unpacked before the inspection was made? _____ Were containers and packing available? _____

What evidence was there of Pilferage before Delivery? _____

Was there sufficient space in Package to Contain Missing Goods? _____ What material Occupied the Remaining Space? _____

Did Comparison of Check with Invoice or Weighing Package, Verify loss? _____ If Released Valuation, Show Weight of Articles Damaged or Short _____

Kind of Container _____ New or Old _____ (Carton, Box, Crate, Etc.) Wired ☐ Corded ☐ Strapped ☐ Nailed ☐ Sealed ☐

Box Maker's Gross Weight Limit _____ Gross Weight of Loaded Carton _____ If Carton Were Flats Glued? _____ Were Seams or Edges Split? _____

How Were Goods Packed? _____

Do you Consider Adequately Packed or Protected? _____ What condition of container or contents indicated loss or damage occurred with carrier? _____

To prevent comparable damage in the future, how in your judgement should they have been packed or prepared for shipment?_____

_____

Did Shipment Have Prior Transportation? _____ If so, Is Merchandise Still Packed in Original Container? _____ Original Point of Shipment _____

No. of Articles	Describe fully nature & extent of loss or damage	Invoice Price
	(If necessary use other side of this form)	

Will there Be Salvage? _____ What Disposition will be made of the Salvage? _____

Consignee _____ Carrier _____

By _____ By _____
                                                    Inspector

This Report is Merely a Statement of Facts and Not an Acknowledgement of Carrier's Liability.

When presenting claims for loss and damage, attach the following documents:

1. This Inspection Report
2. Original Paid Freight Bill
3. Original Bill of Lading

4. Original Invoice or an exact certified copy showing all discounts
5. Your Bill showing nature and amount of claim
6. Shipper's and Consignee's Concealed Loss and Damage Forms,

Claim blanks and other necessary forms to properly present your claim may be obtained from carrier's agent.

8-4 INSPECTION REPORT OF LOSS OR DAMAGE DISCOVERED AFTER DELIVERY

Standard Form for the Handling of Concealed Loss and Concealed Damage Claims

SHIPPERS FORM

INFORMATION REQUIRED FROM SHIPPER IN SUPPORT OF CLAIM FOR CONCEALED LOSS OR CONCEALED DAMAGE

Shipper's Claim No. _____ Consignee's Claim No. _____

Point of Origin _____ Destination _____

Date _____ Number of Packages _____

Shipper _____ Consignee _____

Commodity _____

INFORMATION REQUIRED	ANSWERS
1. Were the goods packed at the Factory, or by you _____	
2. Where were the goods packed? _____	
3. When were the goods packed, if known? _____	
4. If packed at the factory, did you open and examine the goods before reshipment? _____	
5. When you received the goods from the factory, did you place them in your warehouse and leave them in the same place until reshipment? _____	
6. If the goods were moved from place to place in your warehouse, after receiving same from the factory were they handled carefully, or was there a possibility of their becoming damaged while in your possession, before reshipment?_____	
7. Did you deliver shipment to carrier's dock, or did they pick the shipment up at your dock? _____	
8. On what date was delivery made to, or shipment picked up by out-bound carrier? _____	
9. Give name of carrier to whom shipment was delivered or picked up by. _____	

I hereby certify the foregoing statement of facts to be true in every particular, to the best of my knowledge and belief.

Date at _____

_____
(Signature)

Date _____ 19_____

_____
(In what capacity employed)

8-5 CONCEALED LOSS AND CONCEALED DAMAGE—SHIPPER

**Standard Form for the Handling of Concealed Loss
and Concealed Damage Claims**

CONSIGNEE'S FORM

Information Required From Consignee in Support of Claim for Concealed
Loss or Concealed Damage

Shipper's Claim No. _____ Consignee's Claim No. _____

Description of Shipment

Point of Origin _____ Destination _____

Date Received _____ Number of Packages _____

Shipper _____ Consignee _____

Commodity _____

_____

_____

1. When (date and hour) was shipment received at your place of business? _____

2. Name of truck driver, if known _____

3. If not received by truck, state how received _____

4. On what date was loss or damage discovered? _____

5. On what date was carrier notified of loss or damage? _____

6. Kind of container? _____

7. How was package protected against abstraction of or damage to contents (strapped, sealed, or otherwise)? _____

_____

8. Was container examined before opening? _____ Or after opening? _____

9. If condition of container at time of such examination indicated cause of loss or damage, explain fully _____

_____

10. If condition of contents or interior packing indicated loss or damage, explain fully _____

_____

11. If property received did not fill container to capacity, what material occupied the remaining space? _____

12. What condition of container or contents indicated that loss or damage occurred while in possession of carriers?

_____

_____

_____

I hereby certify the foregoing statement of facts to be true in every particular.

Dated at _____   _____
                                                  (Signature)

Date _____ 19_____   _____
                                             (In what capacity employed)

8-6 CONCEALED LOSS AND CONCEALED DAMAGE—CONSIGNEE

WORK SHEET. SUPPLEMENTAL TO CONCEALED LOSS & DAMAGE INSPECTION REPORT.

Date _____ Report No._____

Agency _____

CARTON: Length _____ Height _____ Width _____ New ( ) Used ( ) Wt. _____

Construction _____ Made by _____ at _____

CRATE: Length _____ Height _____ Width _____ New ( ) Used ( ) Wt. _____

Cleats _____ Their position _____

CONSTRUCTION) Top _____ Bottom _____ Sides _____

OF CRATES:) Ends _____

BOX SIZE: Length _____ Height _____ Width _____ Wt. _____

WOOD STOCK USED _____ Diagonal bracing _____ Exterior _____

_____

NAILING _____ Size _____ Kind _____ Spacing _____

CLOSURES: Paper taped _____ Glued _____ Wire bound _____ Steel banded _____ Rope _____

Position of steel banding _____ Of wire banding _____

INTERNAL PACKING OR BRACING: Shredded paper ( ). Inserts & Position _____

_____ Waxed Paper & Position _____

Kimpax ( ). Tufflex ( ). Corroflex ( ). And Position _____

Airspace _____ Internal bracing & Position _____

Additional information _____

_____

Wooden-nailed ( ). Wooden-wire-bound ( ). Cleated veneer ( ). Cleated Fibreboard ( ).

If cartons: Solid ( ) Flutes ( ) Corrugated ( ) Double faced ( ) Double-walled ( )

Box Maker's Certificate _____ Gr. Wt. _____ Gr. Wt. Limit _____

DRUMS OR BARRELS: Steel: Capacity _____ Gauge _____ Date _____

Wooden: Tight ( ) Slack ( )

Fibre ( ). Remarks _____

_____

COST PRICE _____ Materials used in manufacture _____

SHIPPING POINTS: North ( ). South ( ). East ( ). West ( ).

PAST EXPERIENCE ON DAMAGE _____

PROMISED IMPROVEMENTS _____

REMARKS _____

RECEIVING FACILITIES _____

Delivery to: Sidewalk level ( ). Tail gate level ( ). Sidewalk chute to Basement ( ).

Other _____ Does consignee: Hand truck ( ). Conveyor ( ). Fork Lift ( ).

Pallets ( ). Are packages first stored ( ) or moved direct to unpacking facilities ( ).

Do packages receive much handling before being unpacked? _____

Inspector _____

NOTE: Use other side of this sheet for drawings or additional information.

8-7 SUPPLEMENTAL WORKSHEET FOR LOSS AND DAMAGE CLAIMS

O S & D REPORT

[ ] OVER [ ] SHORT [ ] DAMAGE	DATE	
TERMINAL	PRO #	DATE
CARRIER	FREIGHT ROUTE	

CONSIGNEE   DESTINATION

SHIPPER   ORIGIN

NO. OF PKGS.	
CASE NOS.	
DESCRIPTION	
REMARKS	

ACTION TAKEN_____

_____

_____

_____

_____

_____   _____

RECEIVING MANAGER   DATE

8-8 OVERAGE, SHORTAGE, AND DAMAGE REPORT

Date_____

To:_____   Consignee_____

From:_____   _____

Re: Tracer Request   _____

                                     _____

As of this date:

    [] Purchase Order _____ has not been received.
    [] Shortage of_____ has not been received.

Please put a tracer on this shipment and inform me of its
disposition as soon as possible.

Shipper_____   Date Shipped_____

    _____   Bill of Lading #_____

    _____

Carrier_____   Pro #_____

    _____   Date Received_____

    _____

Reply:_____

_____

_____

_____

_____

8-9 TRACER REQUEST

Urgent Tracer

IMMEDIATE REPLY REQUESTED

Date Sent _____

Date Recd. _____

Date Ans. _____

To: _____

From: _____

Consignee: _____ Order Nos. _____

Shipper: _____ Order Nos. _____

In Bound Carrier: _____

Message: _____

_____

Reply: _____

_____

Pls. furnish information you have by return Air Mail.

8-10 SHIPMENT TRACER

Part I

Postal Customer:

The sender of the article described below has made an inquiry regarding delivery of the item. The article was not located at the mailing office. Therefore, we are contacting you to determine if the article has been delivered. Please indicate below if the article has been received. Return the form in the enclosed PREADDRESSED ENVELOPE WHICH REQUIRES NO POSTAGE. Your response will assist the Postal Service in providing improved service. **PLEASE RETURN BOTH PARTS I AND II-A.**

THANK YOU

The Article Was: ☐ Received *(Date if known)* _____ ☐ Not Received ☐ Refused	Date of Reply	Signature of Addressee or Agent
Remarks		

PS Form **1510,** January 1989

U.S. Postal Service

MAIL LOSS/RIFLING REPORT

1. Complaint Date	2. Office Accepting Complaint *(City and State)*	3. Complaint ☐ Loss ☐ Rifling

4. Article Was Mailed By	5. Article Was Addressed To
a. Name	a. Name
b. Return Address As On Article Mailed	b. Address As On Article Mailed
c. City d. State e. ZIP + 4	c. City d. State e. ZIP + 4
f. Day Telephone Number *(Include Area Code)*	f. Day Telephone Number *(Include Area Code)*

6. Article Was Mailed	7. Article Was Sent	8. Type of Mail
a. Date Month Day Year	b. Time ☐ AM *(Hour)* ☐ PM	☐ 1st-Class ☐ Parcel Post ☐ Other *(Specify)* _____	☐ Letter ☐ Parcel ☐ Other *(Specify)* _____

9. Special Services
☐ Special Handling   ☐ Special Delivery   ☐ Certified   ☐ Return Receipt for merchandise
No. _____

10. Place of Mailing ☐ Main Post Office ☐ Station or Branch ☐ Contract Station ☐ Collection Box ☐ Residence or Business	Name And/Or Address of Location Checked	
	City And State of Location Checked	ZIP + 4 For Location Checked

11. Contents Of Article *(Describe in detail, size, color, brand name, serial no., check no., and amount, etc.)*	12. Value $

8-11 TRACER—SPS

Part III

Postmaster *(Office of Address)* Indicate disposition of the Certified article described in Part II-B below
1. a. If Records Indicate Delivery, Show Delivery Date:
b. State Name of Individual, Company, or Organization Accepting Article:
2. If No Record Of Delivery, Forward Parts I And II-A To Addressee: Date _____
3. If No Response Is Received In 15 Days From Addressee, Check ☐ and Return Part III To The Postmaster, Office Of Origin
4. If Addressee Responds, Return All Parts of Form 1510 To Office of Origin.
5. If No Record of Delivery And Addressee Denies Receipt, Conduct Search For Article Before Returning Form To Office of Origin.

PS Form **1510**, January 1989

Part IV

Superintendent Dead Letter Or Parcel Branch Conduct search for article described in Part II-B below		
1.	Branch Serving Mailing Office	
a. Conducted Search On *(Date)*	b. Search Conducted By *(Name)*	c. Article Was ☐ Located ☐ Not Located
2.	Branch Serving Addressee Office	
a. Conducted Search On *(Date)*	b. Search Conducted By *(Name)*	c. Article Was ☐ Located ☐ Not Located
3. If Article Was Located, It Was Forwarded To ☐ Sender ☐ Addressee		

PS Form **1510**, January 1989

Part II-B

U.S. Postal Service

MAIL LOSS/RIFLING REPORT

1. Complaint Date	2. Office Accepting Complaint *(City and State)*	3. Complaint ☐ Loss ☐ Rifling

4. Article Was Mailed By	5. Article Was Addressed To
a. Name	a. Name
b. Return Address As On Article Mailed	b. Address As On Article Mailed
c. City d. State e. ZIP + 4	c. City d. State e. ZIP + 4
f. Day Telephone Number *(Include Area Code)*	f. Day Telephone Number *(Include Area Code)*

6. Article Was Mailed	7. Article Was Sent	8. Type of Mail
a. Date — Month / Day / Year b. Time ☐ AM ☐ PM *(Hour)*	☐ 1st-Class ☐ Parcel Post ☐ Other *(Specify)* _____	☐ Letter ☐ Parcel ☐ Other *(Specify)* _____

9. Special Services

☐ Special Handling   ☐ Special Delivery   ☐ Certified   ☐ Return Receipt for merchandise

No. _____

10. Place of Mailing ☐ Main Post Office ☐ Station or Branch ☐ Contract Station ☐ Collection Box ☐ Residence or Business	Name And/Or Address of Location Checked	
	City And State of Location Checked	ZIP + 4 For Location Checked

11. Contents Of Article *(Describe in detail, size, color, brand name, serial no., check no., and amount, etc.)*	12. Value $

8-11 (Continued)

OVERCHARGE CLAIM

CLAIM NO._____

FROM_____   TO_____

_____   _____

_____   _____

_____   _____

Freight Bill Number_____   Date_____

Shipper_____   Origin_____

Consignee_____   Destination_____

Freight Charges Paid Per Attached Freight Bill $_____._____

Freight Charges For This Shipment Should Be $_____._____

Amount Of Overcharge $_____._____

How Charges Are Assessed:

Description of Freight	Weight	Rate	Charges

Documents Submitted
[] Original Freight Bill
[] Original Invoice
[] Bond of Indemnity
[] Letter
[] Other_____

_____
Traffic Manager

8-12 FREIGHT BILL OVERCHARGE CLAIM

Date:

[Inside Address]
....

....

....

RE: Invoice 330765

[Salutation]

Please find enclosed a copy of your invoice being held in our office for freight substantiation. Our records do not indicate receipt of the items we were invoiced for.

As soon as proof of delivery is received, your invoice will be processed and payment mailed according to terms.

Thank you,

Accounts Payable

8-13 SUBSTANTIATION REQUEST

```
                    ASSIGNMENT OF CLAIM


We hereby assign, transfer, and set over to _____
as assignee, all our rights, title, and interest in and to the ship-
ment hereinafter more particularly described, also all rights as to
all claims for loss, damage, or overcharge as to said shipment, and
we hereby jointly and severally agree to hold harmless any and all
carriers against all liability, loss, damage, and injury which may
be occasioned as the result of payment to said assignee in accord-
ance herewith, as said shipment which

consisted of _____shipped by _____

consigned to _____ consignee,

from _____station

State of _____, to _____station

State of _____, the ___day of _____, 19__

car_____ covered by waybill # _____dated_____

        Assignment dated at _____State of _____
This ___day of _____, 19_____

Witness:


_____        _____
                                      (Signature)
```

8-14 ASSIGNMENT OF CLAIM

BOND OF INDEMNITY

In consideration of the settlement by the_____

_____Company (hereinafter called the Railroad) of the

undersigned's claim, No._____for_____ without requiring

                        original bill of lading,
presentation of the original freight bill,   the undersigned hereby

agrees that the Railroad and/or any connecting carrier participating

in the shipment covered thereby, may pay any and all claims which

                        original bill of lading,
shall be made by the holder of the original freight bill,   not in excess

of the sum paid the undersigned by the Railroad; and in case of payment

by the Railroad, or by any connecting carrier participating in said

                        original bill of lading,
shipment, of any claim made by the holder of the original freight bill,

the undersigned agrees to refund to the Railroad the amount paid by it

in settlement of the undersigned's said claim.

IN WITNESS WHEREÒN, the undersigned has signed this instrument

at Spokane, Wash., this_____ day of_____, 19_____

Claim No._____   _____

8-15 BOND OF INDEMNITY

```
                    SHORTAGE CERTIFICATE

                                    DATE_____
                                    CLAIM NO._____
                                    SHIPPER/INVOICE NO._____

THIS IS TO CERTIFY THAT SHORTAGE OF _____
FROM/TO_____AT_____DATE_____
HAS NOT BEEN RECEIVED OR RETURNED FROM ANY SOURCE TO DATE, AND IN THE EVENT
OF FUTURE RETURN OR DELIVERY _____ HEREBY AGREE
TO NOTIFY THE _____OF THIS RECEIPT.  SHOULD
THE SHORTAGE FOR WHICH THE CLAIM IS PAID BE RECEIVED OR RETURNED FROM ANY
SOURCE _____HEREBY AGREE, VOLUNTARILY, TO EITHER
RETURN THE GOODS TO CARRIER OR, IF ACCEPTABLE, TO RETURN THE GOODS TO
_____ OR, RETURN AMOUNT PAID TO THE
_____.


CONSIGNEE/SHIPPER_____
TITLE     _____


WITNESS  _____
TITLE    _____
DATE     _____
```

8-16 SHORTAGE CERTIFICATE

FREIGHT CLAIMS

ATTENTION: ALL PERSONNEL RESPONSIBLE FOR RECEIVING FREIGHT SHIPMENTS

Failure to follow procedures outlined below indicates a shipment was accepted in good condition and allows no recourse for recovering loss from damage.

RECEIVING FREIGHT

1. *Immediately* upon delivery, count cartons and examine carefully for *exterior* damage.
2. Note any shortage and/or *exterior* damage on the freight bill you sign, and have the driver note it on your copy.
3. Keep your copy of the freight bill.
4. Open all cartons *at once,* and check contents for *concealed* shortages or damage.
5. Note any *concealed* shortage and/or damage on your copy of the freight bill.

REPORTING SHORTAGE OR DAMAGE

6. Notify your buyer in the PURCHASING DEPARTMENT *within 36 hours* so he can arrange for the carrier to inspect the damaged merchandise. If he is away ask for his assistant. (Failure to comply with this requirement may result in voiding the claim.)

CLAIM PROCEDURE

7. Pending inspection, store damaged items, cartons and packing *at the receiving point.*
8. Show the inspector damaged items with cartons and packing and the freight bill. Be sure to keep your copy of the freight bill.
9. Read the inspector's report carefully before signing it. Make certain it requests replacement, *unless* repairs will be completely satisfactory *or* your department agrees to keep the merchandise and accept the damage allowance offered. A new item cannot be ordered from the supplier unless the inspector's report specifies "REPLACE."
10. Immediately forward your copy of the inspection report, along with the freight bill, to: Purchasing Department, 3917 University Way N.E., attention of your buyer.
11. Do not use the damaged merchandise unless you have been given *written* permission by the inspector.
12. Do not surrender the damaged merchandise to the carrier or his agent without obtaining a written receipt, which should then be forwarded to your buyer in the Purchasing Department.
13. Do not return the damaged merchandise to the supplier without a *Return Goods Memorandum* from the Purchasing Department.

PURCHASING DEPARTMENT
3917 University Way N.E.

8-17 SAMPLE CLAIM PROCEDURE

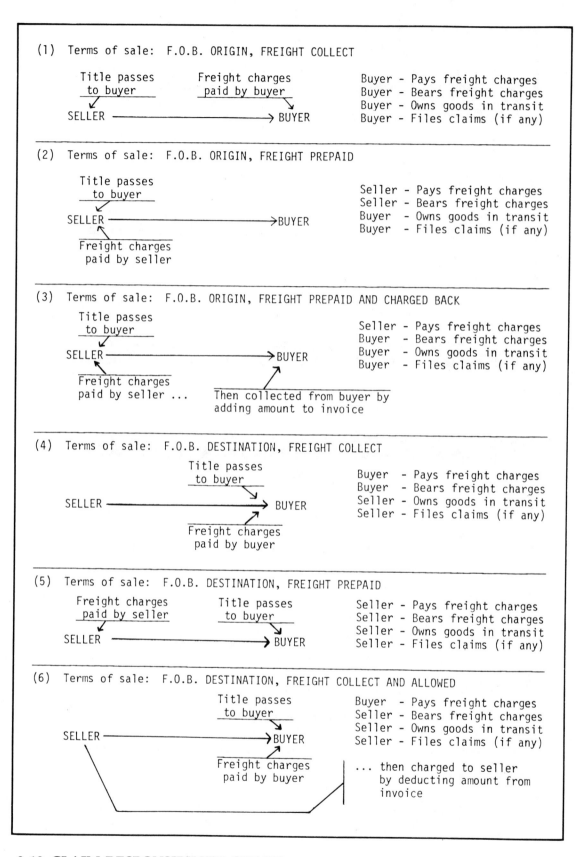

(1) Terms of sale: F.O.B. ORIGIN, FREIGHT COLLECT

Title passes   Freight charges   Buyer - Pays freight charges
  to buyer   paid by buyer   Buyer - Bears freight charges
                                                 Buyer - Owns goods in transit
SELLER ──────────────────────────→ BUYER   Buyer - Files claims (if any)

(2) Terms of sale: F.O.B. ORIGIN, FREIGHT PREPAID

Title passes   Seller - Pays freight charges
  to buyer   Seller - Bears freight charges
                                                 Buyer - Owns goods in transit
SELLER ──────────────────────────→ BUYER   Buyer - Files claims (if any)

Freight charges
paid by seller

(3) Terms of sale: F.O.B. ORIGIN, FREIGHT PREPAID AND CHARGED BACK

Title passes   Seller - Pays freight charges
  to buyer   Buyer - Bears freight charges
                                                 Buyer - Owns goods in transit
SELLER ──────────────────────────→ BUYER   Buyer - Files claims (if any)

Freight charges
paid by seller ...   Then collected from buyer by
                        adding amount to invoice

(4) Terms of sale: F.O.B. DESTINATION, FREIGHT COLLECT

                   Title passes   Buyer - Pays freight charges
                     to buyer   Buyer - Bears freight charges
                                                 Seller - Owns goods in transit
SELLER ──────────────────────────→ BUYER   Seller - Files claims (if any)

                   Freight charges
                   paid by buyer

(5) Terms of sale: F.O.B. DESTINATION, FREIGHT PREPAID

Freight charges   Title passes   Seller - Pays freight charges
  paid by seller   to buyer   Seller - Bears freight charges
                                                 Seller - Owns goods in transit
SELLER ──────────────────────────→ BUYER   Seller - Files claims (if any)

(6) Terms of sale: F.O.B. DESTINATION, FREIGHT COLLECT AND ALLOWED

                   Title passes   Buyer - Pays freight charges
                     to buyer   Seller - Bears freight charges
                                                 Seller - Owns goods in transit
SELLER ──────────────────────────→ BUYER   Seller - Files claims (if any)

                   Freight charges
                   paid by buyer   ... then charged to seller
                                                by deducting amount from
                                                invoice

8-18 CLAIM RESPONSIBILITY CHART

CHECKLIST FOR FILING
DOMESTIC INDEMNITY CLAIMS

TYPE OF MAIL / ACTION	INSURED	COD	REGISTERED	EXPRESS MAIL	EXPRESS MAIL COD
Complete Form 565			✔		
Complete Form 3812	✔	✔			
Complete Form 5690				✔	✔
File Immediately if Damage or Partial Loss	✔	✔	✔	✔	✔
File after 7 days				✔	
File after 15 days			✔		
File after 30 Days (45 if sent SAM or PAL) (75 Days if sent surface to an APO, FPO, or outside our 48 states)	✔				
File after 45 days		✔			✔
File Within 90 Days From Date Article Was Mailed				✔	✔
File Within 1 Year From Date Article Was Mailed	✔	✔	✔		
File at Any Post Office	✔	✔	✔	✔*	✔*
If Complete Loss, Only Sender May File		✔	✔	✔	✔
If Claim is for Damage or Partial Loss, Either Sender or Addressee May File	✔	✔	✔	✔	✔
Submit Original Mailing Receipt	✔	✔	✔	✔	✔
Submit Evidence of Value	✔	✔	✔	✔	✔
Submit Proof of Loss	✔		✔		
Submit Article, Container, Wrapper, and Packaging, if Damage or Partial Loss	✔	✔	✔	✔	✔

✱ *If for the complete loss of Express Mail, the claim must be filed at the post office where the article was mailed.*

8-19 CHECKLIST FOR FILING USPS CLAIMS

Chapter Nine

SAFETY AND HAZARDOUS MATERIALS

The 1990s will see not only tremendous changes in industrial safety and environmental concerns, but also strict enforcement of their rules and regulations. As the Occupational Safety and Health Administration (OSHA) is becoming much more active again, so are environmental agencies, to ensure that safety and health requirements are being met by industry. Because workplace safety is the responsibility of the employer, that responsibility is assumed by management at various levels within an organization—including warehouse and distribution managers.

This chapter covers OSHA's recordkeeping guidelines for occupational injuries and illnesses, the handling of hazardous materials, and samples of local government forms required for storing toxic or hazardous chemicals. Also included are forms and reports that are imperative for creating and maintaining a safer work environment.

OCCUPATIONAL SAFETY AND HEALTH ADMINISTRATION

The Occupational Safety and Health Act of 1970 requires employers to prepare and maintain records of occupational injuries and illnesses. The OSH Act and recordkeeping regulations in Part 1904 of Title 29, Code of Federal Regulations, constitute the framework of OSHA's recordkeeping requirements. Although very detailed, OSHA's recordkeeping is not complicated and only two forms must be maintained.

9-1. LOG AND SUMMARY OF OCCUPATIONAL INJURIES AND ILLNESSES—OSHA NO. 200

The log portion of this form is used for recording and classifying recordable occupational injuries and illnesses and for noting the extent and outcome of each case. The summary portion of the form is used to summarize injuries and illnesses in an organization for the previous calendar year. The organization must keep this form for five years. On the back of the Log and Summary of Occupational Injuries and Illnesses are detailed instructions to each section. Also included in the instructions are definitions of the terms used.

Key Information

- Recordable Cases (e.g., information on all occupational deaths, nonfatal occupational illnesses, and OSHA-defined nonfatal occupational injuries—see side 2 of form for details)
- Case or File Number
- Date of Each Injury or Illness
- Employee Information (e.g., name, occupation, department)
- Description of Injury or Illness
- Company Information
- Extent of and Outcome of Injury
- Type, Extent of, and Outcome of Illness
- Total Number of Each Type of Injury and Illness

9-2. SUPPLEMENTARY RECORD OF OCCUPATIONAL
INJURIES AND ILLNESSES

To supplement the Log and Summary of Occupational Injuries and Illnesses, an organization must maintain a record of each recordable occupational injury or illness. The record must be maintained for a period of at least five years.

Key Information

- Employer Information (see lines 1–3 on sample form)
- Injured or Ill Employee Information (see lines 4–9 on sample form)
- Information Regarding the Accident or Exposure to Occupational Illness Information (see lines 10–13 on sample form)
- Description of Accident or Illness (see lines 14–17)
- Physical/Hospital Information (see lines 18–19)

9-3. GUIDE TO RECORDABILITY OF CASES UNDER THE OCCUPATIONAL
SAFETY AND HEALTH ACT

This chart shows the methodology used and outlines the procedure employers should apply in deciding whether or not to record a particular case.

9-4. GUIDELINES FOR ESTABLISHING WORK RELATIONSHIP FOR OCCUPATIONAL INJURY OR ILLNESS

When an employee is on the employer's premises, a work relationship is presumed. However, when an employee is off the employer's premises, a work relationship must be established. This chart provides a guide for establishing the work relationship of cases of employee injury or illness.

9-5. OCCUPATIONAL ILLNESS OR INJURY REPORT—ANALYSIS

This four-page report is a comprehensive analysis of an occupational illness or injury. It is an excellent tool for compiling and maintaining data on accidents and illnesses and for developing safety plans for future prevention.

Key Information

- Identifying Information On Employer and On the Injured or Ill Employee
- Time and Place of Injury or Illness
- Description of Accident or Exposure
- Medical Attention Given
- Cause of Accident or Illness (see Part 2)
- Future Prevention
- Cost Data (see Part 3)
- Insurance Information (see Part 4)
- Disciplinary Action

9-6. WORKERS' COMPENSATION BOARD FORM C-2—EMPLOYER'S REPORT OF INJURY

This form is used by employers who believe that the employee will lose more than seven days from work, or where the injury results in death or is likely to produce a permanent disability. (This form is used in New York State.)

Key Information

- Workers' Compensation Board (WCB) Case Numbers (if known)
- Employee's Social Security Number
- Employer Information
- Employee Information
- Nature of Injury or Occupational Disease (lines 17–22 on form)
- Fatal Cases (line 23)
- Cause of Accident or Occupational Disease (lines 24–27 on form)

9-7. WORKER'S COMPENSATION BOARD FORM C-2.5—EMPLOYER'S REPORT OF INJURY

This form is used to report only those injuries where there is no lost time from work, but where medical attention is required or when the employer believes there will be no more than seven days of lost time.

Key Information

- Case Numbers (if known)
- Employer Information
- Employee Information
- Accident Information (lines 4–7 on form)
- Nature of Injury or Occupational Disease (lines 11–15 on form)

9-8. WORK INJURY REPORT

This form is used to report as much information as possible concerning a work-related injury. Included in this report is the supervisor's investigation of the accident and corrective action for prevention.

Key Information

- Employee Information
- Description of Injury
- Supervisor's Accident Investigation Report
- Corrective Action Taken

9-9. FIRST AID REPORT

This form is used to report a minor injury, such as a small cut or bruise and the first aid treatment that was administered.

Key Information

- Employee Information
- Nature of Occurrence of Accident or Injury
- Description of Accident or Injury
- Action Taken

9-10. MONTHLY REPORT ON INJURIES AND ACCIDENTS BY DEPARTMENT

This form allows management to review the total number of injuries and accidents for each month and to check for recurring incidents.

Key Information

- Total Accidents or Injuries, by Department
- Total Labor Hours Lost
- Type of Injury or Accident

9-11. ANNUAL SUMMARY OF ACCIDENTS AND INJURIES BY TYPE AND DEPARTMENT

The form shown gives a summary of accidents and injuries for the year and breaks it down by type and department. When recurring incidents happen in the same department, a hazard investigation should be initiated.

Key Information

- Department
- Type of Injury or Accident
- Totals of Each Type of Injury or Accident

9-12. AUTHORIZATION TO RELEASE EMPLOYEE MEDICAL RECORD INFORMATION TO A DESIGNATED REPRESENTATIVE

This letter is used by an employee who is requesting his or her company medical information be released to a doctor, another company, and so on. An employee can request all or part of this transcript to be forwarded.

Key Information

- Name of the Individual or Organization to Receive
- Medical Information
- Description of Information to Be Released
- Restrictions Regarding Release of Information

9-13. NOTICE OF UNSAFE CONDITION REPORTED

The memo shown is from a warehouse manager to the shipping supervisor. It states that an unsafe condition has been reported within the supervisor's area of responsibility.

9-14. NOTICE OF UNSAFE CONDITION OBSERVED

The letter shown is from a warehouse manager to the receiving manager to convey the observation of an unsafe condition in the receiving area.

9-15. JOB SAFETY RECOMMENDATION

The form shown is used to promote job safety awareness. Employees and managers should be encouraged to make recommendations for safer work procedures.

Key Information

- Description of Present Procedure
- Reason for Concern
- Recommendation for Change to Improve Plant Safety
- Supervisor's Comments
- Disposition

9-16. SAFETY MEETING ATTENDANCE RECORD

Taking attendance at a safety meeting confirms the seriousness of the meeting. The form shown is a basic attendance record listing date, subject, and attendants. The completed form should be returned to the person responsible for warehouse safety.

9-17. SAFETY INSPECTION CHECKLIST

This form lists all areas in a warehouse/distribution plant that should be checked for safety. The list serves only as a reminder, so personnel should be alert to observe other unsafe conditions. The back of this form is used for comments or recommendations.

9-18. LOADING DOCK SAFETY CHECKLIST

The loading dock is potentially one of the most likely places where a serious accident can occur. Material handling equipment, trailers, conveyors, and congestion all lead to hazardous conditions. This checklist can help ensure that the dock area is safely maintained and that hazardous conditions are corrected.

Key Information

- Vehicles/Traffic Control Safety (e.g., use of sale equipment, proper training)
- Vehicle Restraining (e.g., safe use and maintenance of restraints)
- Dock Levelers (e.g., adequate dock dimensions and safety features)
- Portable Dock Plates (e.g., adequate capacity, regular inspection)
- Dock Doors (e.g., adequate maintenance)
- Traffic Doors (e.g., sufficient visibility and lighting)
- Weather Sealing (e.g., safety of design)
- Trailer Lifting (e.g., adequate stability for safe operation)
- Other Considerations (e.g., dock lights, scissor lifts, conveyors)

OSHA'S HAZARD COMMUNICATION STANDARD

In 1980, the Occupational Safety and Health Administration issued a standard requiring employers to provide employees with information concerning hazardous chemicals. The Hazard Communication Standard (HCS) is designed so that employers who use chemicals, rather than produce or import them, are not required to evaluate the hazards of those chemicals. Hazard determination is the responsibility of the producers and importers of the materials. Producers and importers of chemicals are then required to provide the hazard information to employers that purchase their products.

9-19. MATERIAL SAFETY DATA SHEET

Material Safety Data Sheets (MSDS) are required to provide detailed information on each hazardous chemical, including its physical and chemical characteristics, and on appropriate safety measures. Chemical manufacturers and importers are required to obtain or develop an MSDS for each hazardous chemical they produce or import and to supply the purchaser with a copy. MSDSs must be readily accessible to employees during their contact with the chemical. There is no specified format for the MSDS, although there are specific information requirements. The form shown was developed by OSHA (OSHA Form 174) and may be used by chemical manufacturers and importers to comply with the rule.

Key Information

- Manufacturers Information (See Section I.)
- Emergency Phone Number (See Section I. This information is needed to provide additional assistance in case of an injury or illness due to chemical handling.)
- Hazardous Ingredients/Identity Information [See Section II. This information should identify all hazardous components and the chemical identity, the permissible exposure limit (OSHA PEL), and the total lung capacity (ACGIH TLV).]
- Physical/Chemical Characteristics (See Section III.)
- Fire and Explosion Hazard Data (See Section IV.)
- Reactivity Data (See Section V.)
- Health Hazard Data (See Section VI.)
- Precautions for Safe Handling and Use (See Section VII.)
- Control Measures (See Section VIII.)

9-20. HAZARDOUS SUBSTANCE INFORMATION FORM

This two-page form is used to give as much information as possible about a hazardous substance, including description of the hazard, recommended protection, and site control. Copies should be readily accessible in all areas where the hazardous substance is handled and stored.

Key Information

- Physical/Chemical Properties (See Section I of form.)
- Hazardous Characteristics (See Section II.)
- Recommended Protection (See Section IV.)
- Recommended Site Control (See Section V.)

9-21. EMPLOYEE INFORMATION REQUEST FORM

In compliance with OSHA's Hazard Communication Standard, an employee has the right to all information concerning the hazardous substance he or she is in contact with. The form shown is used to expedite a request by an employee.

Key Information

- Employee Information
- Description of Toxic/Hazardous Substance
- Description of Employee's Contact with Substance

9-22. HAZARD INVESTIGATION REPORT

The form shown is used in response to a request by an employee or management to investigate a potential work hazard. The main result is to determine if a hazardous condition exists.

Key Information

- Type of Hazard
- How Accident Could Happen
- Results of Possible Accident or Injury
- Investigator's Comments

9-23. HAZARDOUS WASTE MANIFEST

The transportation of hazardous waste has controls at two levels, federal and state. Certain states require additional information not required under federal law. Shippers, transporters, and receivers of hazardous waste should consult with the state in which the hazardous waste is being transported to or from for guidelines. The form shown is required for the state of New York. It has eight parts; the disposer; the generator; and the treatment, storage, or disposal facility (TSD) each mails copies to their state.

Key Information

- Generator's U.S. EPA number (line 1 on form)
- Generator's Information (name, address, phone number)

- State's Additional Information (items A–K on form)
- Description of Hazardous Waste (items 11–14)
- Special Handling Instructions (line 15)
- Transporter's Information (lines 17–18)
- TSD Facility Information (lines 19–20)

9-24. HAZARDOUS MATERIALS WARNING LABELS

When shipping hazardous materials, all packages must be properly marked with warning labels. The chart shown illustrates the appropriate label for different materials.

Key Information

- General Guidelines on the Use of Warning Labels
- UN (United Nations) Class Numbers
- Examples of Domestic and International Labels

9-25. HAZARDOUS MATERIALS WARNING PLACARDS

Motor vehicles, freight containers, and rail cars carrying hazardous materials are required to display warning placards, depending on the class of hazardous materials they are carrying. The chart shown illustrates warning placards and matches them up with their hazard class.

Key Information

- Guidelines on Which Placard to Use for Different Transportation Methods and Different Hazardous Materials
- Hazard Classes (e.g., explosives, poisons)
- International Placarding
- UN (United Nations) and NA (North American) Identification Numbers

9-26. APPLICATION FOR PERMIT TO CONSTRUCT TOXIC/HAZARDOUS MATERIALS STORAGE FACILITY

Before a company can build a toxic/hazardous materials storage facility, a permit to construct is required by their local town or county. To apply for a permit, detailed plans and reports of the project must be provided with the application.

Key Information

- Description/Reason for Permit
- Property Location

- Facility Information
- Contact Person
- Description of Project

9-27. TOXIC LIQUID STORAGE REGISTRATION FORM

For a company to store toxic liquids, it must register with its local county government. Local government requirements vary and should be checked into before planning storage. The form shown is used by a county department of health services to register toxic liquid storage.

Key Information

- Facility/Tank Owner Information
- Tank Number (code chart on form)
- Location
- Cathodic Protection Designation
- Dispenser and Fill Characteristics

9-28. APPLICATION FOR UNDERGROUND FLAMMABLE/COMBUSTIBLE LIQUID TANK

The form shown is an application to obtain a permit for underground storage of flammable/combustible liquids.

Key Information

- Facility Name and Address
- Tank Information (e.g., name of tank manufacturer, type of tank construction material)
- Type of Leak Detection Device
- Source of Water Supply
- Method of Disposal of Flammable/Combustible Liquid

9-29. EMERGENCY RESPONSE OPERATIONS CHART

This chart demonstrates procedures to follow in the event of an accident involving hazardous materials.

9-30. DECISION AID FOR EMERGENCY DECONTAMINATION

This chart demonstrates procedures to follow for decontamination during medical emergencies. When planning for decontamination, procedures should be developed for decontaminating the victim, protecting medical personnel, and disposing of contaminated protective equipment and wash solutions.

9-31. DECISION AID FOR EVALUATING HEALTH AND SAFETY ASPECTS OF DECONTAMINATION METHODS

The chart shown provides questions to consider when deciding on the best decontamination method to use. Decontamination procedures must provide an organized process by which levels of contamination are reduced.

9-32. FLOWCHART FOR HANDLING STORAGE CONTAINERS FOR HAZARDOUS MATERIALS

The chart shown details the proper handling of storage containers for chemicals or hazardous materials. Dashed boxes indicate optional steps.

9-33. PERSONNEL ORGANIZATION FOR INVESTIGATION OF HAZARDOUS WASTE SITE

This chart gives an example of an organizational framework for a hazardous waste site response team. The on-site categories are divided into personnel that are essential for a safe and efficient response. Also listed are optional personnel, who may be included, depending on the size of the operation.

Bureau of Labor Statistics
Log and Summary of Occupational
Injuries and Illnesses

U.S. Department of Labor

NOTE: This form is required by Public Law 91-596 and must be kept in the establishment for 5 years. Failure to maintain and post can result in the issuance of citations and assessment of penalties. *(See posting requirements on the other side of form.)*

RECORDABLE CASES: You are required to record information about every occupational death, every nonfatal occupational illness, and those nonfatal occupational injuries which involve one or more of the following: loss of consciousness, restriction of work or motion, transfer to another job, or medical treatment (other than first aid). *(See definitions on the other side of form.)*

Company Name

Establishment Name

Establishment Address

For Calendar Year 19____

Page ____ of ____

Form Approved
O.M.B. No. 1220-0029
See OMB Disclosure
Statement on reverse

Case or File Number	Date of Injury or Onset of Illness	Employee's Name	Occupation	Department	Description of Injury or Illness
(A)	(B)	(C)	(D)	(E)	(F)

Extent of and Outcome of INJURY

Fatalities	Nonfatal Injuries			
Injury Related	Injuries With Lost Workdays			Injuries Without Lost Workdays
Enter DATE of death. Mo./day/yr. (1)	Enter a CHECK if injury involves days away from work, or days of restricted work activity, or both. (2)	Enter number of DAYS away from work. (3)	Enter number of DAYS of restricted work activity. (4) (5)	Enter a CHECK if no entry was made in columns 1 or 2 but the injury is recordable as defined above. (6)

Type, Extent of, and Outcome of ILLNESS

Type of Illness							Fatalities	Nonfatal Illness				
CHECK Only One Column for Each Illness *(See other side of form for terminations or permanent transfers.)*							Illness Related	Illnesses With Lost Workdays				Illnesses Without Lost Workdays
Occupational skin diseases or disorders (a)	Dust diseases of the lungs (b)	Respiratory conditions due to toxic agents (c)	Poisoning (systemic effects of toxic materials) (d)	Disorders due to physical agents (e)	Disorders associated with repeated trauma (f)	All other occupational illnesses (g)	Enter DATE of death. Mo./day/yr. (8)	Enter a CHECK if illness involves days away from work, or days of restricted work activity, or both. (9)	Enter number of DAYS away from work. (10)	Enter number of DAYS of restricted work activity. (11) (12)		Enter a CHECK if no entry was made in columns 8 or 9. (13)

PREVIOUS PAGE TOTALS

TOTALS (Instructions on other side of form)

Certification of Annual Summary Totals By _____ Title _____ Date _____

OSHA No. 200

POST ONLY THIS PORTION OF THE LAST PAGE NO LATER THAN FEBRUARY 1.

9-1 LOG AND SUMMARY OF OCCUPATIONAL INJURIES AND ILLNESSES—OSHA NO. 200

We estimate that it will take from 4 minutes to 30 minutes to complete a line entry on this form, including time for reviewing instructions; searching, gathering and maintaining the data needed; and completing and reviewing the entry. If you have any comments regarding this estimate or any other aspect of this recordkeeping system, send them to the Bureau of Labor Statistics, Division of Management Systems (1220-0029), Washington, D.C. 20212 and to the Office of Management and Budget, Paperwork Reduction Project (1220-0029), Washington, D.C. 20503.

Instructions for OSHA No. 200

I. Log and Summary of Occupational Injuries and Illnesses

Each employer who is subject to the recordkeeping requirements of the Occupational Safety and Health Act of 1970 must maintain for each establishment a log of all recordable occupational injuries and illnesses. This form (OSHA No. 200) may be used for that purpose. A substitute for the OSHA No. 200 is acceptable if it is as detailed, easily readable, and understandable as the OSHA No. 200.

Enter each recordable case on the log within six (6) workdays after learning of its occurrence. Although other records must be maintained at the establishment to which they refer, it is possible to prepare and maintain the log at another location, using data processing equipment if desired. If the log is prepared elsewhere, a copy updated to within 45 calendar days must be present at all times in the establishment.

Logs must be maintained and retained for five (5) years following the end of the calendar year to which they relate. Logs must be available (normally at the establishment) for inspection and copying by representatives of the Department of Labor, or the Department of Health and Human Services, or States accorded jurisdiction under the Act. Access to the log is also provided to employees, former employees, and their representatives.

II. Changes in Extent of or Outcome of Injury or Illness

If, during the 5-year period the log must be retained, there is a change in an extent and outcome of an injury or illness which affects entries in columns 1, 2, 6, 8, 9, or 13, the first entry should be lined out and a new entry made. For example, if an injured employee at first required only medical treatment but later lost workdays away from work, the check in column 6 should be lined out, and checks entered in columns 2 and 3 and the number of lost workdays entered in column 4.

In another example, if an employee with an occupational illness lost workdays, returned to work, and then died of the illness, any entries in columns 9 through 12 should be lined out and the date of death entered in column 8.

The entire entry for an injury or illness should be lined out if later found to be nonrecordable. For example, an injury which was initially thought to involve medical treatment but later was determined to have involved only first aid.

III. Posting Requirements

A copy of the totals and information following the fold line of the last page for the year must be posted at each establishment in the place or places where notices to employees are customarily posted. This copy must be posted no later than *February 1 and must remain in place until March 1.*

Even though there were no injuries or illnesses during the year, zeros must be entered on the totals line, and the form posted.

The person responsible for the *annual summary totals* shall certify that the totals are true and complete by signing at the bottom of the form.

IV. Instructions for Completing Log and Summary of Occupational Injuries and Illnesses

Column A – CASE OR FILE NUMBER. Self-explanatory.

Column B – DATE OF INJURY OR ONSET OF ILLNESS.

For occupational injuries, enter the date of the work accident which resulted in injury. For occupational illnesses, enter the date of initial diagnosis of illness, or, if absence from work occurred before diagnosis, enter the first day of the absence attributable to the illness which was later diagnosed or recognized.

Columns C through F – Self-explanatory

Columns 1 and 8 – INJURY OR ILLNESS-RELATED DEATHS. Self-explanatory.

Columns 2 and 9 – INJURIES OR ILLNESSES WITH LOST WORKDAYS. Self-explanatory.

Any injury which involves days away from work, or days of restricted work activity, or both must be recorded since it always involves one or more of the criteria for recordability.

Columns 3 and 10 – INJURIES OR ILLNESSES INVOLVING DAYS AWAY FROM WORK. Self-explanatory.

Columns 4 and 11 – LOST WORKDAYS—DAYS AWAY FROM WORK.

Enter the number of workdays (consecutive or not) on which the employee would have worked but could not because of occupational injury or illness. The number of lost workdays should not include the day of injury or onset of illness or any days on which the employee would not have worked even though able to work.

NOTE: For employees not having a regularly scheduled shift, such as certain truck drivers, construction workers, farm labor, casual labor, part-time employees, etc., it may be necessary to estimate the number of lost workdays. Estimates of lost workdays shall be based on prior work history of the employee AND days worked by employees, not ill or injured, working in the department and/or occupation of the ill or injured employee.

Columns 5 and 12 – LOST WORKDAYS—DAYS OF RESTRICTED WORK ACTIVITY.

Enter the number of workdays (consecutive or not) on which because of injury or illness:
(1) the employee was assigned to another job on a temporary basis, or
(2) the employee worked at a permanent job less than full time, or
(3) the employee worked at a permanently assigned job but could not perform all duties normally connected with it.

The number of lost workdays should not include the day of injury or onset of illness or any days on which the employee would not have worked even though able to work.

Columns 6 and 13 – INJURIES OR ILLNESSES WITHOUT LOST WORKDAYS. Self-explanatory.

Columns 7a through 7g – TYPE OF ILLNESS.

Enter a check in only *one* column for each illness.

TERMINATION OR PERMANENT TRANSFER—Place an asterisk to the right of the entry in columns 7a through 7g (type of illness) which represented a termination of employment or permanent transfer.

V. Totals

Add number of entries in columns 1 and 8.

Add number of checks in columns 2, 3, 6, 7, 9, 10, and 13.

Add number of days in columns 4, 5, 11, and 12.

Yearly totals for each column (1-13) are required for posting. Running or page totals may be generated at the discretion of the employer.

If an employee's loss of workdays is continuing at the time the totals are summarized, estimate the number of future workdays the employee will lose and add that estimate to the workdays already lost and include this figure in the annual totals. No further entries are to be made with respect to such cases in the next year's log.

VI. Definitions

OCCUPATIONAL INJURY is any injury such as a cut, fracture, sprain, amputation, etc., which results from a work accident or from an exposure involving a single incident in the work environment.

NOTE: Conditions resulting from animal bites, such as insect or snake bites or from one-time exposure to chemicals, are considered to be injuries.

OCCUPATIONAL ILLNESS of an employee is any abnormal condition or disorder, other than one resulting from an occupational injury, caused by exposure to environmental factors associated with employment. It includes acute and chronic illnesses or diseases which may be caused by inhalation, absorption, ingestion, or direct contact.

The following listing gives the categories of occupational illnesses and disorders that will be utilized for the purpose of classifying recordable illnesses. For purposes of information, examples of each category are given. These are typical examples, however, and are not to be considered the complete listing of the types of illnesses and disorders that are to be counted under each category.

7a   Occupational Skin Diseases or Disorders
Examples: Contact dermatitis, eczema, or rash caused by primary irritants and sensitizers or poisonous plants, oil acne, chrome ulcers, chemical burns or inflammations, etc.

7b   Dust Diseases of the Lungs (Pneumoconioses)
Examples: Silicosis, asbestosis and other asbestos-related diseases, coal worker's pneumoconiosis, byssinosis, siderosis, and other pneumoconioses.

7c   Respiratory Conditions Due to Toxic Agents
Examples: Pneumonitis, pharyngitis, rhinitis or acute congestion due to chemicals, dusts, gases, or fumes; farmer's lung; etc.

7d   Poisoning (Systemic Effect of Toxic Materials)
Examples: Poisoning by lead, mercury, cadmium, arsenic, or other metals, poisoning by carbon monoxide, hydrogen sulfide, or other gases; poisoning by benzol, carbon tetrachloride, or other organic solvents; poisoning by insecticide sprays such as parathion, lead arsenate; poisoning by other chemicals such as formaldehyde, plastics, and resins, etc.

7e   Disorders Due to Physical Agents (Other than Toxic Materials)
Examples: Heatstroke, sunstroke, heat exhaustion, and other effects of environmental heat; freezing, frostbite, and effects of exposure to low temperatures; caisson disease; effects of ionizing radiation (isotopes, X-rays, radium); effects of nonionizing radiation (welding flash, ultraviolet rays, microwaves, sunburn); etc.

7f   Disorders Associated With Repeated Trauma
Examples: Noise-induced hearing loss, synovitis, tendovinitis, an bursitis, Raynaud's phenomena, and other conditions due to repeated motion, vibration, or pressure.

7g   All Other Occupational Illnesses
Examples: Anthrax, brucellosis, infectious hepatitis, malignant and benign tumors, food poisoning, histoplasmosis, coccidioidomycosis, etc.

MEDICAL TREATMENT includes treatment (other than first aid) administered by a physician or by registered professional personnel under the standing orders of a physician. Medical treatment does NOT include first-aid treatment (one-time treatment and subsequent observation of minor scratches, cuts, burns, splinters, and so forth, which do not ordinarily require medical care) even though provided by a physician or registered professional personnel.

ESTABLISHMENT. A single physical location where business is conducted or where services or industrial operations are performed (for example, a factory, mill, store, hotel, restaurant, movie theater, farm, ranch, bank, sales office, warehouse, or central administrative office). Where distinctly separate activities are performed at a single physical location, such as construction activities operated from the same physical location as a lumber yard, each activity shall be treated as a separate establishment.

For firms engaged in activities which may be physically dispersed, such as agriculture, construction, transportation, communications, and electric, gas, and sanitary services, records may be maintained at a place to which employees report each day.

Records for personnel who do not primarily report of work at a single establishment, such as traveling salesmen, technicians, engineers, etc., shall be maintained at the location from which they are paid or the base from which personnel operate to carry out their activities.

WORK ENVIRONMENT is comprised of the physical location, equipment, materials processed or used and the kinds of operations performed in the course of an employee's work, whether on or off the employer's premises.

9-1 (Continued)

Bureau of Labor Statistics
Supplementary Record of
Occupational Injuries and Illnesses

U.S. Department of Labor

This form is required by Public Law 91-596 and must be kept in the establishment for *5 years.* Failure to maintain can result in the issuance of citations and assessment of penalties.	Case or File No.	Form Approved O.M.B. No. 1220-0029

Employer

1. Name

See OMB Disclosure Statement on reverse.

2. Mail address *(No. and street, city or town, State, and zip code)*

3. Location, if different from mail address

Injured or Ill Employee

4. Name *(First, middle, and last)* — Social Security No.

5. Home address *(No. and street, city or town, State, and zip code)*

6. Age

7. Sex: *(Check one)*   Male ☐   Female ☐

8. Occupation *(Enter regular job title, not the specific activity he was performing at time of injury.)*

9. Department *(Enter name of department or division in which the injured person is regularly employed, even though he may have been temporarily working in another department at the time of injury.)*

The Accident or Exposure to Occupational Illness

If accident or exposure occurred on employer's premises, give address of plant or establishment in which it occurred. Do not indicate department or division within the plant or establishment. If accident occurred outside employer's premises at an identifiable address, give that address. If it occurred on a public highway or at any other place which cannot be identified by number and street, please provide place references locating the place of injury as accurately as possible.

10. Place of accident or exposure *(No. and street, city or town, State, and zip code)*

11. Was place of accident or exposure on employer's premises?   Yes ☐   No ☐

12. What was the employee doing when injured? *(Be specific. If he was using tools or equipment or handling material, name them and tell what he was doing with them.)*

13. How did the accident occur? *(Describe fully the events which resulted in the injury or occupational illness. Tell what happened and how it happened. Name any objects or substances involved and tell how they were involved. Give full details on all factors which led or contributed to the accident. Use separate sheet for additional space.)*

Occupational Injury or Occupational Illness

14. Describe the injury or illness in detail and indicate the part of body affected. *(E.g., amputation of right index finger at second joint; fracture of ribs; lead poisoning; dermatitis of left hand, etc.)*

15. Name the object or substance which directly injured the employee. *(For example, the machine or thing he struck against or which struck him; the vapor or poison he inhaled or swallowed; the chemical or radiation which irriatated his skin; or in cases of strains, hernias, etc., the thing he was lifting, pulling, etc.)*

16. Date of injury or initial diagnosis of occupational illness

17. Did employee die? *(Check one)*   Yes ☐   No ☐

Other

18. Name and address of physician

19. If hospitalized, name and address of hospital

Date of report	Prepared by	Official position

9-2 SUPPLEMENTARY RECORD OF OCCUPATIONAL INJURIES AND ILLNESSES

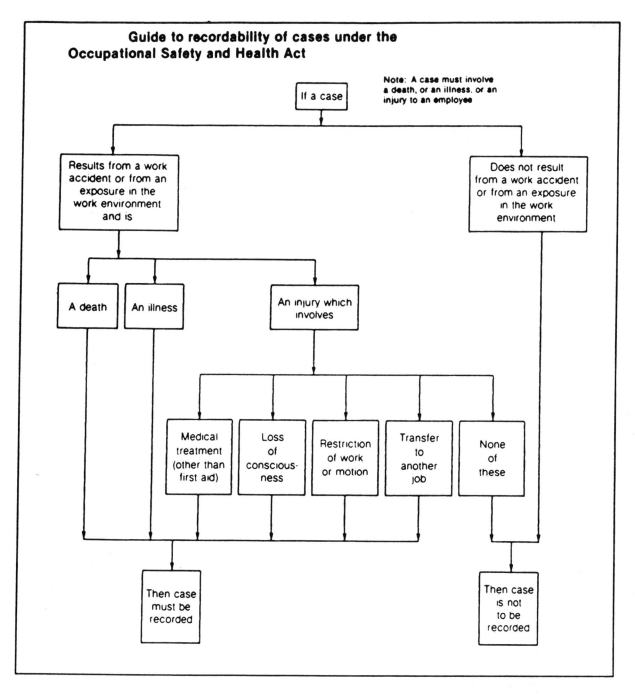

9-3 GUIDE TO RECORDABILITY OF CASES UNDER THE OCCUPATIONAL SAFETY AND HEALTH ACT

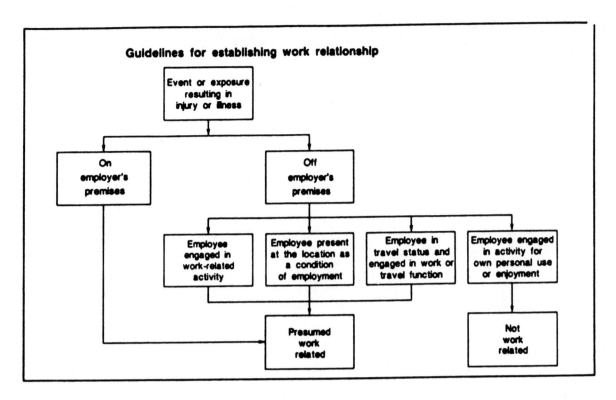

9-4 GUIDELINES FOR ESTABLISHING WORK RELATIONSHIP FOR OCCUPATIONAL INJURY OR ILLNESS

OCCUPATIONAL ILLNESS OR INJURY REPORT-ANALYSIS
Part 1—The Facts

IMPORTANT—FILL OUT PART 1 IMMEDIATELY WHILE ALL DETAILS ARE FRESH AND READILY OBTAINABLE

EMPLOYER

Name	Mail Address	Case or File No.

Location if different from mail address

INJURED OR ILL PERSON

Name	Job Title	Soc. Sec. No.
Home Address	Department	Payroll/Clock No.
Home Phone	Sex ☐ Male ☐ Female	Age

TIME AND PLACE OF INJURY OR ILLNESS

Date of Accident	Time	a.m. p.m.	Place of Accident or Exposure	
Date of initial diagnosis				Employer's Premises ☐ Yes ☐ No
Nature of illness			Part of body affected	Did Employee die? ☐ Yes ☐ No

Indoors

Type and quality of lighting

Type of Flooring: ☐ Concrete ☐ Carpet ☐ Tile ☐ Wood ☐ _____

Condition of floor: ☐ Dry ☐ Wet ☐ Soapy ☐ Fresh Carpeting ☐ Freshly Waxed ☐ _____

Outdoors

Weather Conditions: ☐ Clear ☐ Rainy ☐ Snow ☐ Sleet ☐ Overcast ☐ _____

Type and Condition of Surface

Other conditions which should be noted

DESCRIPTION

Description of Accident or Exposure
(What was Employee doing? How did accident occur?)

(use blank paper if more space is needed)

Diagram of Accident

(use blank paper if more space is needed)

List tools, machinery, chemicals, etc. involved in this injury or illness

Nature of the accident

☐ Fell ☐ Struck by _____
☐ Tripped ☐ Shock
☐ Slipped ☐ Burn
☐ Caught in or between _____

Witnesses:

ACTION TAKEN

Medical Attention Given

☐ Insured was examined by Dr. _____ at _____ am/pm.
☐ on company premises
☐ in Doctor's office
☐ _____

Doctor's full name and address
_____
_____
_____
Phone: _____

☐ Insured was taken to _____ Hospital at _____ am/pm.
☐ by private car
☐ by ambulance
☐ _____

Hospital Address
_____
_____
_____
Was ☐ Released ☐ Admitted

Miscellaneous

☐ First Aid was given by _____
(address) _____
_____

☐ Family was notified by _____
☐ _____
☐ _____
☐ _____

Part 1—The Facts   Prepared by _____ Title _____ Date _____

9-5 OCCUPATIONAL ILLNESS OR INJURY REPORT—ANALYSIS

	WHAT CAUSED THE ACCIDENT OR ILLNESS?	HOW CAN IT BE PREVENTED IN THE FUTURE?
WORKER	☐ Carelessness ☐ Not Alert ☐ Poor Training or Instructions ☐ Unsafe Work Procedure ☐ Physically or Mentally Inadequate for Job ☐ Horseplay ☐ _____ ☐ _____ ☐ _____	
WORKING AREA	☐ Equipment Poorly Placed ☐ Housekeeping—Dirty or Cluttered ☐ Not Enough Working Space ☐ Poor Lighting or Ventilation ☐ _____	
MACHINERY INVOLVED	☐ Defective Machine ☐ Machine Guards not in use ☐ Machine Guards Missing ☐ Unsafe Clothing ☐ _____ ☐ _____ ☐ _____ ☐ _____	
MISCELLANEOUS	☐ Work Procedure Unsafe ☐ Material Used Unsafe ☐ _____ ☐ _____ ☐ _____ ☐ _____ ☐ _____	

	ACTION TO BE TAKEN	WHEN BY WHOM
CONCLUSIONS	1. _____ 2. _____ 3. _____ 4. _____ 5. _____ 6. _____	_____ _____ _____ _____ _____ _____

Part 2—Analysis

Prepared by _____ Title _____ Date _____

Reviewed by _____ Title _____ Date _____

9-5 (Continued)

PERSONS INJURED			
Medical Expenses not covered by Insurance		$ _____	
Lost Time Wages Paid to Injured		_____	
Other (Itemize) _____		_____	
_____		_____	
TOTAL "INJURED PERSON" EXPENSES		$ _____	▶ $

LOST TIME		Man / Per	
Supervisory Time	Man ____ hrs. @ $ ____ Per hr.	$ _____	
Workers Watching or Helping	Man ____ hrs. @ $ ____ Per hr.	_____	
Workers who needed the output or assistance of injured	Man ____ hrs. @ $ ____ Per hr.	_____	
Other _____	Man ____ hrs. @ $ ____ Per hr.	_____	
TOTAL "LOST TIME" EXPENSES (NON-INJURED)		$ _____	▶ $

MAKE-UP TIME			
Cost of overtime required to make up lost production	Man ____ hrs. @ $ ____ Per hr.	$ _____	
Straight time cost of extra people hired to make up production	Man ____ hrs. @ $ ____ Per hr.	_____	
Other _____	Man ____ hrs. @ $ ____ Per hr.	_____	
TOTAL "MAKE-UP TIME" EXPENSES		$ _____	▶ $

MISC. NON-LABOR EXPENSES		
Replacement or repair of damaged machinery	_____	
Replacement of Destroyed Materials	_____	
Additional overhead—heat, light, rental of temporary space	_____	
Value of Contract(s) lost due to accident	_____	
Other _____	_____	
_____	_____	
_____	_____	
_____	_____	
TOTAL MISC. "NON-LABOR" EXPENSES	$ _____	▶ $
	GRAND TOTAL	$ _____

Part 3—Cost Data

Prepared by _____ Title _____ Date _____

Reviewed by _____ Title _____ Date _____

9-5 (Continued)

	ACTION REQUIRED	ACTION TAKEN		
		HOW	WHEN	BY WHOM
INSURANCE	☐ 1. Accident reported to Agent/Carrier			
	☐ 2. Required forms completed and forwarded			
	☐ 3. Repair estimates obtained and forwarded			
	☐ 4. Damage examined by Adjustor			
	☐ 5.			
PREVENTIVE MEASURES	☐ 6. Cause determined and corrected			
	☐ 7. Nature of cause communicated to employees			
	☐ 8. The following operation or procedure changes instituted			
	a. _____			
	b. _____			
	c. _____			
	d. _____			
MISCELLANEOUS ACTION	☐ 9. Reported to Personnel Dept. to be noted in employee's file			
	☐ 10. Cost report sent to the accounting department			
	☐ 11. Damaged equipment and facilities replaced or repaired			
	☐			
	☐			
	☐			
	☐			
	☐			

	ACTION TAKEN AGAINST	REASON FOR ACTION	NATURE OF DISCIPLINE	WHEN TAKEN	BY WHOM
DISCIPLINARY ACTION IF INDICATED					

Part 4—Follow-up Check List

Prepared by _____ Title_____ Date _____

Reviewed by _____ Title_____ Date _____

9-5 (Continued)

STATE OF NEW YORK
WORKERS' COMPENSATION BOARD

EMPLOYER'S REPORT OF INJURY

Send this notice directly to Chairman, Workers' Compensation Board at address shown reverse side within ten (10) days after accident occurs. Copy also should be sent to your insurance carrier.

PLEASE PRINT OR TYPE—INCLUDE ZIP CODE IN ALL ADDRESSES—EMPLOYEE'S SS# MUST BE ENTERED BELOW

W.C.B. CASE NO.	CARRIER CASE NO.	CODE NO.	WC. POLICY NUMBER	DATE OF ACCIDENT	EMPLOYEE'S S. S. NO.
		W204002			

(ENTER CASE NUMBERS, IF KNOWN, IN ABOVE SPACES)

	(a) NAME	(b) MAIL ADDRESS	(c) OSHA CASE OR FILE NO.
1. EMPLOYER			

(d) LOCATION (if different from mail address)		(e) E. R. NO.

2. INSURANCE CARRIER	THE STATE INSURANCE FUND	199 Church Street, New York, N.Y. 10007

3. INJURED PERSON	(First Name) (Middle Initial) (Last Name)	(Home Address Give Number and Street, City, State, Zip Code and Apt. No.)

EMPLOYER

4. Nature of business: (State principal products manufactured or sold or services rendered)_____

ACCIDENT

5. Address where accident occurred *(Include county)*_____

6. Date of accident: _____19___, Day of Week _____ Hour of Day _____ A. M. _____ P. M.
   If occupational illness, date of initial diagnosis: _____19_____

7. (a) Date disability began:_____19___, Hour of Day _____ A. M. _____ P. M.
   (b) Was injured paid in full for this day?_____

8. Name of Department (where regularly employed) and foreman_____

9. When did you or foreman first know of injury?_____
10. Names and addresses of witnesses: _____

INJURED PERSON

11. (a) Marital status: _____ (b) Sex _____
12. Age:_____ 13. Did you have on file employment certificate or permit?_____
14. Occupation: (a) Job title for which employed:_____
    (b) Occupation when injured: _____
15. (a) How long employed by you?_____ (b) Piece or time worker?_____
    (c) Hours per day: _____ (d) Days per week: _____
16. Earnings in your employ: (a) Rate per: Hour $_____ Day $_____ Week $_____ Month $_____
    (b) Total earnings paid during year prior to date of accident: (include bonuses paid, value of board, lodging, etc.)
    _____ $_____ Average per week: $_____
    (c) Bonuses or premiums paid and included in item 16(b) above: $_____ (d) Estimated value of board, lodging, or other advantages in addition to wages: (included in item 16(b) above
    $_____
    (e) Calendar weeks in past 52 in same kind of work as at time of injury:_____

17. State nature of injury and part or parts of body affected: (as "Injury to Chest," etc.)_____

NATURE OF INJURY OR OCCUPATIONAL DISEASE

18. Did you provide medical care?_____ If so, when?_____
19. Name and address of doctor:_____
20. Name and address of hospital:_____
21. Probable length of disability:_____
22. (a) Has employee returned to work?_____ (b) If so, give date:_____
    (c) At what occupation?_____ (d) At what weekly wage? $_____

NOTE: Form C-11 must be filed each time there is any change in the employment status as reported in item 22 above.

FATAL CASES

23. Has injured died?_____ (a) If so, give date of death:_____
    (b) Name and address of nearest relative:_____

CAUSE OF ACCIDENT OR OCCUPATIONAL DISEASE

24. (a) What was employee doing when accident occurred? (Describe briefly as "loading truck," "operating press," "shoveling dirt," "painting with spray gun," "walking downstairs," etc.)_____

    (b) Where did accident occur? (Specify whether on the employer's premises, and indicate if in street, factory yard, on loading platform, in factory. etc.)_____

25. How was accident or occupational disease sustained? (Describe fully, stating whether injured person slipped, fell, was struck, etc., and what factors led up to or contributed to accident. Use additional sheets, if necessary.)_____

26. (a) What specific machine, tool, appliance, gas, liquid, or other substance or object was most closely connected with this accident or occupational disease?_____
    (b) If mechanical apparatus or vehicle, what part of it? (State if gears, pulley, motor, etc.)_____

27. Were mechanical guards or other safeguards (such as goggles) provided?_____ (a) Were they in use at time of accident?_____ (b) Was machine, tool, or object defective?_____ If so, in what way?_____

Enter "X" in this box if accident was reported on Form C-2.1	DATE OF THIS REPORT: _____
Enter "X" in this box if accident was previously reported on Form C-2.5	FIRM NAME:_____
	SIGNED BY :_____
	TEL. NO._____ Official Title

C-2 C-2 C-2 C-2 C-2

9-6 WORKER'S COMPENSATION BOARD FORM C-2—EMPLOYER'S REPORT OF INJURY

STATE OF NEW YORK
WORKERS' COMPENSATION BOARD

EMPLOYER'S REPORT OF INJURY

IMPORTANT: This form is not to be used to report accidents causing death, permanent injury, or loss of time in excess of 7 days. Form C-2 should be used to report such accidents.

Send this notice directly to Chairman, Workers' Compensation Board at address shown on reverse side within ten (10) days after accident occurs. Copy also should be sent to your insurance carrier.

PLEASE PRINT OR TYPE – INCLUDE ZIP CODE IN ALL ADDRESSES – EMPLOYEE'S SS# MUST BE ENTERED BELOW ➡

WCB CASE NO.	CARRIER CASE NO.	CODE NO.	WC. POLICY NUMBER	DATE OF ACCIDENT	EMPLOYEE'S S.S. NO.

(ENTER CASE NUMBERS, IF KNOWN, IN ABOVE SPACES)

	(a) NAME	(b) MAIL ADDRESS	(c) OSHA CASE OR FILE NO.
1. EMPLOYER			
(d) LOCATION (if different from mail address)			**(e) E.R. NO.**

2. INSURANCE CARRIER THE STATE INSURANCE FUND | 199 Church Street, New York, N.Y. 10007

3. INJURED PERSON
(First Name)　(Middle Initial)　(Last Name) | (Home Address Give Number and Street, City, State, Zip Code and Apt. No.)

ACCIDENT

4. (a) Address where accident occurred (*Include county*) _____

　(b) Was this employer's premises　　　Yes ☐　　　No ☐

5. Date of accident: _____ 19___ Day of Week _____ Hour of Day _____ A.M. _____ P.M.
　If occupational illness, date of initial diagnosis: _____ 19___ , Hour of Day _____ A.M. _____ P.M.

6. (a) Date disability began: _____ 19___ ,
　(b) Was injured paid in full for this day? _____

7. Brief description of accident: (state also what employee was doing at time of accident; what machine, object, or substance caused the accident or occupational disease; name any tool, equipment, etc., employee was using)

_____
_____
_____
_____
_____

INJURED PERSON

8. Check (X)　☐ Male　☐ Female

9. Age: _____　10. Occupation: _____

NATURE OF INJURY OR OCCUPATIONAL DISEASE

11. State nature of injury and part or parts of body affected: (as "Injury to Chest," etc.) _____
_____

12. Did you provide medical care? _____ If so, when? _____

13. Name and address of doctor: _____

14. Name and address of hospital: _____

15. (a) Has employee returned to work? _____ (b) If so, give date: _____

EMPLOYER

16. Nature of business: (State principal products manufactured or sold or services rendered) _____

17. Department, where regularly employed: _____

FIRM NAME: _____

TEL. NO. _____　SIGNED BY: _____

Official Title

DATE OF THIS REPORT: _____

C-2.5　　C-2.5　　C-2.5　　C-2.5　　C-2.5

9-7 WORKER'S COMPENSATION BOARD FORM C-2.5—EMPLOYER'S REPORT OF INJURY

```
+--------------------------------------------------------------+
|                                                              |
|                   WORK INJURY REPORT                         |
|                                                              |
|  EMPLOYEE NAME _____   DEPARTMENT _____  |
|                                                              |
|  SUPERVISOR _____    ACCIDENT DATE _____    |
|                                                              |
|  TIME OF ACCIDENT _____    DATE REPORTED _____    |
|                                                              |
|  NATURE OF INJURY _____   |
|                                                              |
|  MEDICAL ATTENTION REQUIRED _____YES _____ NO      |
|                                                              |
+==============================================================+
|                                                              |
|  EMPLOYEE'S STATEMENT ON HOW ACCIDENT OCCURRED _____    |
|                                                              |
|  _____  |
|                                                              |
|  _____  |
|                                                              |
|  _____  |
|                                                              |
|  _____        _____      |
|      EMPLOYEE'S SIGNATURE              DATE                   |
|                                                              |
+==============================================================+
|                                                              |
|  SUPERVISOR'S INVESTIGATION/STATEMENT OF ACCIDENT _____    |
|                                                              |
|  _____  |
|                                                              |
|  _____  |
|                                                              |
|  _____  |
|                                                              |
|  CORRECTIVE/DISCIPLINARY ACTION TAKEN TO PREVENT             |
|  REOCCURRENCE _____    |
|                                                              |
|  _____  |
|                                                              |
|  _____  |
|                                                              |
|  _____  |
|                                                              |
|  _____        _____      |
|      SUPERVISOR'S SIGNATURE            DATE                   |
|                                                              |
+--------------------------------------------------------------+
```

9-8 WORK INJURY REPORT

```
          FIRST AID REPORT


NAME_____DATE_____

DEPARTMENT_____TITLE_____

DATE OF
OCCURRENCE_____TIME_____PLACE_____

NATURE OF
OCCURRENCE_____

_____

_____

EMPLOYEE'S DESCRIPTION OF ACCIDENT/INJURY_____

_____

_____

ACTION TAKEN_____

_____

SENT: BACK TO WORK []  HOME []  DOCTOR [] HOSPITAL []


                        _____

                        SIGNATURE OF SUPERVISOR
```

9-9 FIRST AID REPORT

MONTHLY ACCIDENT/INJURY REPORT

LOCATION:_____   DATE:_____

MONTH:_____   YEAR:_____

DEPARTMENT	FIRST AID	MEDICAL	SPRAINS/ FRACTURES
RECEIVING			
SHIPPING			
WAREHOUSE			
PRODUCTION			
ORDER FILLING			
STORES			
MAINTENANCE			
TOTAL LABOR HOURS LOST_____			

9-10 MONTHLY REPORT ON INJURIES AND ACCIDENTS BY DEPARTMENT

ANNUAL SUMMARY OF ACCIDENTS AND INJURIES

YEAR ENDING_____

TYPE OF INJURY/ ACCIDENT	DEPARTMENT			
CUTS/BURNS				
BACK				
FRACTURES				
SPRAINS				
EYE				
RESPIRATORY				
OTHER				
TOTAL				

TOTAL LABOR-HOURS WORKED_____

TOTAL LABOR-HOURS LOSS_____   PERCENTAGE_____%

9-11 ANNUAL SUMMARY OF ACCIDENTS AND INJURIES BY TYPE AND DEPARTMENT

Sample Authorization Letter for the Release of Employee Medical Record Information to a Designated Representative (Nonmandatory)

I, _____, hereby authorize _____
    (full name of worker/patient)   (individual or

_____ to release to
organization holding the medical records)

_____
(individual or organization authorized to receive the medical

_____, the following medical information from my personal
information)

medical records: _____
    (Describe generally the information desired to be released)

_____

_____

I give my permission for this medical information to be used for the following purpose: _____

_____, but I do not give permission for any other use or re-disclosure of this information.

(Note: Several extra lines are provided below so that you can place additional restrictions on this authorization letter if you want to. You may, however, leave these lines blank. On the other hand, you may want to (1) specify a particular expiration date for this letter (if less than 1 year); (2) describe medical information to be created in the future that you intend to be covered by this authorization letter; or (3) describe portions of the medical information in your records that you do not intend to be released as a result of this letter.)

_____

_____

_____

_____

_____

_____
Full name of Employee or Legal Representative

_____
Signature of Employee or Legal Representative

_____
Date of Signature

9-12 AUTHORIZATION TO RELEASE EMPLOYEE MEDICAL RECORD INFORMATION TO A DESIGNATED REPRESENTATIVE

March 3, 1992

To: Shipping Supervisor

From: Warehouse Manager

It has been brought to my attention that_____

_____

_____

_____

This is not in accordance with proper safety procedures. Please look into this matter and take appropriate action to ensure that all safety regulations are being observed and followed.

Please contact me as to the outcome of this situation.

Signed_____

9-13 NOTICE OF UNSAFE CONDITION REPORTED

May 7, 1992

To: Receiving Supervisor

From: Warehouse Manager

Re: Unsafe Condition on Receiving Platform

When I was in the area of ___The receiving platform___

on ___May 6,___ at about _10_ A.M./P.M., I observed

_____forklifts moving at excessive speed and_____

_____failure of drivers to sound their horns_____

_____when entering doorway to holding floor._____

Please:

    [] correct this situation

    [] see me regarding this matter

    [] _____

Signed_____

9-14 NOTICE OF UNSAFE CONDITION OBSERVED

JOB SAFETY RECOMMENDATION

Date............, 19........ Department..................

Recommendation Made By...................................

PRESENT PROCEDURE/AREA:	REASON FOR SAFETY CONCERN:
_____	_____
_____	_____
_____	_____

RECOMMENDATED MODIFICATION(S):

_____

_____

_____

_____

SUPERVISOR'S RECOMMENDATION AND COMMENTS:

[] APPROVE   [] DISAPPROVE

_____

_____

_____

DISPOSITION: [] Approved, effective....................

[] Disapproved, because..................

....

_____   _____

SIGNATURE OF PLANT MANAGER/SAFETY DIRECTOR   DATE

9-15 JOB SAFETY RECOMMENDATION

SAFETY MEETING ATTENDANCE RECORD

MEETING DATE:_____   LOCATION:_____

MEETING SUBJECT:_____

NAME	NAME

DEPARTMENT	AREA SUPERVISOR

NOTE: UPON COMPLETION, THIS FORM TO BE RETURNED
         TO SAFETY DIRECTOR FOR FILING.

9-16 SAFETY MEETING ATTENDANCE RECORD

SAFETY INSPECTION CHECKLIST

Plant or Department ....   Date ....

This list is intended only as a reminder. Look for other unsafe acts and conditions, and then report them so that corrective action can be taken. Note particularly whether unsafe acts or conditions that have caused accidents have been corrected. Note also whether potential accident causes, marked "X" on previous inspection, have been corrected.

($\sqrt{}$) indicates *Satisfactory*   (X) indicates *Unsatisfactory*

1. FIRE PROTECTION
Extinguishing equipment .... ☐
Standpipes, hoses, sprinkler
   heads, and valves .... ☐
Exits, stairs, and signs .... ☐
Storage of flammable material .... ☐

2. HOUSEKEEPING
Aisles, stairs, and floors .... ☐
Storage and piling of material .... ☐
Wash and locker rooms .... ☐
Light and ventilation .... ☐
Disposal of waste .... ☐
Yards and parking lots .... ☐

3. TOOLS
Power tools, wiring .... ☐
Hand tools .... ☐
Use and storage of tools .... ☐

4. PERSONAL PROTECTIVE EQUIP.
Goggles or face shields .... ☐
Safety shoes .... ☐
Gloves .... ☐
Respirators or gas masks .... ☐
Protective clothing .... ☐

5. MATERIAL HANDLING EQUIP.
Power trucks, hand trucks .... ☐
Elevators .... ☐
Cranes and hoists .... ☐
Conveyors .... ☐
Cables, ropes, chains, slings .... ☐

6. BULLETIN BOARDS
Neat and attractive .... ☐
Display changed regularly .... ☐
Well illuminated .... ☐

7. MACHINERY
Point of operation guards ...... ☐
Belts, pulleys, gears, shafts, etc. ☐
Oiling, cleaning, and adjusting .. ☐
Maintenance and oil leakage .... ☐

8. PRESSURE EQUIPMENT
Steam equipment .... ☐
Air receivers and compressors .. ☐
Gas cylinders and hose .... ☐

9. UNSAFE PRACTICES
Excessive speed of vehicles .... ☐
Improper lifting .... ☐
Smoking in danger areas .... ☐
Horseplay .... ☐
Running in aisles or on stairs ☐
Improper use of air hoses .... ☐
Removing machine or
   other guards .... ☐
Work on unguarded
   moving machinery .... ☐

10. FIRST AID
First aid kits and rooms ..... ☐
Stretchers and fire blankets .... ☐
Emergency showers .... ☐
All injuries reported .... ☐

11. MISCELLANEOUS
Acids and caustics .... ☐
New processes, chemicals,
   and solvents .... ☐
Dusts, vapors, or fumes .... ☐
Ladders and scaffolds .... ☐

Signed ....

USE REVERSE SIDE FOR DETAILED COMMENTS OR RECOMMENDATIONS

9-17 SAFETY INSPECTION CHECKLIST

Loading Dock Safety Checklist

Provided as a service to industry by Rite-Hite Corporation.

Date _____

Company Name _____

Plant Name _____ Plant Location _____

Dock examined/Door numbers _____

Company representative completing checklist:

Name _____ Title _____

A. Vehicles/Traffic Control

1. Do forklifts have the following safety equipment?
   - ☐ Seat belt   ☐ Load backrest
   - ☐ Headlight   ☐ Backup alarm
   - ☐ Horn   ☐ Overhead guard
   - ☐ Tilt indicator
   - ☐ On-board fire extinguisher
   - ☐ Other _____

	Yes	No
2. Are the following in use?		
Driver candidate screening	☐	☐
Driver training/licensing	☐	☐
Periodic driver retraining	☐	☐
Vehicle maintenance records	☐	☐
Written vehicle safety rules	☐	☐

	Yes	No
3. Is the dock kept clear of loads of materials?	☐	☐
4. Are there convex mirrors at blind corners?	☐	☐
5. Is forklift cross traffic over dock levelers restricted?	☐	☐
6. Is pedestrian traffic restricted in the dock area?	☐	☐
7. Is there a clearly marked pedestrian walkway?	☐	☐
8. Are guardrails used to define the pedestrian walkway?	☐	☐

9. Comments/recommendations

_____
_____
_____
_____
_____

B. Vehicle restraining

	Yes	No
1. If vehicle restraints are used:		
a. Are all dock workers trained in the use of the restraints?	☐	☐
b. Are the restraints used consistently?	☐	☐
c. Are there warning signs and lights inside and out to tell when a trailer is secured and when it is not?	☐	☐
d. Are the outdoor signal lights clearly visible even in fog or bright sunlight?	☐	☐
e. Can the restraints secure trailers regardless of the height of their ICC bars?	☐	☐
f. Can the restraints secure all trailers with I-beam, round, or other common ICC bar shapes?	☐	☐
g. Does the restraint sound an alarm when a trailer cannot be secured because its ICC bar is missing or out of place?	☐	☐

RITE-HITE

9-18 LOADING DOCK SAFETY CHECKLIST

h. Are dock personnel specifically trained to watch for trailers with unusual rear-end assemblies (e.g. sloping steel back plates and hydraulic tailgates) that can cause a restraint to give a signal that the trailer is engaged even when it is not safely engaged? ☐ ☐

i. Are dock personnel specifically trained to observe the safe engagement of all unusual rear-end assemblies? ☐ ☐

j. Do the restraints receive regular planned maintenance? ☐ ☐

k. Do restraints need repairs or replacement? (List door numbers.)

_____

l. Comments/recommendations

_____

_____

2. If wheel chocks are used: Yes No

a. Are dock workers, rather than truckers, responsible for placing chocks? ☐ ☐

b. Are all dock workers trained in proper chocking procedures? ☐ ☐

c. Are chocks of suitable design and construction? ☐ ☐

d. Are there two chocks for each position? ☐ ☐

e. Are all trailers chocked on both sides? ☐ ☐

f. Are chocks chained to the building? ☐ ☐

g. Are warning signs in use? ☐ ☐

h. Are driveways kept clear of ice and snow to help keep chocks from slipping? ☐ ☐

i. Comments/recommendations

_____

_____

C. Dock levelers

Yes No

1. Are the dock levelers working properly? ☐ ☐

2. Are levelers long enough to provide a gentle grade into trailers of all heights? ☐ ☐

3. Is leveler width adequate when servicing wider trailers? ☐ ☐

4. Do platform width and configuration allow safe handling of end loads? ☐ ☐

5. Is leveler capacity adequate given typical load weights, lift truck speeds, ramp inclines and frequency of use? ☐ ☐

6. Do levelers have the following safety features?
Working-range toe guards ☐ ☐
Full-range toe guards ☐ ☐
Ramp free-fall protection ☐ ☐
Automatic recycling ☐ ☐

7. Do levelers receive regular planned maintenance? ☐ ☐

8. Do levelers need repair or replacement? (List door numbers.)

_____

_____

9. Comments/recommendations _____

_____

_____

D. Portable dock plates

Yes No

1. Is plate length adequate? ☐ ☐

2. Is plate capacity adequate? ☐ ☐

3. Are plates of suitable design and materials? ☐ ☐

4. Do plates have curbed sides? ☐ ☐

5. Do plates have suitable anchor stops? ☐ ☐

6. Are plates moved by lift trucks rather than by hand? ☐ ☐

7. Are plates stored away from traffic? ☐ ☐

8. Are plates inspected regularly? ☐ ☐

9. Do plates need repair or replacement? (List door numbers.)

_____

_____

10. Comments/recommendations

_____

_____

9-18 (Continued)

E. Dock Doors

	Yes	No
1. Are doors large enough to admit all loads without obstruction?	☐	☐
2. Are door rails protected by bumper posts?	☐	☐
3. Do doors receive regular planned maintenance?	☐	☐

4. Which doors (if any) need repair or replacement?

_____

_____

5. Comments/recommendations

_____

_____

F. Traffic Doors

	Yes	No
1. Are doors wide enough to handle all loads and minimize damage.	☐	☐
2. Does door arrangement allow safe lift truck and pedestrian traffic?	☐	☐
3. Are visibility and lighting adequate on both sides of all doors?	☐	☐

4. Which doors (if any) need repair or replacement?

_____

_____

5. Comments/recommendations

_____

_____

G. Weather sealing

	Yes	No
1. Are the seals or shelters effective in excluding moisture and debris from the dock?	☐	☐
2. Are seals or shelters sized to provide an effective seal against all types of trailers?	☐	☐
3. Are seals or shelters designed so that they will not obstruct loading and unloading?	☐	☐

4. Are dock levelers weather sealed along the sides and back?	☐	☐
5. In addition to seals or shelters, would an air curtain solve a problem?	☐	☐

6. Do seals or shelters need repair or replacement? (List door numbers.)

_____

_____

7. Comments/recommendations

_____

_____

H. Trailer Lifting

1. How are low-bed trailers elevated for loading/unloading?

☐ Wheel risers ☐ Concrete ramps
☐ Trailer-mounted jacks
☐ Truck levelers

	Yes	No
2. Do lifting devices provide adequate stability?	☐	☐
3. Are trailers secured with vehicle restraints when elevated?	☐	☐

4. Do lifting devices need repair or replacement? (List door numbers.)

_____

_____

5. Comments/recommendations

_____

_____

I. Other Considerations

	Yes	No
1. Dock lights		
a. Is lighting adequate inside trailers?	☐	☐
b. Is the lift mechanism properly shielded?	☐	☐
2. Scissors lifts		
a. Are all appropriate workers trained in safe operating procedures?	☐	☐
b. Is the lift mechanism properly shielded?	☐	☐
c. Are guardrails and chock ramps in place and in good repair?	☐	☐

9-18 (Continued)

3. Conveyors
   a. Are all appropriate workers trained in safe operating procedures? ☐ ☐
   b. Are necessary safeguards in place to protect against pinch points, jam-ups and runaway material? ☐ ☐
   c. Are crossovers provided? ☐ ☐
   d. Are emergency stop buttons in place and properly located? ☐ ☐

4. Strapping
   a. Are proper tools available for applying strapping? ☐ ☐
   b. Do workers cut strapping using only cutters equipped with a holddown device? ☐ ☐
   c. Do workers wear hand, foot and face protection when applying and cutting strapping? ☐ ☐
   d. Are all appropriate workers trained in safe strapping techniques? ☐ ☐

5. Manual handling
   a. Is the dock designed so as to minimize manual lifting and carrying? ☐ ☐
   b. Are dock workers trained in safe lifting and manual handling techniques? ☐ ☐

6. Miscellaneous
                                                  Yes No
   a. Are pallets regularly inspected? ☐ ☐
   b. Are dock bumpers in good repair? ☐ ☐
   c. Is the dock kept clean and free of clutter? ☐ ☐
   d. Are housekeeping inspections performed periodically? ☐ ☐
   e. Are anti-skid floor surfaces, mats or runners used where appropriate? ☐ ☐

   f. Are stairways or ladders provided for access to ground level from the dock? ☐ ☐
   g. Is the trailer landing strip in good condition? ☐ ☐
   h. Are dock approaches free of potholes or deteriorated pavement? ☐ ☐
   i. Are dock approaches and outdoor stairs kept clear of ice and snow? ☐ ☐
   j. Are dock positions marked with lines or lights for accurate trailer spotting? ☐ ☐
   k. Do all dock workers wear personal protective equipment as required by company policy? ☐ ☐
   l. Is safety training provided for all dock employees? ☐ ☐
   m. Are periodic safety refresher courses offered? ☐ ☐

J. General comments/recommendations

_____
_____
_____
_____
_____

For additional copies of this Loading Dock Safety Checklist, write to Rite-Hite Corporation, 8900 Arbon Drive, P.O. Box 23043, Milwaukee, WI 53223-0043.
For more information on loading dock safety, write for a complimentary copy of Rite-Hite's Dock Safety Guide.

This loading dock safety checklist is provided as a service by Rite-Hite Corporation, Milwaukee, Wis. It is intended as an aid to safety evaluation of loading dock equipment and operations. However, it is not intended as a complete guide to loading dock hazard identification. Therefore, Rite-Hite Corporation makes no guarantees as to nor assumes any liability for the sufficiency or completeness of this document. It may be necessary under particular circumstances to evaluate other dock equipment and procedures in addition to those included in the checklist. For information on U.S. loading dock safety requirements, consult OSHA Safety and Health Standards (29 CFR 1910). In other countries, consult the applicable national or provincial occupational health and safety codes.

RITE·HITE

Contact: Rite-Hite Corporation, 8900 N. Arbon Drive, P.O. Box 23043, Milwaukee, WI 53223
(414) 355-2600 ● 1-800-456-0600 ● FAX (414) 355-9248
Rite-Hite® is a registered trademark of the Rite-Hite Corporation.

9-18 (Continued)

Material Safety Data Sheet

May be used to comply with
OSHA's Hazard Communication Standard,
29 CFR 1910.1200. Standard must be
consulted for specific requirements.

U.S. Department of Labor

Occupational Safety and Health Administration
(Non-Mandatory Form)
Form Approved
OMB No. 1218-0072

IDENTITY (As Used on Label and List)	Note: Blank spaces are not permitted. If any item is not applicable, or no information is available, the space must be marked to indicate that.

Section I

Manufacturer's Name	Emergency Telephone Number
Address (Number, Street, City, State, and ZIP Code)	Telephone Number for Information
	Date Prepared
	Signature of Preparer (optional)

Section II — Hazardous Ingredients/Identity Information

Hazardous Components (Specific Chemical Identity; Common Name(s))	OSHA PEL	ACGIH TLV	Other Limits Recommended	% (optional)

Section III — Physical/Chemical Characteristics

Boiling Point		Specific Gravity (H_2O = 1)	
Vapor Pressure (mm Hg.)		Melting Point	
Vapor Density (AIR = 1)		Evaporation Rate (Butyl Acetate = 1)	

Solubility in Water

Appearance and Odor

Section IV — Fire and Explosion Hazard Data

Flash Point (Method Used)	Flammable Limits	LEL	UEL

Extinguishing Media

Special Fire Fighting Procedures

Unusual Fire and Explosion Hazards

9-19 MATERIAL SAFETY DATA SHEET

Section V — Reactivity Data

Stability	Unstable		Conditions to Avoid
	Stable		

Incompatibility (*Materials to Avoid*)

Hazardous Decomposition or Byproducts

Hazardous Polymerization	May Occur		Conditions to Avoid
	Will Not Occur		

Section VI — Health Hazard Data

Route(s) of Entry:	Inhalation?	Skin?	Ingestion?

Health Hazards (*Acute and Chronic*)

Carcinogenicity:	NTP?	IARC Monographs?	OSHA Regulated?

Signs and Symptoms of Exposure

Medical Conditions
Generally Aggravated by Exposure

Emergency and First Aid Procedures

Section VII — Precautions for Safe Handling and Use

Steps to Be Taken in Case Material Is Released or Spilled

Waste Disposal Method

Precautions to Be Taken in Handling and Storing

Other Precautions

Section VIII — Control Measures

Respiratory Protection (*Specify Type*)

Ventilation	Local Exhaust		Special	
	Mechanical (*General*)		Other	

Protective Gloves		Eye Protection

Other Protective Clothing or Equipment

Work/Hygienic Practices

9-19 (Continued)

COMMON NAME:_____CHEMICAL NAME:_____

I. PHYSICAL/CHEMICAL PROPERTIES

SOURCE

Natural physical state: Gas____ Liquid____ Solid____ _____
(at ambient temps of 20°C-25°C)

Molecular weight	_____	g/g-mole	_____
Density[a]	_____	g/ml	
Specific gravity[a]	_____ @ _____	°F/°C	_____
Solubility: water	_____ @ _____	°F/°C	_____
Solubility[b]: _____	_____ @ _____	°F/°C	_____
Boiling point	_____	°F/°C	_____
Melting point	_____	°F/°C	_____
Vapor pressure	_____ mmHg @ _____	°F/°C	_____
Vapor density	_____ @ _____	°F/°C	_____
Flash point	_____	°F/°C	_____

(open cup_____; closed cup_____)

Other: _____ _____ _____

II. HAZARDOUS CHARACTERISTICS

A. TOXICOLOGICAL HAZARD	HAZARD?		CONCENTRATIONS (PEL, TLV, other)	SOURCE
Inhalation	Yes	No	_____	_____
Ingestion	Yes	No	_____	_____
Skin/eye absorption	Yes	No	_____	_____
Skin/eye contact	Yes	No	_____	_____
Carcinogenic	Yes	No	_____	_____
Teratogenic	Yes	No	_____	_____
Mutagenic	Yes	No	_____	_____
Aquatic	Yes	No	_____	_____
Other: _____	Yes	No	_____	_____

B. TOXICOLOGICAL HAZARD	HAZARD?		CONCENTRATIONS	SOURCE
Combustibility	Yes	No	_____	_____
Toxic byproduct(s):	Yes	No		
_____			_____	_____
_____			_____	_____
Flammability	Yes	No		
LFL			_____	_____
UFL			_____	_____
Explosivity	Yes	No		
LEL			_____	_____
UEL			_____	_____

_____

[a]Only one is necessary.

[b]For organic compounds, recovery of spilled material by solvent extraction may require solubility data.

9-20 HAZARDOUS SUBSTANCE INFORMATION FORM

C. REACTIVITY HAZARD   HAZARD?   CONCENTRATIONS   SOURCE

                         Yes No

Reactivities:

_____   _____   _____

_____   _____   _____

D. CORROSIVITY HAZARD   HAZARD?   CONCENTRATIONS   SOURCE

   ph _____   Yes No

   Neutralizing agent:

_____   _____   _____

_____   _____   _____

E. RADIOACTIVE HAZARD   HAZARD?   EXPOSURE RATE   SOURCE

   Background   Yes No   _____   _____

   Alpha particles   Yes No   _____   _____

   Beta particles   Yes No   _____   _____

   Gamma radiation   Yes No   _____   _____

III. DESCRIPTION OF INCIDENT:

Quantity involved _____

Release information _____

_____

Monitoring/sampling recommended _____

_____

IV. RECOMMENDED PROTECTION:

Worker _____

_____

Public _____

_____

V. RECOMMENDED SITE CONTROL:

Hotline _____

_____

Decontamination line _____

_____

Command Post location _____

_____

VI. REFERENCES FOR SOURCES:

_____

_____

_____

_____

_____

_____

_____

_____

9-20 (Continued)

EMPLOYEE INFORMATION REQUEST FORM

NAME_____ JOB TITLE_____

DEPARTMENT_____ SUPERVISOR_____

===

DESCRIPTION OF THE TOXIC SUBSTANCE YOU ARE EXPOSED TO:

TRADE NAME_____

CHEMICAL NAME OR INGREDIENTS (IF KNOWN)_____

_____

MANUFACTURER (NAME AND ADDRESS, IF KNOWN)_____

_____

DOES SUBSTANCE HAVE A LABEL?_____YES _____NO
IF YES, ATTACH A LABEL OR A COPY OF INFORMATION ON LABEL.

PHSYICAL FORM OF SUBSTANCE: _____SOLID _____LIQUID_____ GAS

_____DUST _____OTHER

ADDITIONAL INFORMATION WHICH WILL IDENTIFY THE SUBSTANCE:

_____

_____

IN WHICH WAY(S) DO YOU COME IN CONTACT WITH THIS SUBSTANCE?

_____

_____

	RECEIVED BY:
SIGNATURE:_____	SAFETY DIRECTOR:_____
DATE:_____	DATE:_____

9-21 EMPLOYEE INFORMATION REQUEST FORM

HAZARD INVESTIGATION REPORT

DATE_____   INVESTIGATION NO._____

DEPARTMENT_____   REQUESTED BY_____

REASON FOR INVESTIGATION_____

_____

_____

DESCRIPTION/NAME OF POTENTIALLY HAZARDOUS EQUIPMENT OR

MATERIALS_____

_____

DESCRIBE HOW AN ACCIDENT COULD HAPPEN_____

_____

ACCIDENT/INJURY THAT COULD OCCUR_____

_____

HOW PROBABLE IS THE EVENT OF AN ACCIDENT/INJURY

HAPPENING DUE TO THIS SITUATION?_____

_____

INVESTIGATOR'S COMMENTS/RECOMMENDATIONS_____

_____

_____
SIGNATURE OF INVESTIGATOR

9-22 HAZARD INVESTIGATION REPORT

STATE OF NEW YORK
DEPARTMENT OF ENVIRONMENTAL CONSERVATION
DIVISION OF HAZARDOUS SUBSTANCES REGULATION

HAZARDOUS WASTE MANIFEST
P.O. Box 12820, Albany, New York 12212

Please print or type. Do not Staple.

Form Approved. OMB No. 2050-0039. Expires 9-30-91

UNIFORM HAZARDOUS WASTE MANIFEST	1. Generator's US EPA No.	Manifest Document No.	2. Page 1 of	Information in the shaded areas is not required by Federal Law.

3. Generator's Name and Mailing Address

A. State Manifest Document No.
NY B 212825 7

4. Generator's Phone (   )

B. Generator's ID

5. Transporter 1 (Company Name)	6. US EPA ID Number	C. State Transporter's ID
		D. Transporter's Phone ( )
7. Transporter 2 (Company Name)	8. US EPA ID Number	E. State Transporter's ID
		F. Transporter's Phone ( )
9. Designated Facility Name and Site Address	10. US EPA ID Number	G. State Facility's ID
		H. Facility's Phone ( )

11. US DOT Description (Including Proper Shipping Name, Hazard Class and ID Number)	12. Containers		13. Total Quantity	14. Unit Wt/Vol	I. Waste No.
	No.	Type			
a.					EPA ———— STATE
b.					EPA ———— STATE
c.					EPA ———— STATE
d.					EPA ———— STATE

J. Additional Descriptions for Materials listed Above		K. Handling Codes for Wastes Listed Above	
a c		a ☐ c ☐	
b d		b ☐ d ☐	

15. Special Handling Instructions and Additional Information

16. GENERATOR'S CERTIFICATION: I hereby declare that the contents of this consignment are fully and accurately described above by proper shipping name and are classified, packed, marked and labeled, and are in all respects in proper condition for transport by highway according to applicable international and national government regulations and state laws and regulations.

If I am a large quantity generator, I certify that I have program in place to reduce the volume and toxicity of waste generated to the degree I have determined to be economically practicable and that I have selected the practicable method treatment, storage, or disposal currently available to me which minimizes the present and future threat to human health and the environment; OR if I am a small generator, I have made a good faith effort to minimize my waste and select the best waste management method that is available to me and that I can afford.

Printed/Typed Name	Signature	Mo.	Day	Year

17. Transporter 1 (Acknowledgement of Receipt of Materials)				
Printed/Typed Name	Signature	Mo.	Day	Year

18. Transporter 2 (Acknowledgement of Receipt of Materials)				
Printed/Typed Name	Signature	Mo.	Day	Year

19. Discrepancy Indication Space

20. Facility Owner or Operator: Certification of receipt of hazardous materials covered by this manifest except as noted in Item 19.

Printed/Typed Name	Signature	Mo.	Day	Year

NY B 212825 7

Left margin: In case of emergency or spill immediately call the National Response Center (800) 424-8802 and the N.Y. Dept. of Environmental Conservation (518) 457-7362.

Left side labels: GENERATOR / TRANSPORTER / FACILITY

EPA Form 8700-22 (Rev. 9-88) Previous editions are obsolete.

COPY 1—Disposer State—Mailed by TSD Facility

9-23 HAZARDOUS WASTE MANIFEST

Hazardous Materials Warning Labels

DOMESTIC LABELING

General Guidelines on Use of Labels
(CFR, Title 49, Transportation, Parts 100-177)

- Labels illustrated above are normally for *domestic shipments*. However, some air carriers *may* require the use of International Civil Aviation Organization (ICAO) labels.

- Domestic Warning Labels *may* display UN Class Number, Division Number (and Compatibility Group for Explosives only.) Sec. 172.407(g).

- Any person who offers a hazardous material for transportation MUST label the package, if required. [Sec. 172.400(a)].

- The Hazardous Materials Tables, Sec. 172.101 and 172.102, identify the proper label(s) for the hazardous materials listed.

- Label(s), when required, must be printed on or affixed to the surface of the package near the proper shipping name. [Sec. 172.406(a)].

- When two or more different labels are required, display them next to each other. [Sec. 172.406(c)].

- Labels may be affixed to packages (even when not required by regulations) provided each label represents a hazard of the material in the package. [Sec. 172-401].

Check the Appropriate Regulations

Domestic or International Shipment

UN Class Numbers

Class 1—Explosives

Class 2—Gases (compressed, liquified or dissolved under pressure)

Class 3—Flammable liquids

Class 4—Flammable solids or substances

Class 5—Oxidizing substances
Division 5.1-Oxidizing substances or agents.
Division 5.2-Organic peroxides.

Class 6—Poisonous and infectious substances

Class 7—Radioactive substances

Class 8—Corrosives

Class 9—Miscellaneous dangerous substances

INTERNATIONAL LABELING

Substance liable to Spontaneous Combustion

Poisonous Substance

Poisonous Substance

Infectious Substance

EXAMPLES OF INTERNATIONAL LABELS

- These are examples of International Labels not presently used for domestic shipments.

- Text, when used Internationally *may* be in the language of the country of origin.

- Most of the domestic labels (illustrated above) *may* be used Internationally.

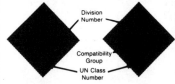

EXAMPLES OF EXPLOSIVE LABELS

- The NUMERICAL DESIGNATION represents the CLASS or DIVISION.

- ALPHABETICAL DESIGNATION represents the COMPATIBILITY GROUP (for Explosives Only)

- DIVISION NUMBERS and COMPATIBILITY GROUP combinations can result in over 30 different "Explosives" labels (see IMDG Code/ICAO).

For complete details, refer to one or more of the following:
- Code of Federal Regulations, Title 49, Transportation. Parts 100-199. [All Modes]
- International Civil Aviation Organization (ICAO) Technical Instructions for the Safe Transport of Dangerous Goods by air. [Air]
- International Maritime Organization (IMO) Dangerous Goods Code. [Water]
- "Transportation of Dangerous Goods Regulations" of Transport Canada. [All Modes]

U.S. Department of Transportation

Research and Special Programs Administration

Washington, D.C. 20590

CHART 8
REV. FEBRUARY 1986

9-24 HAZARDOUS MATERIALS WARNING LABELS CHART

Hazardous Materials Warning Placards

DOMESTIC PLACARDING

Illustration numbers in each square (1 through 18) refer to TABLES 1 and 2 below.

| 1 | 2 | 3 | 4 POISON GAS 2 | 5 FLAMMABLE GAS 2 | 6 NON-FLAMMABLE GAS 2 | 7 CHLORINE 2 |

| 8 | 9 FLAMMABLE 3 | 10 COMBUSTIBLE 3 | 11 FLAMMABLE SOLID | 12 FLAMMABLE SOLID | 13 OXIDIZER | 14 ORGANIC PEROXIDE 5 |

| 15 POISON 6 | 16 RADIOACTIVE 7 | 17 CORROSIVE 8 | 18 DANGEROUS | |

(WHITE) SQUARE BACKGROUND FOR PLACARD

HIGHWAY
- Used for "HIGHWAY ROUTE CONTROLLED QUANTITY OF RADIOACTIVE MATERIALS". (Sec. 172.507)

RAIL
- Used for RAIL SHIPMENTS—"EXPLOSIVE A." "POISON GAS" and "POISON GAS-RESIDUE" placards. (Sec. 172.510(a))

TABLE 1

HAZARD CLASSES	*NO.
Class A explosives	1
Class B explosives	2
Poison A	4
Flammable solid (DANGEROUS WHEN WET label only)	12
Radioactive material (YELLOW III label)	16
Radioactive material:	
Uranium hexafluoride fissile (containing more than 1.0% U^{235})	16 & 17
Uranium hexafluoride, low-specific activity (containing 1.0% or less U^{235})	16 & 17

NOTE: For details on the use of Tables 1 and 2, see Sec. 172.504 (See footnotes at bottom of tables.)

Guidelines
(CFR, Title 49, Transportation, Parts 100-177)

- Placard *motor vehicles, freight containers*, and *rail cars* containing *any quantity* of hazardous materials listed in TABLE 1.
- Placard *motor vehicles, freight containers* and *rail cars* containing 1,000 pounds or more gross weight of hazardous materials classes listed in TABLE 2.
- Placard *freight containers* 640 cubic feet or more containing *any quantity* of hazardous material classes listed in TABLES 1 and/or 2 when offered for transportation by air or water. Under 640 cubic feet see Sec. 172.512(b).

CAUTION
CHECK EACH SHIPMENT FOR COMPLIANCE WITH THE APPROPRIATE HAZARDOUS MATERIALS REGULATIONS:
Proper Classification   Marking   Placarding
Packaging   Labeling   Documentation
PRIOR TO OFFERING FOR SHIPMENT

TABLE 2

HAZARD CLASSES	*NO.
Class C explosives	18
Blasting agent	3
Nonflammable gas	6
Nonflammable gas (Chlorine)	7
Nonflammable gas (Fluorine)	15
Nonflammable gas (Oxygen, cryogenic liquid)	8
Flammable gas	5
Combustible liquid	10
Flammable liquid	9
Flammable solid	11
Oxidizer	13
Organic peroxide	14
Poison B	15
Corrosive material	17
Irritating material	18

INTERNATIONAL PLACARDING

- Most international placards are similar (color and pictorial symbol(s) to the Domestic placards illustrated above.
- International placards are enlarged ICAO or IMO labels (See International Labeling—Otherside).
- Placard MUST correspond to *hazard class* of material.

- Placard *ANY QUANTITY* of hazardous materials when loaded in FREIGHT CONTAINERS, PORTABLE TANKS, RAIL CARS and HIGHWAY VEHICLES.
- International placards *may be used in addition* to DOT placards for international shipments.

When required, *Subsidiary Risk placards* must be displayed in the same manner as *Primary Risk placards*. Class numbers are *not shown* on Subsidiary Risk placards.

- COMPATIBILITY GROUP DESIGNATORS *must be* displayed on EXPLOSIVES PLACARDS.
- UN CLASS NUMBERS and DIVISION NUMBERS *MUST* be displayed on hazard class placards when required.

UN and NA Identification Numbers

- The four digit UN or NA numbers must be displayed on all hazardous materials packages for which identification numbers are assigned. Example: ACETONE UN 1090.
- UN (United Nations) or NA (North American) numbers are found in the Hazardous Materials Tables, Sec. 172.101 and 172.102 (CFR, Title 49, Parts 100-199)
- Identification numbers may not be displayed on "POISON GAS," "RADIOACTIVE" or "EXPLOSIVE" placards. (Sec. 172.334)
- UN numbers are displayed in the same manner for both Domestic and International shipments.
- NA numbers are used only in the USA and Canada.

When hazardous materials are transported in Tank Cars, Cargo Tanks and Portable Tanks, UN or NA numbers *must* be displayed on:

PLACARDS OR ORANGE PANELS

and

Appropriate Placard must be used.

EUROPEAN NUMBERING SYSTEM—

Top Number—Hazard Index (Identification of Danger, 2 or 3 figures) Example: 33 = highly inflammable liquid.

Bottom Number—UN Number of substance Example: 1088 ACETAL

For more complete details on identification Numbers see Sec. 172.300 through 172.338.

9-25 HAZARDOUS MATERIALS WARNING PLACARDS

<table>
<tr><td colspan="2">

SUFFOLK CO. DEPT. OF HEALTH SERVICES

-- APPLICATION --

PERMIT TO CONSTRUCT

TOXIC/HAZARDOUS MATERIALS STORAGE FACILITY

</td><td>

Permit requested for: (check all that apply)

☐ above ground tank   ☐ upgrade exstg. facility

☐ underground tank   ☐ transfer facility

☐ drum/portable cont.   ☐ re-piping

☐ vapor recovery   ☐ dry bulk

☐ other:

</td></tr>
</table>

NOTICE*   Construction may not take place without a valid Permit to Construct. Plans will not be reviewed without a completed application.

Property Tax Map No.   District _____   Section _____ . ___   Block ___   Lot _____ . ___

Facility Name: _____   Facility owner: _____

Address: _____   Owner's address: _____

     (no.)   (street)   (no)   (street)

Community: _____   Community: _____

State: _____ Zip: _____   State: _____ Zip: _____

Phone: _____   Phone: _____

Person to contact for this project: _____   Phone: _____

Address (if different from owner) _____

                                 (no.)   (street)

                                 (city)   (state)   (zip)

Briefly describe project:

I CERTIFY THAT ALL INFORMATION SUPPLIED HEREON AND ATTACHED HERETO IS TRUE TO THE BEST OF MY KNOWLEDGE

_____   _____   _____

     applicants signature   print name   date

-- OFFICIAL USE ONLY --

This application with attached plans and reports has been reviewed and approved for construction and the permit expires* on _____.

Approving engineer _____   Date _____

SCDHS JOB NO. _____   FAC. ID.NO. _____

9-26 APPLICATION FOR PERMIT TO CONSTRUCT TOXIC/HAZARDOUS MATERIALS STORAGE FACILITY

SUFFOLK COUNTY DEPARTMENT OF HEALTH SERVICE
TOXIC LIQUID STORAGE REGISTRATION FORM

OFFICIAL USE ONLY

New _____
Change _____
Add _____

Fac. Ref. No.

Principal Property Tax Code

District | Section | Block | Lot

Facility Name | No. | Street | Community | State | Zip | Phone No.

Tank Owner | No. | Street | Community | State | Zip | Phone No.

*- Designates cathodic protection

Write mat'l. number in left column

1- GASOLINE
2- #2 FUEL OIL
3- #4 FUEL OIL
4- #6 FUEL OIL
5- KEROSENE
6- WASTE OIL
7- DIESEL
8- ORG. SOLVENT
9- IND. WASTES
10- MOTOR OIL
11- TRANS FLUID
12- ANTIFREEZE
13- CAUSTIC
14- METHANOL
15- DRUM STOR.
Other Material (Specify)

TANK NUMBER	ABOVEGROUND	UNDERGROUND	INDOORS	OUTDOORS	CAPACITY (GALLONS)	#	YEAR INSTALLED	PLAIN STEEL	FIBERGLAS	BUFFHIDE*	BUFFHIDE	STIP-3	ALPHA	OTHER	FIBERGLAS	BUFFHIDE*	BUFFHIDE	STIP-3	OTHER	SUBMERSIBLE	SUCTION	GRAVITY	OTHER	PUMPED	GRAVITY	OTHER	OFFICIAL USE ONLY

SINGLE WALLED | DOUBLE WALLED | DISPENSER FILL

I certify that information on this application and all attachments have been reviewed and that, based on my inquiry of those persons immediately responsible for obtaining the information contained in this application, I believe that the information is true, accurate, and complete. I understand that false statements made herein are punishable as a Class A misdemeanor pursuant to Section 210.45 of the Penal Law.

Date | Print Name | Signature | Title

Receipt No. _____

Amt. of Fee _____

9-27 TOXIC LIQUID STORAGE REGISTRATION FORM

SUFFOLK COUNTY DEPARTMENT OF HEALTH SERVICES
15 Horseblock Place, Farmingville, New York 11738

APPLICATION FOR UNDERGROUND FLAMMABLE/COMBUSTIBLE LIQUID TANK

	OFFICIAL USE ONLY
FACILITY NAME_____	PLAN APPROVAL NO._____
ADDRESS (DEED LOCATION)_____	DATE_____
_____	REQUIRED FEE_____
HAMLET_____ TOWN_____	RECEIPT NO._____

BRAND/SUPPLIER_____

NAME OF CONTRACTOR_____ LICENSE NO._____

ADDRESS_____ PHONE NO._____

DEPTH TO GROUNDWATER_____ DEWATERING PERMIT_____
(IF GROUNDWATER PRESENT IN TANK EXCAVATION)

TANK INFORMATION

TANK NO.	MANUFACTURER	TANK CONSTRUCTION STEEL/FIBERGLASS	SIZE GALLONS	PRODUCT	FOR H.D. USE ONLY
1					
2					
3					
4					
5					
6					

TYPE OF LEAK DETECTION DEVICE_____ TYPE OF PIPING_____

WATER SUPPLY: PUBLIC_____ PRIVATE_____ SEWERAGE SYSTEM: PUBLIC_____ PRIVATE_____

BUILDING DEPARTMENT_____ FIRE DISTRICT_____

DE-COMMISSION TANKS: 1) NUMBER_____ 2) SIZE GALLONS_____ 3) TYPE_____

4) METHOD OF DISPOSAL_____ 5) LOCATION_____

I CERTIFY THAT ALL INFORMATION SUPPLIED HEREON AND ATTACHED HERETO IS TRUE TO THE BEST OF MY KNOWLEDGE.

_____	_____
SIGNATURE OF APPLICANT	PRINTED NAME OF APPLICANT
_____	_____
COMPANY NAME AND ADDRESS	DATE

9-28 APPLICATION FOR UNDERGROUND FLAMMABLE/COMBUSTIBLE LIQUID TANK

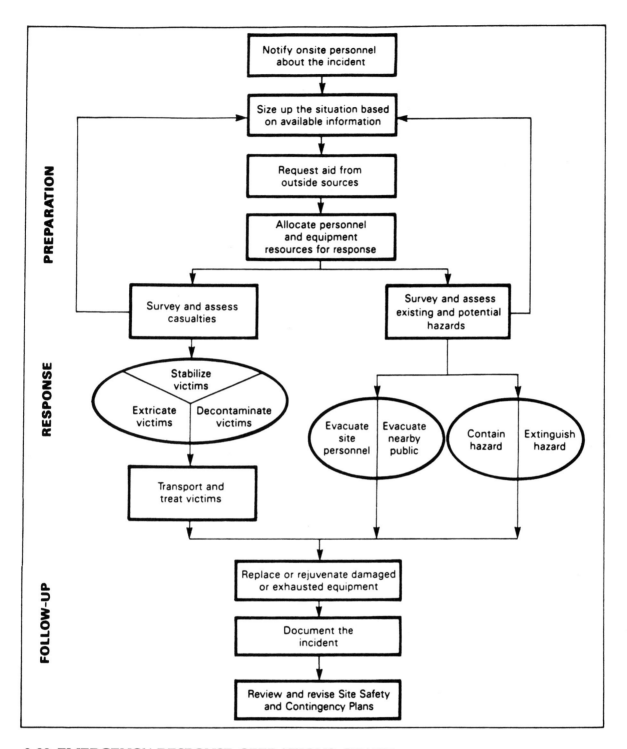

9-29 EMERGENCY RESPONSE OPERATIONS CHART

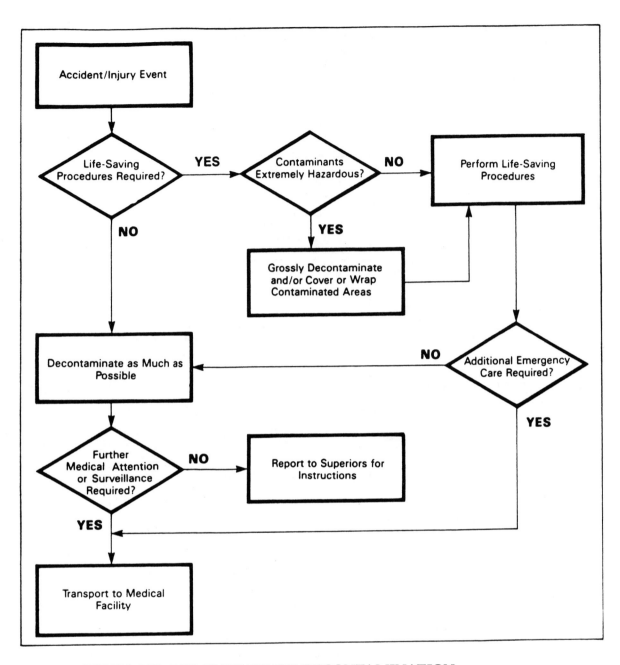

9-30 DECISION AID FOR EMERGENCY DECONTAMINATION

242

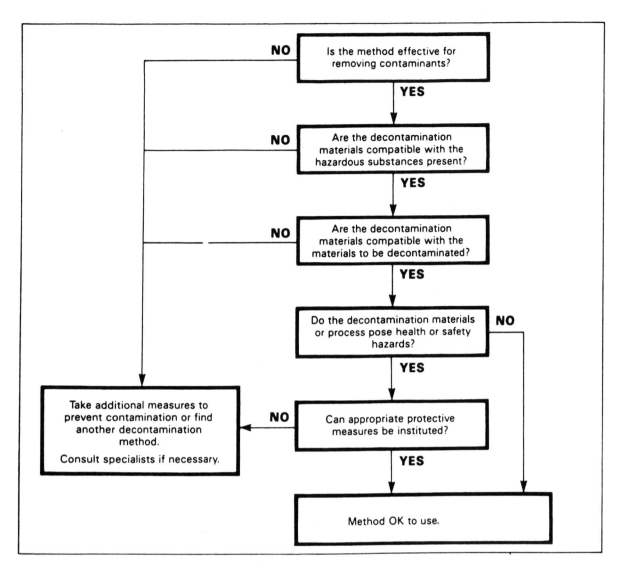

9-31 DECISION AID FOR EVALUATION HEALTH AND SAFETY ASPECTS OF DECONTAMINATION METHODS

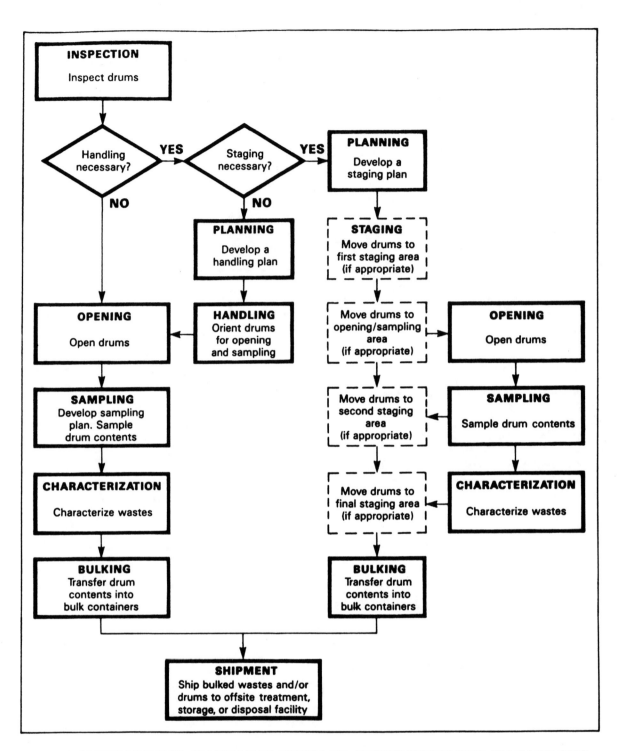

9-32 FLOWCHART FOR HANDLING STORAGE CONTAINERS FOR HAZARDOUS MATERIALS

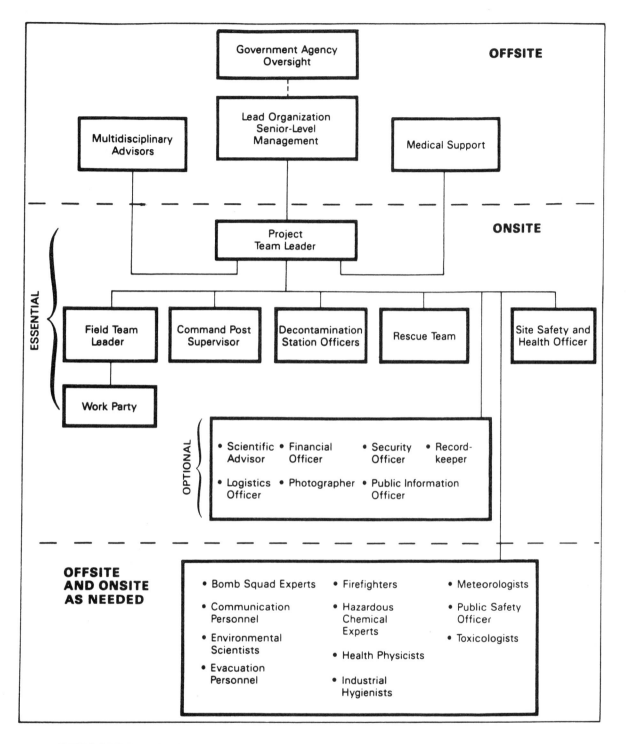

9-33 PERSONNEL ORGANIZATION FOR INVESTIGATION OF HAZARDOUS WASTE SITE

Chapter Ten

VEHICLE AND
EQUIPMENT MAINTENANCE

Automation has increased productivity tenfold, and, although very expensive to acquire, usually pays for itself many times over. However, downtime is expensive, as are repairs. That is why every effort should be made to maintain all vehicles and equipment in top running condition. One of the best ways to do this is to keep excellent records.

This chapter details forms and reports on fleet maintenance, driver's logs, and materials handling equipment. By keeping up to date on the status of all equipment, including hours used and service record, maintenance personnel can monitor component deterioration and achieve maximum product life.

10-1. DRIVER'S DAILY REPORT

This form is used to ensure that the truck has all the basics checked before leaving the yard. On returning to the yard, the driver completes mileage information and records any problems with the vehicle. If there is a problem, the driver completes a vehicle work order and turns it in to service.

Key Information

- Truck Number
- Water/Oil/Fuel Added
- Mileage Record

- Item Check (i.e., safety and maintenance equipment)
- Remarks

10-2. DRIVER'S VEHICLE INSPECTION REPORT—BASIC

The form shown is used by a trucking company to report any problems with their trucks. One section is checked for safety-related service, another for nonsafety-related service. Included on this form is a section for the mechanic's description of work performed.

Key Information

- Vehicle Number
- Safety/Nonsafety-Related Service
- Work Performed

10-3. DRIVER'S VEHICLE INSPECTION REPORT—DETAILED

This report provides the driver with a checklist of all major items on the tractor and trailer. It is handed in daily, and repairs should be made immediately.

Key Information

- Mileage
- Tractor/Trailer Number
- Checklist of Problem Areas

10-4. DRIVER'S VEHICLE CONDITION REPORT

This form is required by the Federal Department of Transportation's Motor Carrier Safety Regulations for interstate motor carriers. The driver of the vehicle states whether or not a problem is detected with the tractor or trailer which affects the safe operation of the vehicle.

Key Information

- Tractor/Trailer Number
- Do Detect/Do Not Detect Deficiency
- Indication and Location of Problem
- Defects Corrected/Need Not Be Corrected
- Signature of Driver and Representative

10-5. DRIVER'S DAILY LOG AND REPORT

The front of this form acts as a delivery log, and a daily report is on the back. The report is a checklist of equipment that is inspected daily by the driver.

Key Information

- Truck/Trailer Number
- Delivery Schedule
- Mileage Record
- Layover Time
- Expenses
- Condition of Equipment Checklist
- Remarks

10-6. VEHICLE WORK ORDER

This form is used to initiate repair work needed on a vehicle. The bottom portion is for mechanic's information.

Key Information

- Requested/Approved by
- Vehicle Number
- Priority Status
- Authorization Number
- Description of Work Requested
- Description of Problem
- Estimated Labor/Parts Cost

10-7. TRUCK SERVICE RECORD

This record is a master log of all routine service and repair work performed on a specific truck. Trucks should be brought in at periodic intervals for routine service, regardless of condition.

Key Information

- Truck Number
- Mileage
- Description of Service Performed

10-8. VEHICLE DAILY TRAVEL DIARY AND MEMORANDUM

This form logs the daily travels of a company vehicle, whether truck, van, or automobile.

Key Information

- Vehicle Number
- Department

- Locations Traveled
- Miles
- Memorandum (e.g., purpose of trip)

10-9. LEASED VEHICLE MILEAGE RECORD

The form shown records the mileage for a leased vehicle with a per state breakdown.

Key Information

- Pro Number
- Truck/Trailer Number
- Trip Information
- Mileage by State
- Summary of Miles

10-10. VEHICLE ACCIDENT REPORT

A vehicle accident report should be kept in every company vehicle at all times. If an accident occurs, the driver must record as much information as possible on the other vehicle involved. This information will be needed to fill out insurance forms. It is advisable to call the police and have them file a report. A primary reason for this, unfortunately, is to protect the company against a bogus lawsuit later on.

Key Information

- Company Vehicle Information
- Accident Date and Location
- Description of Accident
- Description of Damage
- Driver Information
- Second Vehicle Information
- Information on the Driver of Second Vehicle

10-11. LIFT TRUCK MAINTENANCE LOG

This log keeps track of how many hours a lift truck is running and what maintenance has been performed.

Key Information

- Truck Number
- Hours Running

- Hours Charged
- Description of Maintenance or Service Performed

10-12. FORKLIFT SERVICE REPORT

This form is used by a mechanic to report routine or emergency service performed on a forklift. Included on this form is a checklist of services performed and a section for comments.

Key Information

- Forklift Identification Number
- Mileage/Hours
- Date of Last Service
- Reason for Service
- Checklist of Services Performed

10-13. LIFT TRUCK STATUS LOG

The form shown helps a supervisor or manager keep track of the location of lift trucks at all times. A manager can allocate a specific number of trucks to certain sections of the warehouse, depending on need.

Key Information

- Vehicle Number
- Location
- Time

10-14. DAILY BATTERY RECORD

This form records the condition of a battery on a daily basis, allowing maintenance to monitor its ability to run equipment.

Key Information

- Battery Number
- Specific Gravity
- Repairs and Capacity Tests

DRIVERS DAILY REPORT

DATE _____ TRUCK NO. _____ EMP. # _____ DRIVER _____

_____ QTS. WATER ADDED   ENDING HUBOMETER _____

_____ QTS. OIL ADDED   BEGINNING HUBOMET _____

_____ GALS FUEL ADDED   MILES TRAVELED _____

CHECK ITEMS IN TRUCK BEFORE LEAVING LOT

_____ JACK

_____ WHEEL WRENCH

_____ SAFETY EQUIPMENT (Triangle, Flags, Fusee's)

IF ANY OF ABOVE ARE MISSING, IT MUST BE REPORTED TO SHOP FOREMAN BEFORE LEAVING LOT.

IF YOU TURNED IN A WORK ORDER YESTERDAY, WAS IT REPAIRED TO YOUR SATISFACTION.

                    Circle one: YES   NO

REMARKS _____

_____

_____

10-1 DRIVER'S DAILY REPORT

VEHICLE INSPECTION REPORT

Vehicle No._____   Date_____

==

DRIVER REPORT

[ ] Condition of this vehicle is satisfactory

[ ] This vehicle requires safety related service

[ ] This vehicle requires non safety related service

Detailed description of service required:_____

_____

_____

_____

_____   _____
Driver's Signature   Date

==

MECHANIC'S REPORT OF WORK PERFORMED:_____

_____

_____

_____

_____   _____
Mechanic's Signature   Date

10-2 DRIVER'S VEHICLE INSPECTION REPORT—BASIC

DRIVER'S INSPECTION REPORT

DATE _____   TRACTOR NO._____

MILEAGE _____   TRAILER NO._____

CHECK ALL ITEMS APPROVED AND USE X TO INDICATE PROBLEM

	GENERAL OUTER CONDITION	OIL AND WATER LEVELS	
	FRAME	BATTERY	
	LEAKS	COOLING SYSTEM	
	TIRES	HEATER AND DEFROSTER	
	AXLES (FRONT AND REAR)	WINDSHIELD WIPERS	
	EXHAUST SYSTEM	STEERING	
	HOSES	HORN	
	HOOK-UP AND FIFTH WHEEL	ELECTRICAL	
	FUEL TANK	AIR SYSTEM	
	SAFETY ACCESSORIES	EMERGENCY SIGNALS	
	MIRRORS	FUSES	

COMMENTS_____

_____

_____

_____

_____   _____

DRIVER'S SIGNATURE   DATE

10-3 DRIVER'S VEHICLE INSPECTION REPORT—DETAILED

DRIVERS VEHICLE CONDITION REPORT

AS REQUIRED BY THE D.O.T. FEDERAL MOTOR CARRIER SAFETY REGULATIONS, I SUBMIT THE FOLLOWING

DATE _____   TRACTOR NO. _____   TRAILOR NO. _____

(   ) I DETECT NO DEFECT OR DEFICIENCY IN THIS MOTOR VEHICLE AS WOULD BE LIKELY TO AFFECT THE SAFETY OF ITS OPERATION OR RESULT IN ITS MECHANICAL BREAKDOWN.

(   ) I DETECT THE FOLLOWING DEFECT OR DEFICIENCIES IN THIS MOTOR VEHICLE THAT WOULD BE LIKELY TO AFFECT THE SAFETY OF ITS OPERATION OR RESULT IN ITS MECHANICAL BREAKDOWN. INDICATE WHETHER DEFECT ARE ON TRACTOR OR TRAILER-USE SUFFICIENT DETAIL TO LOCATE FOR MECHANIC.

_____

_____

_____

(   ) ABOVE DEFECTS CORRECTED   DRIVER _____
(   ) ABOVE DEFECTS NEED NOT BE CORRECTED   CERTIFIED
FOR SAFE OPERATION OF VEHICLE   REPRESENTATIVE _R Tim M°Ghirie_

           DRIVER _____

10-4 DRIVER'S VEHICLE CONDITION REPORT

TRUCK NO. _____ TRAILER NO. _____ NAME _____ DATE _____

TIME IN	STOPS	TIME OUT	SPEEDOMETER FINISH			
			SPEEDOMETER START			
			MILEAGE TODAY			
			LAYOVER TIME			
			TOWN	FROM	TO	TOTAL
						HRS.
						HRS.

TOWN DEL.	WEIGHT	TIME	EXPENSES

REMARKS: TANDEM   SINGLE

IMPORTANT: DRIVER'S DAILY REPORT OF THE MECHANICAL CONDITION OF THE VEHICLE AS RECOMMENDED BY F M A
EACH OF THE FOLLOWING ITEMS SHOULD BE INSPECTED DAILY BY THE DRIVER
DEFECTIVE ITEMS SHOULD BE REPAIRED IMMEDIATELY

EQUIPMENT	DEFECTIVE	O.K.	EQUIPMENT	DEFECTIVE	O.K.
AIR LINES			HEAD LIGHTS		
BRAKES			STOP LIGHTS		
BRAKE WARNING DEVICE			TAIL LIGHTS		
FIRE EXTINGUISHER			CLEARANCE LIGHTS		
FLAGS - FLARES - FUSES			REFLECTORS		
SPARE BULBS AND FUSES			TURN INDICATORS		
SPARE SEALED BEAM			MIRRORS		
WINDSHIELD WIPERS			SPEEDOMETER		
DEFROSTERS			TIRES		
HORN			STEERING		
			MOTOR		

REMARKS: _____

_____

_____

10-5 DRIVER'S DAILY LOG AND REPORT

VEHICLE WORK ORDER		B2 1672
REQUESTED BY	APPROVED BY	VEHICLE NUMBER
DATE	PRIORITY [ ] URGENT [ ] SAFETY [ ] ROUTINE	AUTHORIZATION NUMBER

WORK REQUESTED

SPACE BELOW FOR MECHANIC'S USE ONLY

PROBLEM

PARTS NEEDED	ESTIMATED LABOR COST	ESTIMATED PARTS COST

COMMENTS

10-6 VEHICLE WORK ORDER

TRUCK SERVICE RECORD

TRUCK NUMBER_____

DATE	MILEAGE	SERVICE PERFORMED	MECHANIC

10-7 TRUCK SERVICE RECORD

DATE	LOCATIONS		MILES		MEMORANDUM
	FROM	TO	START	FINISH	

VEHICLE DAILY TRAVEL DIARY AND MEMORANDUM

VEHICLE NO._____   DEPARTMENT_____

10-8 VEHICLE DAILY TRAVEL DIARY AND MEMORANDUM

LEASED VEHICLE MILEAGE RECORD (IVMR)
W. C. McQuaide, Inc.

PRO # _____

TRUCK # _____   DRIVER NAME _____   EMP # _____

TRAILER # _____   LEASED OWNER # _____   - _____

DATE TRIP STARTED _____   DATE TRIP ENDED _____

TIME TRIP STARTED _____   TIME TRIP ENDED _____

TRIP ORIGIN _____   TRIP DESTINATION _____

ROUTE OF TRAVEL _____

_____

MILEAGE BY STATES: STATES NOT LISTED:

****

DC_____   *NY_____   NY PERMIT# _____ *

DE_____   *OH TAX_____   OH PERMIT# _____ *   _____   _____

****

IL_____   OH TAX FREE _____   _____   _____

IL_____   PA_____   _____   _____

KY_____   SC_____   ***************************************

MD_____   VA_____   *ENDING MILES _____ *

MI_____   WV_____   *BEGINNING MILES _____ *

NJ_____   *TOTAL MILES _____ *

****

CREDIT FOR OH TURNPIKE REQUIRES ORIGINAL TNPK. RECEIPT ATTACHED
CREDIT FOR FUEL PURCHASED REQUIRES ORIGINAL FUEL RECEIPT ATTACHED
BEGINNING MILES MUST EQUAL THE LAST TRIP'S ENDING MILES
ALL MILEAGE IS TO BE OBTAINED FROM THE TRUCK'S HUBOMETER
MILEAGE BY STATES MUST EQUAL TOTAL HUBOMETER MILES
ALL OF THE ABOVE INFORMATION MUST BE FILLED IN. LEAVE NO BLANKS.

10-9 LEASED VEHICLE MILEAGE RECORD

VEHICLE ACCIDENT REPORT

OWNER'S NAME	NUMBER & STREET

CITY	STATE & ZIP	LICENSE PLATE NUMBER

MAKE	YEAR	MODEL	COLOR	ODOMETER

ACCIDENT DATE	TIME [ ] AM [ ] PM	COUNTY

STREET	CROSS STREET [ ]N [ ]S [ ]E [ ]W

ACCIDENT DESCRIPTION

VEHICLE TOWED? [ ] YES [ ] NO	DESCRIBE DAMAGE

OPERATOR'S NAME	EMPLOYEE NO.	DEPARTMENT

LICENSE NO.	SIGNATURE	DATE

SECOND VEHICLE IDENTIFICATION NUMBER	LICENSE PLATE NO.

MAKE	YEAR	MODEL	COLOR

OPERATOR'S NAME	LICENSE NUMBER

ADDRESS

10-10 VEHICLE ACCIDENT REPORT

LIFT TRUCK MAINTENANCE LOG

Date_____

Truck #	Hours On	Hours Charged	Maintenance/Service

10-11 LIFT TRUCK MAINTENANCE LOG

```
+--------------------------------------------------------------------+
|                                              NO. 1143              |
|        SERVICE REPORT                                               |
|                                                                    |
|    FORKLIFT ID NO._____      DATE_____         |
|                                                                    |
|    MILEAGE/HOURS_____                                   |
|                                                                    |
|    DATE OF LAST SERVICE_____    MILEAGE/HOURS_____       |
|                                                                    |
|    IS THIS A ROUTINE SERVICE  [] YES  [] NO  IF NO, EXPLAIN         |
|    PROBLEM:                                                         |
|             _____          |
|                                                                    |
|    _____      |
|                                                                    |
|    _____      |
+--------------------------------------------------------------------+
|                                                                    |
|    SERVICE PERFORMED (CHECK ALL THAT APPLY)                         |
|                                                                    |
|    [] CHANGE OIL AND FILTERS       [] INSPECT HORN                  |
|    [] LUBRICATE CHASSIS            [] INSPECT ALL LIGHTS            |
|    [] TOP OFF ALL FLUID LEVELS     [] INSPECT ALL HOSES            |
|    [] CHECK AND ADJUST BELTS       [] TEST COOLING SYSTEM          |
|    [] CHECK AND ADJUST BRAKES      [] INSPECT TIRES                |
+--------------------------------------------------------------------+
|                                                                    |
|    PARTS REPAIRED/REPLACED_____      |
|                                                                    |
|    _____      |
|                                                                    |
|    _____      |
|                                                                    |
|    COMMENTS:_____      |
|                                                                    |
|    _____      |
|                                                                    |
|    _____      |
|                                                                    |
|                          _____            |
|                            MECHANIC'S SIGNATURE                     |
+--------------------------------------------------------------------+
```

10-12 FORKLIFT SERVICE REPORT

LIFT TRUCK STATUS LOG

DATE: _____   PAGE _____ OF _____

VEHICLE #	LOCATION	TIME	LOCATION	TIME	LOCATION	TIME	TOTAL
		_|_ TO _|_		_|_ TO _|_		_|_ TO _|_	
		_|_ TO _|_		_|_ TO _|_		_|_ TO _|_	
		_|_ TO _|_		_|_ TO _|_		_|_ TO _|_	
		_|_ TO _|_		_|_ TO _|_		_|_ TO _|_	
		_|_ TO _|_		_|_ TO _|_		_|_ TO _|_	
		_|_ TO _|_		_|_ TO _|_		_|_ TO _|_	
		_|_ TO _|_		_|_ TO _|_		_|_ TO _|_	
		_|_ TO _|_		_|_ TO _|_		_|_ TO _|_	
		_|_ TO _|_		_|_ TO _|_		_|_ TO _|_	
		_|_ TO _|_		_|_ TO _|_		_|_ TO _|_	
		_|_ TO _|_		_|_ TO _|_		_|_ TO _|_	

10-13 LIFT TRUCK STATUS LOG

DAILY BATTERY RECORD

Battery Number_____

Week of_____Year_____

Date	Specific Gravity In	Gravity Out	Water Added	Operator

Repairs and Capacity Tests

Date	Repair/Comments	% Capacity

10-14 DAILY BATTERY RECORD

Chapter Eleven

WAREHOUSE
PERSONNEL MANAGEMENT

The most important area of operations in a company, is its personnel. Before any department can function properly, a strong management-labor relationship must exist. Maintaining employee records, notifying and informing personnel, and interdepartmental communications are three vital areas of management concern. This chapter deals with forms and reports involving hiring new employees, evaluating current personnel, disciplinary action, and other important work-related records.

11-1. PERSONNEL REQUISITION

The form shown is used when a department has a need to either replace or add personnel. It is filled out detailing as much information as possible, in order for the personnel department to fill the position with the best candidate.

Key Information

- Description of Job Needed
- Reason for Need
- Job Requirements (e.g., educational, experience)
- Approved by (requisitioner's signature)

11-2. EMPLOYMENT APPLICATION—BASIC

This form acquires all the basic information needed from a potential employee. Included on this application is a blocked-off section, which lists additional questions that an employer can ask if they are an occupational necessity.

Key Information

- Applicant Information
- Employment History
- Military Record
- Education
- Blocked-off Area (personal questions pertaining to marital status, physical defects, criminal record, etc.)

11-3. EMPLOYMENT APPLICATION—DETAILED

The form shown is a much more detailed employment application that includes space for interviewer's comments, any tests administered, and results of a reference check.

Key Information

- Applicant's Personal Information
- Education
- Employment History
- Names of Personal References
- Military Record
- Blocked-off Area of Special Questions
- Interviewer's Comments
- Test(s) Scores/Comments
- Reference Check Results

11-4. EMPLOYMENT INTERVIEW GUIDE

This form is a guide for the interviewer to use when conducting an interview. It is very comprehensive and allows the interviewer to record various information concerning the applicant.

Key Information

- Work History
- Financial (e.g., income, goals)
- Education
- Personal and Social
- Additional Questions (must be legally permissible)

11-5. PREEMPLOYMENT REFERENCE CHECK

This form is sent to applicant's previous employer, to verify the information that the applicant listed is correct and to get a rating on his or her performance.

Key Information

- Applicant's Stated Information
- Reason for Separation
- Rating of Characteristics Pertaining to Employee's Work

11-6. PREEMPLOYMENT REFERENCE CHECK BY TELEPHONE

The form shown is a guide used when calling the applicant's previous employer. Checking a reference by telephone is time consuming, but the end result is a truer perspective of the applicant.

Key Information

- Verification of Applicant's Information
- Applicant's Relationship with Previous Employer
- Summary/Additional Information

11-7. NEW EMPLOYEE DATA CARD

This data card is filled out by a new employee and is similar to an employment application. A copy of this data card is sent to employee's department head, and personnel files the original in employee's record folder.

Key Information

- Employee Information
- Physical/Medical Information
- Education
- Employment History
- Military Record

11-8. PERSONNEL RECORD UPDATE

This form is used by personnel periodically to update an employee's file.

Key Information

- Any Physical Defects/Illnesses Since Last Update
- Additional Schooling/Training
- New Memberships/Awards

11-9. EMPLOYMENT HISTORY FILE

The form shown is a folder containing an employee's records. On the front of the folder is the employee's personal information and employment history with company, and the back serves as an employment termination record.

Key Information

- Personal Data
- Employment History
- Termination Record (e.g., reason for termination, recommendation for reemployment)

11-10. EMPLOYEE EVALUATION FORM

The form shown is used to evaluate an employee by examining many different abilities and characteristics, instead of evaluating on an overall level. This helps to spot areas where an employee is weak or strong, so these areas can be improved or used more effectively. A completed evaluation form should be discussed with the employee, so decisions on improvement or better utilization can be made.

Key Information

- Rating of Traits, Abilities, and Characteristics
- Overall Evaluation
- Major Weak/Strong Points
- Recommendations

11-11. EXECUTIVE EVALUATION FORM

The form shown is used to evaluate executive, administrative, and professional personnel. It is an excellent form to use when making a decision on promoting a supervisor or manager.

Key Information

- Employee Information
- Evaluation of Work Performance (Section A)
- Evaluation of Supervisory Performance (Section B)
- Evaluation of Factors Affecting Job Performance (Section C)
- Overall Evaluation (Section D)
- Potential (Section E)
- Employee's Comments

11-12. EMPLOYEE ATTENDANCE RECORD

The form shown is used to maintain employee attendance data. On the date employee is absent, record the code listing reason. This form is ideal for keeping track of sick days and vacation time used by each employee.

Key Information

- Employee Information
- Sick/Vacation Time Due
- Reason for Absence
- Yearly Summary

11-13. EMPLOYEE LATENESS REPORT

This report should be made in triplicate, with original for employee's supervisor, one copy for personnel, and one copy for the payroll department.

Key Information

- Employee Information
- Whether Employee Had Prior Approval for Lateness
- Reason for Lateness
- Action to Be Taken

11-14. EMPLOYEE ABSENCE REPORT

This form is used to report an employee absence, including reason for absence, and when employee will return to work.

Key Information

- Employee Information
- Date of Return
- Reason for Absence
- Reason Explained

11-15. DAILY DEPARTMENTAL ABSENCE REPORT

This report logs all daily absences within a department and determines if production will be affected.

Key Information

- Employees Absent
- Reason for Absence
- Date Expected Back
- Affect on Production
- Whether Job Is Being Covered
- How Will Work Be Made Up

11-16. OVERTIME REQUEST AND APPROVAL

This form is used by the head of the warehouse or distribution department to obtain permission to run an employee on overtime.

Key Information

- Employee Information
- Reason for Overtime
- Approved/Denied by (signature)
- Reason for Denial

11-17. EMPLOYEE OVERTIME PERMIT

The form shown authorizes overtime for an employee per day, project, contract, and so on. A copy of this permit should be sent to the payroll department showing authorization.

Key Information

- Employee Information
- Overtime Hours Authorized
- Details of Overtime Approval (e.g., what department, which shift)
- Comments

11-18. EMPLOYEE CHANGE OF STATUS REPORT

The form shown is used to report any changes in an employee's job status, whether department, shift, or rate.

Key Information

- Employee Information
- Job Change from/to

- Reason for Change
- Authorized/Approved by (signature)

11-19. VACATION REQUEST AND APPROVAL

This form is used to schedule vacation times for employees to maintain adequate production levels and output. Employees with the longest seniority are given first choice. To schedule correctly, a manager must consider the time periods involved and should be aware of busy or slow weeks for the company.

Key Information

- Entitled Vacation Time
- Preferred Choices
- Approved Vacation Time

11-20. VACATION SCHEDULE

The form shown is a folder containing employees' vacation information. The outside of the folder is used to record the entire vacation schedule of all employees.

Key Information

- Employee's Name
- Payroll Number or Department
- Vacation Time Due

11-21. EMPLOYEE WARNING NOTICE

The form shown is used to notify an employee that he or she has violated company policy. A copy is given to the employee, department head, and to personnel. If a company is unionized, a copy must be sent to the shop steward.

Key Information

- Employee Information
- Nature of Violation
- Company/Employee Statement

11-22. EMPLOYEE WARNING REPORT

This form is more detailed than a warning notice. It includes an area to describe disciplinary action to be taken.

Key Information

- Employee Information
- Nature of Violation
- Company Remarks
- Employee's Statement Regarding the Violation
- Action to Be Taken

11-23. SECURITY INCIDENT REPORT

The form shown is used to report a security incident, either by an employee or nonemployee. An incident can be theft, damage to corporate property, civil disorder, and so on.

Key Information

- Nature of Incident
- Incident Reported to
- Description of Incident
- Action Taken

11-24. EMPLOYEE EXIT INTERVIEW

This form is an in-depth examination of termination of an employee. It gives the employer complete knowledge of the circumstances involving the termination, whether resignation or discharge. The form allows an employer to examine the justification of discharge or the employee's justification in resigning. Is there a problem within the company? With management? Has the employee received proper training? Is the relationship worth salvaging? The employee exit interview is an excellent form to not only evaluate the employee, but also the company.

Key Information

- Type of Termination
- Reason for Termination (e.g., resignation, discharge), with Details
- Sample Exit Interview Questions
- Summary Questions (e.g., employee's likes, dislikes)
- Interviewer's Evaluation of Employee's Reason for Separation
- Interviewer's Recommendation for Salvage

11-25. EMPLOYEE SEPARATION NOTICE

When an employee resigns or is discharged, a separation notice should be completed, with copies sent to the personnel department and to payroll.

Key Information

- Employee Information
- Effective Date of Separation
- Reason for Separation
- Comments

PERSONNEL REQUISITION

To Requisitioner: The Civil Rights Act of 1964 prohibits discrimination in employment because of race, color, creed, religion, sex or national origin. Federal law also prohibits other types of discrimination such as age and citizenship. The laws of most States also prohibit some or all of the above types of discrimination as well as some additional types such as discrimination based upon ancestry, marital status or physical or mental handicap or disability. Any expressions of limitations in these areas expressed in this requisition should be warranted by a bona fide occupational qualification or other legally permissible reason.

DATE _____

FROM _____   _____
                                 NAME   DEPARTMENT

I. DESCRIPTION OF NEED

DATE NEEDED	NUMBER OF EMPLOYEES	JOB TITLE	JOB CLASSIFICATION NUMBER	HIRING SALARY RANGE	JOB SALARY RANGE

PERMANENT _____ TEMPORARY _____   If temporary, for how long? _____   **WHICH SHIFT?** _____

PART TIME _____ FULL TIME _____   If part time, what hours or days? _____

II. REASON FOR NEED

REPLACEMENT: YES ___ NO ___ If yes, person(s) replaced _____   **ADDITION:** YES ___ NO ___ If yes, state reasons _____

_____   _____

_____   _____

III. REQUIREMENTS

EDUCATION: GRADE SCHOOL _____ HIGH SCHOOL _____ COLLEGE _____ COMMERCIAL _____ OTHER _____

EXPERIENCE: Please indicate, clearly, what is absolutely required as a prerequisite.

REQUIRED _____

_____

_____

DESIRABLE _____

_____

_____

_____

ANY OTHER REQUIREMENTS: _____

_____

_____

_____

DATE _____   APPROVED BY _____

_____

DO NOT WRITE BELOW THIS LINE

DATE FILLED _____ By WHOM _____

11-1 PERSONNEL REQUISITION

<table>
<tr><td colspan="2">FOR OFFICE USE ONLY</td></tr>
<tr><td>Possible Work
Locations</td><td>Possible
Positions</td></tr>
<tr><td></td><td></td></tr>
</table>

EMPLOYMENT APPLICATION

(Short Form)

(PLEASE PRINT PLAINLY)

<table>
<tr><td colspan="2">FOR OFFICE USE ONLY</td></tr>
<tr><td>Work
Location _____</td><td>Rate _____</td></tr>
<tr><td>Position _____</td><td>Date _____</td></tr>
</table>

Position(s) applied for _____

Were you previously employed by us? _____ If yes, when? _____

If your application is considered favorably, on what date will you be available for work? _____ 19 _____

PERSONAL

Date _____

Name _____ Social Security No. _____
 Last   First   Middle

Present address _____ Telephone No. _____
 No.   Street   City   State   Zip

Are you legally eligible for employment in the U.S.A.? _____ Are you of the legal age to work? _____

List below present and past employment, beginning with your most recent

Name and Address of Company and Type of Business	From		To		Weekly Starting Salary	Weekly Last Salary	Reason for Leaving	Name of Supervisor
	Mo.	Yr.	Mo.	Yr.				
Describe the work you did:								
Telephone								

Name and Address of Company and Type of Business	From		To		Weekly Starting Salary	Weekly Last Salary	Reason for Leaving	Name of Supervisor
	Mo.	Yr.	Mo.	Yr.				
Describe the work you did:								
Telephone								

Name and Address of Company and Type of Business	From		To		Weekly Starting Salary	Weekly Last Salary	Reason for Leaving	Name of Supervisor
	Mo.	Yr.	Mo.	Yr.				
Describe the work you did:								
Telephone								

I hereby give permission to contact the employers listed above concerning my prior work experience.

Signed _____

If there is a particular employer(s), you do not wish us to contact, please indicate which one(s). _____

MILITARY SERVICE RECORD

Were you in U.S. Armed Forces? Yes _____ No _____ If yes, what Branch? _____

11-2 EMPLOYMENT APPLICATION—BASIC

© Copyright 1971, 1972, 1973, 1976, 1978, 1979, 1982, 1983, 1985—V.W. EIMICKE ASSOCIATES, INC., Bronxville, N.Y.

EDUCATION

Encircle last year completed

Describe any other training or education

Elementary School	5	6	7	8	_____
High School	1	2	3	4	_____
College	1	2	3	4	_____

PLEASE READ AND SIGN BELOW

The facts set forth in my application for employment are true and complete. I understand that if employed, any false statement on this application may result in my dismissal. I further understand that this application is not and is not intended to be a contract of employment, nor does this application obligate the employer in any way if the employer decides to employ me. You are hereby authorized to make any investigation of my personal history and financial and credit record through any investigative or credit agencies or bureaus of your choice.

In making this application for employment I authorize you to make an investigative consumer report whereby information is obtained through personal interviews with my neighbors, friends, or others with whom I am acquainted. This inquiry, if made, may include information as to my character, general reputation, personal characteristics and mode of living. I understand that I have the right to make a written request within a reasonable period of time to receive additional, detailed information about the nature and scope of any such investigative report that is made.

_____
Signature of Applicant

To Applicant: READ THIS INTRODUCTION CAREFULLY BEFORE ANSWERING ANY QUESTIONS IN THIS BLOCKED-OFF AREA. The Civil Rights Act of 1964 prohibits discrimination in employment because of race, color, creed, religion, sex or national origin. Federal law also prohibits other types of discrimination such as age. The laws of most States also prohibit some or all of the above types of discrimination as well as some additional types such as discrimination based upon ancestry, marital status or physical or mental handicap or disability.

DO NOT ANSWER ANY QUESTION CONTAINED IN THIS BLOCKED-OFF AREA UNLESS THE EMPLOYER HAS CHECKED THE BOX NEXT TO THE QUESTION, thereby indicating that for the position for which you are applying the requested information is needed for a legally permissible reason, including, without limitation, national security requirements, a bona fide occupational qualification or business necessity.

☐ Are you over the age of eighteen? _____ If no, hire is subject to verification that you are of minimum legal age.

☐ How do you wish to be addressed? Mr. ___Mrs. ___Miss___ Ms _____

☐ Sex: M _____F _____ • ☐ Height: _____ ft. _____ in. ☐ Weight _____ lbs.

☐ Marital Status: Single _____Engaged_____Married_____Separated_____Divorced_____Widowed _____

☐ Date of Marriage _____ ☐ Number of dependents including yourself _____

☐ Are you a citizen of the U.S.A.? _____ ☐ What is your present Selective Service classification? _____

☐ Have you ever been bonded? _____If yes, on what jobs? _____

☐ Have you ever been convicted of a crime, excluding misdemeanors and summary offenses, in the past ten years which has not been

annulled or expunged or sealed by a court? _____If yes, describe in full _____

☐ Do you have any physical condition which may limit your ability to perform the particular job for which you are applying? _____

If yes, describe such condition and explain how you can perform the job for which you are applying in spite of it. _____

_____

_____

☐ Do you have any physical defects which preclude you from performing certain kinds of work? _____ If yes, describe such

defects and specific work limitations. _____

☐ Have you had a major illness in the past 5 years? _____If yes, describe _____

☐ Have you received compensation for injuries? _____If yes, describe _____ ___

Employer may list other bona fide occupational questions on lines below:

☐ _____

☐ _____

This *"Employment Application"* is prepared for general use throughout the United States. Our legal counsel has advised us that the material outside the blocked-off area complied with all Federal and State fair employment practice laws and with the Fair Credit Reporting Act. However, the various fair employment practice laws and related statutes and the interpretations of them change frequently, and neither V.W. Eimicke Associates, Inc. nor its counsel assume any responsibility for the inclusion in this *"Employment Application"* of any questions that may violate local and/or State and/or Federal laws. Users should consult their counsel about any legal question they may have with respect to the use of this form.

11-2 (Continued)

APPLICATION FOR EMPLOYMENT

(PLEASE PRINT PLAINLY)

PERSONAL

Date _____

Name _____ Social Security No. _____
      Last   First   Middle

Present address _____ Telephone No. _____
      No.   Street   City   State   Zip

Are you legally eligible for employment in the U.S.A.? Yes___ No___ (If yes, verification will be required.)

Are you of the legal age to work? _____

Position(s) applied for _____

Were you previously employed by us?_____ If yes, when? _____

If your application is considered favorably, on what date will you be available for work? _____ 19_____

Are there any other experiences, skills, or qualifications which will be of special benefit in the job for which you are applying? (Applicant should not list any information that Federal and/or State law precludes obtaining in the pre-employment stage.) _____

_____

_____

_____

RECORD OF EDUCATION

School	Name and Address of School	Course of Study	Check Last Year Completed				Did You Graduate?	List Diploma or Degree
Elementary			5	6	7	8	☐ Yes ☐ No	
High			1	2	3	4	☐ Yes ☐ No	
College			1	2	3	4	☐ Yes ☐ No	
Other (Specify)			1	2	3	4	☐ Yes ☐ No	

(Turn to Next Page)

11-3 EMPLOYMENT APPLICATION—DETAILED

List below present and past employment, beginning with your most recent

I

Name and Address of Company and Type of Business	From		To		Weekly Starting Salary	Weekly Last Salary	Reason for Leaving	Name of Supervisor
	Mo.	Yr.	Mo.	Yr.				
	Describe the work you did:							
Telephone								

II

Name and Address of Company and Type of Business	From		To		Weekly Starting Salary	Weekly Last Salary	Reason for Leaving	Name of Supervisor
	Mo.	Yr.	Mo.	Yr.				
	Describe the work you did:							
Telephone								

III

Name and Address of Company and Type of Business	From		To		Weekly Starting Salary	Weekly Last Salary	Reason for Leaving	Name of Supervisor
	Mo.	Yr.	Mo.	Yr.				
	Describe the work you did:							
Telephone								

IV

Name and Address of Company and Type of Business	From		To		Weekly Starting Salary	Weekly Last Salary	Reason for Leaving	Name of Supervisor
	Mo.	Yr.	Mo.	Yr.				
	Describe the work you did:							
Telephone								

I hereby give permission to contact the employers listed above concerning my prior work experience.

Signed _____

If there is a particular employer(s), you do not wish us to contact, please indicate which one(s). _____

_____

PERSONAL REFERENCES (Not Former Employers or Relatives)

Name and Occupation	Address	Phone Number

MILITARY SERVICE RECORD

Were you in U.S. Armed Forces? Yes_____ No_____ If yes, what Branch?_____

Did you receive any training in the U.S. Armed Forces that is relevant to the position applied for?_____

_____

11-3 (Continued)

PLEASE READ AND SIGN BELOW

The facts set forth in my application for employment are true and complete. I understand that if employed, any false statement on this application may result in my dismissal. I further understand that this application is not and is not intended to be a contract of employment, nor does this application obligate the employer in any way if the employer decides to employ me. I understand and agree that my employment is at-will and can be terminated by either party with or without notice, at any time, for any reason or no reason. No one other than an officer of the Company has any authority to enter into any agreement for employment for any specified period of time or to make any agreement contrary to the foregoing and then only in a writing signed by an officer. You are hereby authorized to make any investigation of my personal history and financial and credit record through any investigative or credit agencies or bureaus of your choice.

In making this application for employment I authorize you to make an investigative consumer report whereby information is obtained through personal interviews with my neighbors, friends, or others with whom I am acquainted. This inquiry, if made, may include information as to my character, general reputation, personal characteristics and mode of living. I understand that I have the right to make a written request within a reasonable period of time to receive additional, detailed information about the nature and scope of any such investigative report that is made.

_____
Signature of Applicant

To Applicant: READ THIS INTRODUCTION CAREFULLY BEFORE ANSWERING ANY QUESTIONS IN THIS BLOCKED-OFF AREA. The Civil Rights Act of 1964 prohibits discrimination in employment because of race, color, creed, religion, sex or national origin. Federal law also prohibits other types of discrimination such as age and citizenship. The laws of most States also prohibit some or all of the above types of discrimination as well as some additional types such as discrimination based upon ancestry, marital status or physical or mental handicap or disability. The Fair Credit Reporting Act imposes restrictions with respect to credit data.

DO NOT ANSWER ANY QUESTION CONTAINED IN THIS BLOCKED-OFF AREA UNLESS THE EMPLOYER HAS CHECKED THE BOX NEXT TO THE QUESTION, thereby indicating that for the position for which you are applying the requested information is needed for a legally permissible reason, including, without limitation, national security requirements, a bona fide occupational qualification or business necessity.

☐ How long have you lived at present address? _____

☐ Previous address _____ How long did you live there? _____
                No.   Street   City   State   Zip

☐ Are you over the age of eighteen? _____ If no, hire is subject to verification that you are of minimum legal age.

☐ How do you wish to be addressed? Mr.____ Mrs.____ Miss____ Ms.____

☐ Sex: M_____ F_____   ☐ Height:_____ ft._____ in.   ☐ Weight:_____ lbs.

☐ Marital Status: Single _____ Engaged _____ Married _____ Separated _____ Divorced _____ Widowed _____

☐ Date of Marriage _____ ☐ Number of dependents including yourself _____ ☐ Are you a citizen of the U.S.A.? _____

☐ What is your present Selective Service classification? _____

☐ Are you a Vietnam veteran?_____

☐ Indicate dates you attended school:

Elementary _____ High School _____ College _____
          From   To   From   To   From   To

Other (Specify type of school) _____
                                                    From   To

☐ Have you ever been bonded?_____ If yes, on what jobs? _____

☐ Have you ever been convicted of a crime, excluding misdemeanors and summary offenses, in the past ten years which has not been annulled or expunged or sealed by a court?_____ If yes, describe in full _____

☐ Do you have any physical condition which may limit your ability to perform the particular job for which you are applying? _____

If yes, describe such condition and explain how you can perform the job for which you are applying in spite of it. _____

_____

☐ Do you have any physical defects which preclude you from performing certain kinds of work? _____ If yes, describe such

defects and specific work limitations. _____

☐ Have you had a major illness in the past 5 years? _____ If yes, describe _____

_____

☐ Have you received compensation for injuries?_____ If yes, describe _____

_____

☐ List any friends or relatives working for us, other than spouse _____
                                                                      Name(s)

Employer may list other bona fide occupational questions on lines below:

☐ _____

☐ _____

—3—

11-3 (Continued)

APPLICANT — Do not write on this page
FOR INTERVIEWER'S USE

INTERVIEWER	DATE	COMMENTS

FOR TEST ADMINISTRATOR'S USE

TESTS ADMINISTERED	DATE	RAW SCORE	RATING	COMMENTS AND INTERPRETATION

REFERENCE CHECK

*Position Number	RESULTS OF REFERENCE CHECK	*Position Number	RESULTS OF REFERENCE CHECK
I		IV	
II			
III			

*See Page 2

—4—

11-3 (Continued)

EMPLOYMENT INTERVIEW GUIDE

NAME OF APPLICANT _____ DATE _____

CANDIDATE FOR _____
                                                    Job Title

This EMPLOYMENT INTERVIEW GUIDE has been designed to aid in the selection of employees by making each interview more objective. The Guide is only a guide, intended for broad general use. The Interviewer need not ask any of the indicated questions if they are not deemed relevant to the position being applied for; or the Interviewer may decide to ask additional questions during the interview; these questions and the candidate's answers to them should be recorded in the space provided on page 4 of this GUIDE.

Questions within parentheses are provided to assist the Interviewer in interpreting the applicant's answers and should prove helpful in suggesting additional questions.

Although the candidate's answers should be noted during the interview, the Interviewer should review the GUIDE, after the applicant has left, and should expand answers wherever necessary. Finally, the Interviewer should summarize the interview by completing an EMPLOYMENT INTERVIEW REPORT (V.W. EIMICKE ASSOCIATES, INC. FORM 103).

PART 1. WORK HISTORY

1. Please describe in detail the kind of work you did in your last position.

(Secure this information about the other positions held by the applicant, as well. Account for at least 12 years or the entire time since leaving school if the candidate left school recently.) _____

_____

_____

_____

_____

_____

_____

_____

_____

_____

_____

_____

(Will previous work experience be helpful in the position for which applicant is being considered? Has each change of position been to a better and more responsible job? If unemployed at any time, how did applicant manage?)

2. How did you obtain each job? _____

_____

(Is applicant self-reliant? Is applicant resourceful? Is applicant creative in approach?)

3. What salary increases or promotions did you receive? _____

_____

(Were these based on good work? Did applicant advance more quickly than others?)

4. (a) May we contact your former employers for references? _____
   (b) Has a former employer ever refused to give you a recommendation? _____
   (Is there evidence of good will toward former employers?)

5. What experiences have you had in handling people? In supervising others? _____

_____

(Is there indication of leadership potential? Is applicant people oriented?)

6. What did you like best about the jobs you have had in the past? _____

_____

11-4 EMPLOYMENT INTERVIEW GUIDE

7. What did you especially dislike? _____

_____

(Is there justification for the dislikes?)

8. Why did you leave each of your former jobs? (If currently employed, also ask: Why do you want to leave your present job?) _____

_____

(Are answers reasonable and consistent? Is there evidence of good will toward former employers?)

9. Describe the type of criticism most frequently made of your work by former employers _____

_____

(Does applicant welcome constructive criticism? Is applicant objective about himself/herself? Does applicant maintain a serious attitude toward work?)

10. Compare interview findings with the data in the Employment Section of the Application for Employment Form for inconsistencies or omissions.

PART II. FINANCIAL

1. Have you ever held a part-time job to supplement the income from your full-time job?_____
   If yes, describe the type of work: _____

_____

2. (a) What position do you want to hold 10 years from now?_____

_____

   (b) How do you plan to achieve these goals?_____

_____

(Are applicant's goals realistic? Does applicant appear to be strongly motivated? Can our Company provide the sought after opportunities.)

PART III. EDUCATION

1. How will your schooling help you to be successful in the job for which you are being considered?

_____

_____

2. Did you work part-time while at school? If yes, describe the type of work: _____

_____

3. What courses did you like best? _____

4. What courses did you like least? _____

5. Were your grades average, below average or above average? _____
   Can you give me more detail on this? _____

_____

(Was applicant a good student?)

6. Have you continued your education in any way since leaving school?_____ If yes,how?

_____

7. Have you had any special training courses in connection with any of your jobs?_____
   If yes, describe: _____

_____

(What is applicant's attitude toward Company training?)

11-4 (Continued)

PART IV. PERSONAL AND SOCIAL

1. In what school-sponsored activities, e.g., clubs, sports, newspapers, etc. did you participate? (Applicant should be told not to name any activities that suggest the race, religion, national origin or ancestry of their members and any other information that Federal and State law precludes obtaining in the pre-employment stage.) _____

_____

(What motivated the participation?)

2. What offices if any did you hold in these clubs or athletic organizations? _____

(Does applicant like to be a leader?)

3. When you were a student what did you do during vacation periods? _____

(Was the activity purposeful?)

4. To what clubs or social groups do you now belong? (Applicant should be told not to name any organizations that suggest the race, religion, national origin or ancestry of their members and any other information that Federal and State law precludes obtaining in the pre-employment stage.) _____

_____

5. What part have you taken in your clubs or organizations? _____

(Were leadership qualities demonstrated?)

6. What do you do in your spare time? _____

_____

On vacations? _____
(Does applicant have many friends? What do sparetime activities reveal about applicant?)

7. What kind of books do you enjoy reading? _____

(How much reading is done?)

8. Which newspapers and magazines do you read regularly? _____

9. How do you usually entertain your friends? _____

_____

(Is there indication of moderation in drinking? Does applicant gamble?)

10. What do you usually do evenings at home? _____

(Is leisure time well spent?)

11. What do you believe are your strongest qualities? _____

_____

12. What are your weak points? In what areas is improvement needed? _____

11-4 (Continued)

13. (a) Why do you want to work for our Company? _____
_____
_____

(b) What do you know about our Company? _____
_____
_____

(c) Why do you want this job? _____
_____

(Are reasons satisfactory? Does applicant have a true picture of our Company? Is estimate of worth to our Company realistic? Can our Company satisfy applicant's needs?)

OTHER QUESTIONS

To Interviewer:

The Civil Rights Act of 1964 prohibits discrimination in employment because of race, color, creed, religion, sex or national origin. Federal law also prohibits other types of discrimination such as age and citizenship. The laws of most States also prohibit some or all of the above types of discrimination as well as some additional types such as discrimination based upon ancestry, marital status or physical or mental handicap or disability.

DO NOT ASK ANY OF THE QUESTIONS THAT FOLLOW UNLESS YOU KNOW IT IS LEGALLY PERMISSIBLE FOR YOU TO DO SO.

1. Do you have any physical defects which preclude you from performing certain kinds of work? _____
If yes, describe such defects and specific work limitations. _____
_____

2. What illnesses, accidents or operations have you had during the past ten years? _____
_____
_____

3. Have you ever received compensation for injuries? _____ If yes, describe: _____
_____

(Does applicant appear to be a generally healthy person? Does applicant appear to be energetic?)

4. Do you have any debts other than those for current living expenses? _____ If yes, explain:
_____

(How were these incurred? Is there a financial problem? Is there indication of poor financial planning?)

5. Have you maintained a systematic savings program? _____
(Does applicant save regularly and sufficiently?)

6. Do you have any other sources of income in addition to salary, e.g., earnings by your spouse, real estate, business interests, dividends on securities? _____ If yes, explain: _____
_____

(How will this income affect applicant's attitude toward this job?)

7. Do you own your own home? _____ If yes, describe: _____
_____

8. Do you own a car(s)? _____ If yes, describe: _____
_____

11-4 (Continued)

PRE-EMPLOYMENT REFERENCE CHECK

_____19_____

_____

_____

_____

Attention: _____

The applicant named below has told us that he/she previously worked for your Company. We would appreciate your furnishing us with as much of the information requested below as possible. We assure you that any information you may give will be treated confidentially.

An early reply will be greatly appreciated.

Sincerely yours,

_____
Title

Co. Name: _____

Co. Address: _____

APPLICANT'S NAME _____

SOCIAL SECURITY/
INSURANCE NUMBER* _____

DATES IN YOUR EMPLOY: FROM_____ TO_____ SALARY: $_____ PER_____

POSITION HELD _____

Is the information listed above correct? YES_____ NO_____ If no, please supply the correct information below.

_____

_____

Why did applicant leave your Company?_____

Would you re-employ? YES_____ NO_____ If no, why not?_____

_____

_____

Please rate applicant on the following characteristics:

	POOR	FAIR	AVERAGE	VERY GOOD	EXCELLENT
QUALITY OF WORK					
QUANTITY OF WORK					
SUITABILITY FOR POSITION					
**PERSONAL APPEARANCE					
ATTENDANCE					
DEPENDABILITY					
COOPERATIVENESS					
CREATIVENESS					

** If relevant to the particular job.

DATE_____   SIGNED_____

TITLE

11-5 PREEMPLOYMENT REFERENCE CHECK

TELEPHONE PRE-EMPLOYMENT REFERENCE CHECK GUIDE

APPLICANT _____
  Name   Soc. Sec. Number

CANDIDATE FOR _____
                              Job Title
DATE OF   CHECKED
REF. CHECK _____ BY _____

PREVIOUS ⎧ COMPANY NAME _____
EMPLOYER ⎨ ADDRESS _____
         ⎪   No.   Street   City   State   Telephone
         ⎪ PERSON
         ⎩ TALKED TO _____
                              Name   Title

INTRODUCE YOURSELF BY NAME, TITLE AND COMPANY

(Name of applicant) has applied for employment with us and has told us that he/she previously worked for your Organization. I should like to verify some information given us. Do you have time to answer a few questions? (If not, get a definite time to recall.)

1. Was applicant employed by your Organization? YES _____ NO _____

2. Applicant states that employment was from _____ to _____

   Is that correct? YES ____ NO ____. If not, show correct dates: from _____ to _____

3. What was applicant's job when starting to work for you? _____

4. What was applicant's job when leaving? _____

5. Applicant states earnings of $ _____ per _____ Is that correct? YES ____ NO _____

   If not, show actual rate $ _____ per _____

6. What did you think of the quality of applicant's work? _____

   _____

   _____

   _____

(PLEASE SEE REVERSE SIDE)

11-6 PREEMPLOYMENT REFERENCE CHECK BY TELEPHONE

7. How hard did applicant work? _____
   _____

8. Was applicant regular and punctual in attendance? YES _____ NO _____

9. How did applicant get along with others? _____
   _____
   _____

10. Did applicant follow instructions? YES _____ NO _____

11. Did applicant have any domestic or personal trouble which
    interfered with work? YES _____ NO _____ Any financial difficulties? YES _____ NO _____
    Any drinking or gambling problems? YES _____ NO _____
    If yes, explain: _____
    _____
    _____
    _____

12. Why did applicant leave your Organization? _____
    _____
    _____
    _____

13. Would you re-employ? YES _____ NO _____   If not, why not? _____
    _____
    _____

14. In summing up, what would you say are applicant's strong points? _____
    _____

    Weak points? _____
    _____

Additional information _____
_____
_____
_____
_____

11-6 (Continued)

NEW-EMPLOYEE DATA CARD

Name_____ Social Security No. _____
      Last   First   Middle

WELCOME! We deeply appreciate your interest in our organization and assure you that we are sincerely interested in your qualifications. Your cooperation in completing this card fully and accurately will supply us with information required for our benefits program.

IN CASE OF EMERGENCY NOTIFY

Name_____ Telephone No._____

Address_____
      No.   Street   City   State   Zip

ADDRESS

Present address_____ Telephone No._____
      No.   Street   City   State   Zip

Previous address_____ Telephone No._____
      No.   Street   City   State   Zip

How long have you lived at your present address?_____ How long at previous address?_____

PERSONAL

*Date of birth_____ *Sex: M_____ F_____ *Height:_____ft._____in. *Weight:_____lbs.
      Month Day Year

*Marital Status: ☐ Single ☐ Engaged ☐ Married ☐ Separated ☐ Divorced ☐ Widowed Date of marriage_____

Name of spouse _____ Where employed_____

*Dependent children (Names and ages) _____

_____ Number of dependents including yourself_____

Are you a citizen of the U.S.A.?_____ If no, do you have the legal right to remain permanently in the U.S.A?_____

If no, Visa Number_____ Have you been convicted of a crime in the past ten years, excluding

misdemeanors and summary offenses?_____ If yes, describe in full_____

_____

List any friends or relatives working for us _____

---

*PHYSICAL/MEDICAL

Describe your general health: ☐ Poor ☐ Fair ☐ Average ☐ Good ☐ Excellent

Do you have any physical or mental condition which may limit your ability to perform certain kinds of work?_____

If yes, describe such defect(s) and specific work limitations _____

_____

Have you had a major illness in the past 5 years? _____ If yes, describe_____

_____

Have you received compensation for injuries?_____ If yes, describe _____

RECORD OF EDUCATION

School	Name and Address of School	Course of Study	Years Attended From	Years Attended To	Check Last Year Completed	Did You Graduate?	List Diploma or Degree
Elementary		✕			5 6 7 8	☐ Yes ☐ No	✕
High					1 2 3 4	☐ Yes ☐ No	
College					1 2 3 4	☐ Yes ☐ No	
Other (Specify)					1 2 3 4	☐ Yes ☐ No	

* See **Important Notice** on reverse.

(Side tab: Name / Last / First / Middle)

11-7 NEW EMPLOYEE DATA CARD

EMPLOYMENT HISTORY List below all past employment, beginning with most recent

Name and Address of Company and Type of Business	From		To		Weekly Starting Salary	Weekly Last Salary	Reason for Leaving	Name of Supervisor
	Mo.	Yr.	Mo.	Yr.				
Telephone	Describe the work you did:							

Name and Address of Company and Type of Business	From		To		Weekly Starting Salary	Weekly Last Salary	Reason for Leaving	Name of Supervisor
	Mo.	Yr.	Mo.	Yr.				
Telephone	Describe the work you did:							

Name and Address of Company and Type of Business	From		To		Weekly Starting Salary	Weekly Last Salary	Reason for Leaving	Name of Supervisor
	Mo.	Yr.	Mo.	Yr.				
Telephone	Describe the work you did:							

Name and Address of Company and Type of Business	From		To		Weekly Starting Salary	Weekly Last Salary	Reason for Leaving	Name of Supervisor
	Mo.	Yr.	Mo.	Yr.				
Telephone	Describe the work you did:							

MILITARY SERVICE RECORD

Were you in U.S. Armed Forces? Yes _____ No _____ If yes, what Branch? _____

Dates of duty: From _____ To _____ Rank at discharge _____
   Month   Day   Year   Month   Day   Year

List duties in the service including special training _____

_____

Have you taken any training under the G.I. Bill of Rights? _____ If yes, what training did you take? _____

_____ What is your present Selective Service classification? _____

> Summarize here any additional experiences and/or skills you may have.
>
>
>
> List any civic, business or professional organizations of which you are a member. (Exclude reference to organizations denoting national origin, race, color or religion)

The facts set forth above are true and complete to the best of my knowledge.

_____   _____
           Date   Signature

11-7 (Continued)

PERSONNEL RECORD UPDATE

NAME _____ DEPARTMENT _____ DATE _____

In order that we may keep our personnel records up-to-date, please show below any changes since

_____. Show Changes Only.
Date of Last Update

_____

Address _____ Phone _____
     No.   Street   City   State   Zip

*Marital Status: Engaged _____ Married _____ Separated _____ Divorced _____ Widowed _____

Number of Dependents   Number of   Their
Including Yourself _____ Children _____ Ages _____

Does your Wife/
Husband Work? _____ Where _____

*Describe any physical defects you have developed since last update which might limit your effectiveness on this job
_____

Describe any major illness you have had since last update which might limit your effectiveness on this job _____
_____

If you received compensation for injuries since last update, explain _____
_____

Selective Service Classification _____

ADDITIONAL SCHOOLING OR SPECIAL TRAINING

DATE	SCHOOL OR AGENCY	NAME OF COURSE AND BRIEF DESCRIPTION

New memberships in technical or professional societies _____
_____

New professional offices or honors _____
_____

Any other changes you would like us to note_____
_____
_____

Employee's Signature _____ Reviewed by _____
     Sign Your Name   Supervisor

NOTE TO SUPERVISOR: Describe on the reverse side any special projects or assignments which you feel have aided this
    employee's development and increased his value to the Company.

*The Civil Rights Act of 1964 prohibits employment discrimination on the basis of sex. The laws of some States prohibit employment discrimination on the basis of marital status or against the handicapped.

11-8 PERSONNEL RECORD UPDATE

Personnel ENVELO-FILE®

PRINT EMPLOYEE'S NAME ON TAB

ADDRESS ___ NO. ___ STREET ___ CITY ___ STATE ___ ZIP ___ TELEPHONE

YEARS OF SERVICE

| | 1 | 2 | 3 | 4 | 5 | 6 | 7 | 8 | 9 | 10 | 11 | 12 | 13 | 14 | 15 | 16 | 17 | 18 | 19 | 20 | 21 | 22 | 23 | 24 | 25 | OVER 25 |

ADDRESS ___ NO. ___ STREET ___ CITY ___ STATE ___ ZIP ___ TELEPHONE

*DATE OF BIRTH ___ *SEX: M. ___ F. ___ SOCIAL SECURITY NUMBER

ADDRESS ___ NO. ___ STREET ___ CITY ___ STATE ___ ZIP ___ TELEPHONE

*CITIZEN OF U.S.A. YES ___ NO ___ *MARITAL STATUS: SINGLE ___ ENGAGED ___ MARRIED ___ SEPARATED ___ WIDOWED ___ DIVORCED ___

IN EMERGENCY NOTIFY

NO. OF DEPENDENTS INCLUDING SELF ___ *JOB RELATED PHYSICAL DISABILITIES ___

ADDRESS ___ NO. ___ STREET ___ CITY ___ STATE ___ ZIP ___ TELEPHONE

EDUCATION: GRADE SCHOOL ___ HIGH SCHOOL ___ COLLEGE ___ SPECIAL TRAINING ___

RELATIVES OR FRIENDS WORKING FOR COMPANY ___ NAME ___ RELATIONSHIP

COMPANY TRAINING ___

NAME ___ RELATIONSHIP

PARTICIPATION IN: CREDIT UNION ___ DATE JOINED ___ GROUP INSURANCE ___ DATE ELIGIBLE ___ PENSION PLAN ___ DATE ELIGIBLE ___ DATE JOINED ___ DATE ELIGIBLE ___ DATE JOINED ___

*CREDIT DATA

UNION MEMBER: YES ___ NO ___ DATE OF JOINING ___

EMPLOYMENT HISTORY

DATES		POSITION	DEPARTMENT	RATE OF PAY		GRADE OF WORK	REASON FOR CHANGE OR TERMINATION
FROM	TO			AMOUNT	PER		

*THE CIVIL RIGHTS ACT OF 1964 PROHIBITS DISCRIMINATION IN EMPLOYMENT BECAUSE OF RACE, COLOR, CREED, RELIGION, SEX OR NATIONAL ORIGIN. FEDERAL LAW ALSO PROHIBITS OTHER TYPES OF DISCRIMINATION SUCH AS AGE AND CITIZENSHIP. THE LAWS OF MOST STATES ALSO PROHIBIT SOME OR ALL OF THE ABOVE TYPES OF DISCRIMINATION AS WELL AS SOME ADDITIONAL TYPES SUCH AS DISCRIMINATION BASED UPON ANCESTRY, MARITAL STATUS, OR PHYSICAL OR MENTAL HANDICAP OR DISABILITY. THE FAIR CREDIT REPORTING ACT IMPOSES RESTRICTIONS WITH RESPECT TO CREDIT DATA.

11-9 EMPLOYMENT HISTORY FILE

SPECIAL INFORMATION

TERMINATION RECORD

VOLUNTARY	INVOLUNTARY	DETAILED STATEMENT OF REASON FOR TERMINATION
BETTER JOB ____	CO. RELOCATION ____	
FAMILY ____	CO. REORGANIZATION ____	
GENERAL DISSATISFACTION ____	END OF TEMPORARY PERIOD ____	
ILLNESS ____	INCOMPETENCE ____	
INSUFFICIENT PAY ____	LACK OF WORK ____	
RELOCATION ____	MISCONDUCT ____	
OTHER ____	TRADE DISPUTE ____	
UNKNOWN ____	RETIREMENT ____	
	DEATH ____	
	OTHER ____	

RECOMMENDED FOR REEMPLOYMENT?

YES ____ NO ____

11-9 (Continued)

EMPLOYEE EVALUATION FORM

NAME: _____ DATE: _____

DEPARTMENT: _____ JOB TITLE: _____

Purposes of this Employee Evaluation:

To take a personal inventory, to pin-point weaknesses and strengths and to outline and agree upon a practical improvement program. Periodically conducted, these Evaluations will provide a history of development and progress.

Instructions:

Listed below are a number of traits, abilities and characteristics that are important for success in business. Place an "X" mark on each rating scale, over the descriptive phrase which most nearly describes the person being rated. (If this form is being used for self-evaluation, you will be describing yourself.)

Carefully evaluate each of the qualities separately.

Two common mistakes in rating are: (1) A tendency to rate nearly everyone as "average" on every trait instead of being more critical in judgment. The rater should use the ends of the scale as well as the middle, and (2) The "Halo Effect," i.e., a tendency to rate the same individual "excellent" on every trait or "poor" on every trait based on the *overall* picture one has of the person being rated. However, each person has strong points and weak points and these should be indicated on the rating scale.

ACCURACY is the correctness of work duties performed.

Makes frequent errors.	Careless; makes recurrent errors.	Usually accurate; makes only average number of mistakes.	Requires little supervision; is exact and precise most of the time.	Requires absolute minimum of supervision; is almost always accurate.

ALERTNESS is the ability to grasp instructions, to meet changing conditions and to solve novel or problem situations.

Slow to "catch on."	Requires more than average instructions and explanations.	Grasps instructions with average ability.	Usually quick to understand and learn.	Exceptionally keen and alert.

CREATIVITY is talent for having new ideas, for finding new and better ways of doing things and for being imaginative.

Rarely has a new idea; is unimaginative.	Occasionally comes up with a new idea.	Has average imagination; has reasonable number of new ideas.	Frequently suggests new ways of doing things; is very imaginative.	Continually seeks new and better ways of doing things; is extremely imaginative.

11-10 EMPLOYEE EVALUATION FORM

*FRIENDLINESS is the sociability and warmth which an individual imparts in his/her behavior toward customers, other employees, his/her supervisor and the persons he/she may supervise.

Very distant and aloof.	Approachable; friendly once known by others.	Warm; friendly; sociable.	Very sociable and out-going.	Extremely sociable; excellent at establishing good will.

PERSONALITY is an individual's behavior characteristics or his/her personal suitability for the job.

Personality unsatisfactory for this job.	Personality questionable for this job.	Personality satisfactory for this job.	Very desirable personality for this job.	Outstanding personality for this job.

*PERSONAL APPEARANCE is the personal impression an individual makes on others. (Consider cleanliness, grooming, neatness and appropriateness of dress on the job.)

Very untidy; poor taste in dress.	Sometimes untidy and careless about personal appearance.	Generally neat and clean; satisfactory personal appearance.	Careful about personal appearance; good taste in dress.	Unusually well groomed; very neat; excellent taste in dress.

PHYSICAL FITNESS is the ability to work consistently and with only moderate fatigue. (Consider physical alertness and energy.)

Tires easily; is weak and frail.	Frequently tires and is slow.	Meets physical and energy job requirements.	Energetic; seldom tires.	Excellent health; no fatigue.

ATTENDANCE is faithfulness in coming to work daily and conforming to work hours.

Often absent without good excuse and/or frequently reports for work late.	Lax in attendance and/or reporting for work on time.	Usually present and on time.	Very prompt; regular in attendance.	Always regular and prompt; volunteers for overtime when needed.

HOUSEKEEPING is the orderliness and cleanliness in which an individual keeps his/her work area.

Disorderly or untidy.	Some tendency to be careless and untidy.	Ordinarily keeps work area fairly neat.	Quite conscientious about neatness and cleanliness.	Unusually neat, clean and orderly.

* If relevant to the particular job.

11-10 (Continued)

DEPENDABILITY is the ability to do required jobs well with a minimum of supervision.

Requires close supervision; is unreliable.	Sometimes requires prompting.	Usually takes care of necessary tasks and completes with reasonable promptness.	Requires little supervision; is reliable.	Requires absolute minimum of supervision.

DRIVE is the desire to attain goals, to achieve.

Has poorly defined goals and acts without purpose; puts forth practically no effort.	Sets goals too low; puts forth little effort to achieve.	Has average goals and usually puts forth effort to reach these.	Strives hard; has high desire to achieve.	Sets high goals and strives incessantly to reach these.

JOB KNOWLEDGE is the information concerning work duties which an individual should know for a satisfactory job performance.

Poorly informed about work duties.	Lacks knowledge of some phases of work.	Moderately informed; can answer most common questions.	Understands all phases of work.	Has complete mastery of all phases of job.

QUANTITY OF WORK is the amount of work an individual does in a work day.

Does not meet minimum requirements.	Does just enough to get by.	Volume of work is satisfactory.	Very industrious; does more than is required.	Superior work production record.

STABILITY is the ability to withstand pressure and to remain calm in crisis situations.

Goes "to pieces" under pressure; is "jumpy" and nervous.	Occasionally "blows up" under pressure; is easily irritated.	Has average tolerance for crises; usually remains calm.	Tolerates most pressure; very good tolerance for crises.	Thrives under pressure; really enjoys solving crises.

COURTESY is the polite attention an individual gives other people.

Blunt; discourteous; antagonistic.	Sometimes tactless.	Agreeable and pleasant.	Always very polite and willing to help.	Inspiring to others in being courteous and very pleasant.

11-10 (Continued)

297

OVERALL EVALUATION in comparison with other employees with the same length of service on this job:

Definitely unsatisfactory.	Substandard but making progress.	Doing an average job.	Definitely above average.	Outstanding.

COMMENTS

Major weak points are—	Major strong points are—
1. _____	1. _____
2. _____	2. _____
3. _____	3. _____
and these can be strengthened by doing the following:	and these can be used more effectively by doing the following:

Rated by _____ _____
  (Name)   (Title)

(If not used as a self-evaluation form, the employee should sign below)

A copy of this Report has been given to me and has been discussed with me.

_____ _____
(Employee's Signature)   (Date)

11-10 (Continued)

Employee
Performance
Evaluation

For Executive, Administrative, and Professional Personnel

Employee Information

Name

Last	First	Middle

Employment Numbers/S.S. Number   In-Service Date

Department   Location

Job Title   Job Code

Supervisor's Name

Last	First	Middle

Date of Last Evaluation   Date of This Evaluation

Purposes of this Performance Evaluation

To take a personal inventory, to pinpoint strengths and weaknesses, and to review past objectives and corresponding accomplishments so as to identify areas where performance can be improved for the benefit of both the employee and the company; and to formulate and agree a practical improvement program of specific challenges.

Prepared by:

Name   Title

Signature   Date

Reviewed by:

Name   Title

Signature   Date

Date discussed with employee

Form 200

11-11 EXECUTIVE EVALUATION FORM

Instructions for Sections A, B, and C. Sections A, B, and C require rating the employee on characteristics pertinent to job performance. Carefully evaluate each of the characteristics, separately, based on recurring day-to-day performance since the last review and not on recent or isolated, exceptional events. For each characteristic, rate the employee poor, fair, average, good, or excellent using these rating definitions and check the appropriate box.

Poor: Definitely below acceptable standards; performance of job requirements is consistently deficient.

Fair: Improvement is needed to meet acceptable standards; performance of job requirement is inconsistent.

Average: Meets acceptable standards; performance of job requirements is consistent.

Good: Above acceptable standards; performance usually exceeds job requirements.

Excellent: Outstanding; unquestionably above acceptable standards; performance consistently exceeds job requirements.

Two common mistakes in rating are: (1) A tendency to rate nearly everyone as "average" on every characteristic instead of being more critical in judgment. The evaluator should use the ends of the scale as well as the middle. (2) The "halo effect," i.e., a tendency to rate the same individual "excellent" on every characteristic or "poor" on every characteristic based on the overall picture one has of the person being evaluated. However, each person has strong and weak points and these should be indicated on the rating scales.

Section A.		Poor	Fair	Average	Good	Excellent
Work Performance	**Knowledge** Understanding of fundamentals, skills, methods, and procedures required in present job.	☐	☐	☐	☐	☐
	Planning Development of methods and work organization to efficiently perform overall work load.	☐	☐	☐	☐	☐
	Application Insure consistent job performance to complete overall work load.	☐	☐	☐	☐	☐
	Accuracy Absence of mistakes and errors in job performance.	☐	☐	☐	☐	☐
	Thoroughness Attention to requisite detail, to completeness; avoidance of superficiality.	☐	☐	☐	☐	☐
	Quality Overall quality of work.	☐	☐	☐	☐	☐
	Quantity Overall quantity of work.	☐	☐	☐	☐	☐

11-11 (Continued)

Section B.		Poor	Fair	Average	Good	Excellent
Supervisory Performance	**Organization** Division of total operation into efficient interdependent components.	☐	☐	☐	☐	☐
	Personnel Selection Identification of job-required characteristics in prospective employees.	☐	☐	☐	☐	☐
	Training Development of personnel efficiency.	☐	☐	☐	☐	☐
	Follow-Up Monitoring that instructions, schedules, etc. are being followed.	☐	☐	☐	☐	☐
	Economy Minimization of controllable costs; optimum utilization of resources.	☐	☐	☐	☐	☐
	Safety Orientation toward safe working practices and health standards.	☐	☐	☐	☐	☐
	Leadership Establishment of personnel team effort toward common objectives.	☐	☐	☐	☐	☐

Section C.		Poor	Fair	Average	Good	Excellent
Factors Affecting Job Performance	**Adaptability** Alteration of activities, plans, etc. to accommodate new or changed situations.	☐	☐	☐	☐	☐
	Analysis Examination of a problem leading to identification of its component parts and their relations.	☐	☐	☐	☐	☐
	Attendance	☐	☐	☐	☐	☐
	Cooperation Working effectively with others to achieve common goals.	☐	☐	☐	☐	☐
	Creativeness Improvement of methods, procedures, etc. by new ideas.	☐	☐	☐	☐	☐
	Expression Oral and written presentation of ideas.	☐	☐	☐	☐	☐
	Health	☐	☐	☐	☐	☐
	Initiative Self-confident, enthusiastic performance of a task with a minimum of instruction.	☐	☐	☐	☐	☐
	Judgment Formation of a sound opinion by careful study of available facts and options.	☐	☐	☐	☐	☐
	Perseverance Maintenance of position in spite of opposition or discouragement.	☐	☐	☐	☐	☐
	Reliability Dependability; instills full confidence.	☐	☐	☐	☐	☐

11-11 (Continued)

Continued on next page

Section D.

Overall Evaluation in Present Position

The supervisor should discuss the incumbent's strong points as well as limitations with a view toward improving the employee's performance. Objectives—concentrating on the fundamentals, skills, methods and procedures required in the present job—should be presented and accepted as *challenges,* and these challenges should be clearly understood by supervisor and employee through effective face-to-face discussion.

Major strengths:

Major Weaknesses:

Past Objectives and Accomplishments (The specific major challenges that were set with the employee for the past evaluation period and the corresponding accomplishments. Indicate any factors outside the employee's control that affected accomplishments.)

Objectives:

Accomplishments:

Future Objectives (The specific major challenges that have been agreed with the employee for the next period.)

Section E.

Potential

☐ Properly placed.

☐ Not properly placed; should be terminated.

☐ Promotable now to the position indicated below.

☐ Promotable to the position indicated below with additional training and experience.

Job Title

Comments:

Employee's Comments

(After you have reviewed this form and discussed it with your supervisor, please state briefly your comments regarding this evaluation. If you have no comments please state "none.")

Employee's Signature   Date

11-11 (Continued)

EMPLOYEE ATTENDANCE RECORD

NAME _____
LAST   FIRST   MIDDLE

DATE OF BIRTH _____   DATE OF HIRE _____   DEPARTMENT _____

SOCIAL SECURITY NUMBER _____   SICK DAYS DUE _____   CLOCK NUMBER _____

19 ___   VACATION TIME DUE _____

	1	2	3	4	5	6	7	8	9	10	11	12	13	14	15	16	17	18	19	20	21	22	23	24	25	26	27	28	29	30	31
JAN																															
FEB																															
MAR																															
APR																															
MAY																															
JUN																															
JUL																															
AUG																															
SEP																															
OCT																															
NOV																															
DEC																															

ABSENCE SUMMARY

A	AO	D	DF	H	J	LA	SF	SS	V	X	EO

YEARLY TOTALS
USE REVERSE SIDE
FOR ADDITIONAL NOTES

A = ACCIDENT ON DUTY
AO = ACCIDENT OFF DUTY
D = DISCIPLINE

DF = DEATH IN FAMILY
H = HOLIDAY
J = JURY DUTY

LA = LEAVE OF ABSENCE
SF = SICKNESS IN FAMILY
SS = SICKNESS-SELF

V = VACATION
X = UNEXCUSED ABSENCE
EO = EXCUSED (OTHER)

11-12 EMPLOYEE ATTENDANCE RECORD

© Copyright, 1965, 1977, V.W. EIMICKE ASSOCIATES, INC., Bronxville, N.Y.

303

TO: _____   _____
               NAME OF SUPERVISOR   DEPARTMENT

To be prepared in triplicate. Original for employee's supervisor.
One copy for personnel records and one copy for Payroll Dept.

EMPLOYEE LATENESS REPORT

EMPLOYEE NAME _____

CLOCK OR PAYROLL
NUMBER _____ DEPT. _____

ADDRESS _____ PHONE _____ SHIFT _____

DUE TO REPORT _____ WILL REPORT _____

PRIOR APPROVAL: ☐ NO ☐ YES BY _____

WAS COMPANY NOTIFIED: ☐ YES ☐ NO

If Yes, Time: _____ Date _____

PERSON REPORTING LATENESS: _____ PHONE _____

REASON FOR LATENESS: _____

_____

_____

_____ ACTION TO BE TAKEN _____

☐ None   Other: _____

☐ Time to be made up   _____

☐ Deduct from payroll   _____

DATE _____ RECORDED BY _____

11-13 EMPLOYEE LATENESS REPORT

TO: _____   _____

NAME OF SUPERVISOR   DEPARTMENT

To be prepared in duplicate. Original for absentee's supervisor.
Copy for personnel records.

ABSENCE REPORT

CLOCK OR
PAYROLL
NAME_____NUMBER_____DEPT._____

ADDRESS_____PHONE_____SHIFT_____

LAST DAY WORKED_____WILL RETURN IN APPROXIMATELY_____DAYS

PERSON REPORTING ABSENCE_____PHONE_____

REPORTED TO:	BY PHONE	BY MESSENGER	OTHER MEANS	DATE	HOUR

REASON FOR ABSENCE

(CHECK APPROPRIATE REASON)

ACCIDENT ON DUTY		HOLIDAY		SICKNESS—SELF	
ACCIDENT OFF DUTY		JURY DUTY		VACATION	
DISCIPLINE		LEAVE OF ABSENCE		UNEXCUSED ABSENCE	
DEATH IN FAMILY		SICKNESS IN FAMILY		EXCUSED (OTHER)	

NAME OF HOSPITAL_____NAME OF DOCTOR_____

REASON FOR ABSENCE EXPLAINED (AS REQUIRED)_____

_____

_____

_____

DATE_____   REPORT RECORDED BY_____

PERSONNEL DEPARTMENT

11-14 EMPLOYEE ABSENCE REPORT

DAILY DEPARTMENTAL ABSENCE REPORT

Department: _____ **Shift:** _____ **Name of Supervisor:** _____

	Reason for Absence	Excused?	Employee's Job Title	Absent since	Expected back on	Under a Doctor's care?
1.		☐ Yes ☐ No				
2.		☐ Yes ☐ No				
3.		☐ Yes ☐ No				
4.		☐ Yes ☐ No				
5.		☐ Yes ☐ No				
6.		☐ Yes ☐ No				

	Is job being covered?	If job is being covered, Indicate how and by whom	If job is not covered, how will work be made up?
1.	☐ Yes ☐ No		
2.	☐ Yes ☐ No		
3.	☐ Yes ☐ No		
4.	☐ Yes ☐ No		
5.	☐ Yes ☐ No		
6.	☐ Yes ☐ No		

REPORT PREPARED BY _____

Date _____

11-15 DAILY DEPARTMENTAL ABSENCE REPORT

OVERTIME REQUEST AND APPROVAL

Date_____

Request Employee _____

Payroll or
Timeclock No. _____ Dept. _____ Shift _____

be permitted to work _____ hours on _____
　　　　　　　　　　　　　　　　　　　　　　　　(Date)

☐ Overtime　　　　　☐ Make-up Time

on Job No. _____ Describe _____

_____

_____

_____

Reason for request _____

_____

_____

_____

Request prepared by _____
　　　　　　　　　　　　　　　　(Signature)

Approved by _____ Date _____
　　　　　　　　　　(Signature)

Request denied by _____ Date _____
　　　　　　　　　　(Signature)

Reason _____

_____

11-16 OVERTIME REQUEST AND APPROVAL

DATE_____   EMPLOYEE OVERTIME PERMIT

NAME:	DEPARTMENT:
EMPLOYEE NUMBER:	PAYROLL CLASSIFICATION:
OVERTIME HOURS AUTHORIZED:	APPROVED BY:

OVERTIME APPROVED FOR:

[ ] DEPARTMENT_____   [ ] JOB LOT_____

[ ] SHIFT_____   [ ] PROJECT NUMBER_____

[ ] CONTRACT_____   [ ] OTHER _____

COMMENTS:_____

_____

_____

DEPARTMENT SUPERVISOR	PAYROLL DEPARTMENT

A COPY OF THIS PERMIT MUST BE SUBMITTED WITH EMPLOYEE'S
TIME RECORD OR OVERTIME WILL NOT BE PAID

11-17 EMPLOYEE OVERTIME PERMIT

EMPLOYEE CHANGE OF STATUS REPORT

Please enter the following change(s) as of _____

Name _____

Clock or
Payroll No. _____

Social Security/
Insurance No.* _____

FROM

Job	Dept.	Shift	Rate

TO

Job	Dept.	Shift	Rate

REASON FOR CHANGE:

☐ Hired
☐ Re-hired
☐ Promotion
☐ Demotion
☐ Transfer
☐ Merit Increase

☐ Length of Service Increase
☐ Re-evaluation of Existing Job
☐ Resignation
☐ Retirement
☐ Layoff
☐ Discharge

☐ Leave of Absence to _____
                          Date

Other reason or explanation: _____
_____
_____
_____

AUTHORIZED BY _____ APPROVED BY _____

Prepare in triplicate: (1) Personnel   (2) Payroll   (3) Employee's Department

11-18 EMPLOYEE CHANGE OF STATUS REPORT

VACATION REQUEST AND APPROVAL

Date_____

To:_____
(Employee's Name)

Dept. _____

In accordance with our Company policy, as of_____, you have been in our employ_____ year(s) and are
(date)   months

entitled to_____ week(s) vacation.
day(s)

To assist in scheduling vacations, please indicate your first, second, and third choice for vacation time below and return

both copies of this form to your supervisor by_____. One copy will be returned to you indicating approved vaca-

tion time.

PERSONNEL DEPARTMENT

	First Choice		Second Choice		Third Choice	
	*Start	Return	Start	Return	Start	Return
1st week or days						
2nd week						
3rd week						
4th week						
5th week						

Signed_____

Date_____

We are happy to approve your vacation time as follows:

Day(s) of _____
Week(s)

_____

Have a wonderful time!

Signed_____
PERSONNEL DEPARTMENT

*Since normal vacation weeks start on Monday, please use Monday dates.

11-19 VACATION REQUEST AND APPROVAL

© Copyright 1972 V.W. Eimicke Associates, Inc., Bronxville, N.Y. 10708

VACATION SCHEDULE ENVELO-FILE®

Year _____

Please note instructions for use on reverse side.

Employee's Name	Payroll No. or DEPT.	Years Service	Vacation Time Due	*JAN	FEB	MAR	APR	MAY	JUN	JUL	AUG	SEP	OCT	NOV	DEC

* Since normal vacation weeks start on Monday, please use Monday dates.

11-20 VACATION SCHEDULE

```
+---------------------------------------------------------------+
|                  EMPLOYEE WARNING NOTICE                      |
|                  ========================                     |
|                                                               |
|   EMPLOYEE'S NAME_____ DEPARTMENT_____       |
|   CLOCK or                                                     |
|   PAYROLL NO._____ DATE OF WARNING_____       |
+---------------------------------------------------------------+
|                                                               |
|                   [] ATTENDANCE    [] TARDINESS               |
|        TYPE                                                    |
|                   [] SAFETY        [] DISOBEDIENCE            |
|         OF                                                     |
|                   [] CARELESSNESS  [] WORK QUALITY           |
|       VIOLATION                                               |
|                   [] OTHER (EXPLAIN)_____          |
|                                                               |
|                      _____          |
|                                                               |
|   DATE OF VIOLATION_____   TIME OF VIOLATION_____      |
|                                                               |
|   PLACE VIOLATION OCCURRED_____       |
|                                                               |
|   [] FIRST WARNING  [] SECOND WARNING  [] THIRD WARNING       |
+---------------------------------------------------------------+
|        COMPANY STATEMENT      |     EMPLOYEE STATEMENT         |
|     _____    |   _____      |
|     _____    |   _____      |
|     _____    |   _____      |
|     _____    |   _____      |
|                                                               |
|     I HAVE READ THIS WARNING NOTICE AND UNDERSTAND IT          |
|   _____       _____      |
|     SUPERVISOR'S SIGNATURE         EMPLOYEE'S SIGNATURE        |
+---------------------------------------------------------------+
```

11-21 EMPLOYEE WARNING NOTICE

EMPLOYEE WARNING RECORD

Employee's Name _____

Clock or Payroll No. _____ Dept. _____

Shift _____ Time _____ a.m. p.m.

Date of Warning _____

WARNING

Date of Violation _____

Time of Violation _____

Place Violation Occurred _____

NATURE OF VIOLATION ▶

☐ Substandard Work   ☐ Conduct   ☐ Tardiness   ☐ Uncooperative

☐ Carelessness   ☐ Disobedience   ☐ _____

COMPANY REMARKS

HAS EMPLOYEE BEEN WARNED PREVIOUSLY?	Form of Warning	WHEN WARNED and BY WHOM		
		1st Warning	2nd Warning	3rd Warning
☐ YES ☐ NO	Oral			
	Written			

EMPLOYEE'S REMARKS RE: VIOLATION

The absence of any statement on the part of the EMPLOYEE indicates his/her agreement with the report as stated.

I have entered my version of the matter above.

Employee's Signature _____ Date _____

ACTION TO BE TAKEN

Approved By _____

Name   Title   Date

I have read this "warning" and understand it.

Employee's Signature _____ Date _____

Signature of person who prepared warning   Title   Date

DISTRIBUTION OF COPIES

☐ Employee   ☐ Personnel Department

☐ Foreman or Supervisor   ☐ Plant Manager

Supervisor's Signature   Date

11-22 EMPLOYEE WARNING REPORT

© Copyright 1970, 1978,—V.W. Eimicke Associates, Inc., Bronxville, N.Y.

```
┌─────────────────────────────────────────────────────┐
│              SECURITY INCIDENT REPORT               │
├──────────┬──────────────────────────────────────────┤
│ NATURE   │  _____    │
│   of     │                                          │
│ INCIDENT │  _____    │
├──────────┴──────────────────────────────────────────┤
│  DATE_____   TIME NOTIFIED_____    │
│                                                      │
│  POLICE NOTIFIED  [] YES [] NO   IF YES, ENTER TIME  │
│                                  NOTIFIED_____  │
│                                                      │
│  POLICEMAN_____PRECINCT#_____SHIELD#_____  │
├──────────────────────────────────────────────────────┤
│  DETAILED DESCRIPTION OF INCIDENT_____   │
│  _____    │
│  _____    │
│  _____    │
│  _____    │
├──────────────────────────────────────────────────────┤
│  EMPLOYEE(S)/PERSON(S) INVOLVED:                     │
│                                                      │
│  _____   _____  │
│   LAST  MIDDLE  FIRST          LAST  MIDDLE  FIRST    │
│  _____   _____  │
│   LAST  MIDDLE  FIRST          LAST  MIDDLE  FIRST    │
├──────────────────────────────────────────────────────┤
│  ACTION TAKEN_____   │
│  _____    │
│  _____    │
│  _____    │
├──────────────────────────────────────────────────────┤
│  _____   _____  _____  │
│  NAME OF PERSON PREPARING REPORT    TITLE     DATE   │
└──────────────────────────────────────────────────────┘
```

11-23 SECURITY INCIDENT REPORT

EMPLOYEE EXIT INTERVIEW

Date_____

Name_____ Department_____

Social Security No._____ Job Title _____

Supervisor's Name _____ Date Hired_____ Date Separated_____

TYPE OF TERMINATION: Retirement_____   Resignation_____   Discharge_____   Layoff_____

I. STATED REASON FOR SEPARATION
(Please check the reason that applies)

RESIGNATION	DISCHARGE	LAYOFF
_____ Physical Condition	Inadequate:	_____ Temporary Work
_____ Family	_____ Ability	_____ Reduction of Staff
_____ Returning to School	_____ Suitability for Position	_____ Other Reason: _____
_____ Secured Better Position	_____ Drive	_____
_____ Going into Business for Self	_____ Efficiency	_____
Disliked:	_____ Cooperation	_____
_____ Hours	_____ Dishonesty	_____
_____ Supervisor	_____ Rules Violation	
_____ Type of Work	_____ Absenteeism	**RETIREMENT**
_____ Wages	_____ Tardiness	_____ Age
_____ Working Conditions	_____ Inadequate Safety Consciousness	_____ Medical
_____ Other Reason: _____	_____ Other Reason: _____	
_____	_____	
_____	_____	
_____	_____	

Complete when employee has RESIGNED:

New Employer _____ Location _____

Nature of new work _____ Pay _____ Hours_____

Complete in DISCHARGE cases:

When was employee notified? _____ How was employee notified? _____

Complete in LAYOFF cases:

Was employee offered transfer? Yes_____ No_____

To which department?_____To which job? _____

Why was transfer refused? _____

11-24 EMPLOYEE EXIT INTERVIEW

II. PATTERNED INTERVIEW

This patterned interview has been designed to assist the interviewer to (1) evaluate the true reason for separation, and (2) make recommendations for salvage.

SELECTION

What kind of work have you been doing in our Company? _____

_____

_____

What type of work did you do prior to joining our Company? _____

_____

_____

(Is previous work related to work assignment in our Company? Does previous work suggest salvage possibilities?)

What type of work do you like best? _____

Least? _____ Why? _____

_____

(Do answers suggest improper selection?)

TRAINING

Who explained your job to you? _____ How? _____

_____

(Was job training adequate?)

When you began work with this Company, who introduced you to the people with whom you would be working? _____

_____

(Was orientation adequate?)

FINANCIAL

How do you feel about your pay? _____

(Is attitude realistic?)

How do you feel about your progress with our Company? _____

_____

_____

(Is attitude realistic?)

11-24 (Continued)

SUPERVISION

How do you feel about your supervisor? _____

_____

_____

(Was quality of supervision adequate? Was quantity of supervision adequate?)

Did you take any complaints to your supervisor?   Yes_____   No_____

If yes, how were they handled? _____

_____

(Is there evidence of proper supervision?)

Have you had any troubles with your supervisor?   Yes_____   No_____

If yes, describe: _____

_____

(Is there evidence of proper supervision?)

SUMMARY

What did you like best about your job? _____

_____

What did you like least about your job? _____

_____

What did you like best about the Company? _____

_____

What did you like least about the Company? _____

_____

Why are you really leaving? _____

_____

_____

(Is this the true reason? Is salvage possible? Is salvage desirable?)

11-24 (Continued)

(If salvage seems possible and desirable)

Would you be willing to stay with our Company under a more satisfactory arrangement?   Yes_____   No_____

What changes would be required? _____

_____

_____

(Are these reasonable? Is the proposition workable?)

_____

Interviewer's evaluation of true reason for separation:

_____

_____

_____

_____

_____

_____

_____

_____

_____

_____

Interviewer's recommendation for salvage (if salvage is possible and desirable)

_____

_____

_____

_____

_____

_____

_____

_____

_____

_____

_____
Interviewer's Signature

11-24 (Continued)

```
+-----------------------------------------------------------------+
|                                                                 |
|    EMPLOYEE SEPARATION NOTICE        DATE_____        |
|                                                                 |
+-------------------------------+---------------------------------+
|  NAME:                        |  DEPARTMENT:                    |
+-------------------------------+---------------------------------+
|  EFFECTIVE DATE:              |  EMPLOYEE NO.:                  |
+-------------------------------+---------------------------------+
|                                                                 |
|  REASON FOR SEPARATION:   [] DISCHARGE    [] LAYOFF             |
|                                                                 |
|                           [] LEAVE OF ABSENCE                   |
|                                                                 |
|                           [] RESIGNED    [] OTHER              |
|                                                                 |
+-----------------------------------------------------------------+
|                                                                 |
|  COMMENTS: _____         |
|                                                                 |
|            _____         |
|                                                                 |
|            _____         |
|                                                                 |
|            _____         |
|                                                                 |
+-----------------------------------------------------------------+
|  _____    _____       |
|  DEPARTMENT SUPERVISOR            PERSONNEL MANAGER             |
|                                                                 |
|         THIS FORM MUST BE COMPLETED AND FILED                   |
|        WITH THE PAYROLL DEPARTMENT IMMEDIATELY                  |
|             UPON SEPARATION OF EMPLOYEE                         |
|                                                                 |
+-----------------------------------------------------------------+
```

11-25 EMPLOYEE SEPARATION NOTICE

Appendix

UNIFORM COMMERCIAL CODE

ARTICLE 7   WAREHOUSE RECEIPTS, BILLS OF
LADING, AND OTHER DOCUMENTS OF TITLE

PART 1   GENERAL

Sec. 7-101.   Short Title

This Article shall be known and may be cited as Uniform Commercial Code—Documents of Title.

Sec. 7-102.   Definitions and Index of Definitions

(1) In this Article, unless the context otherwise requires:
   (a) "Bailee" means the person who by a warehouse receipt, bill of lading, or other document of title acknowledges possession of goods and contracts to deliver them.
   (b) "Consignee" means the person named in a bill to whom or to whose order the bill promises delivery.
   (c) "Consignor" means the person named in a bill as the person from whom the goods have been received for shipment.
   (d) "Delivery order" means a written order to deliver goods directed to a warehouseman, carrier or other person who in the ordinary course of business issues warehouse receipts or bills of lading.
   (e) "Document" means document of title as defined in the general definitions in Article 1 (Section 1-201).

(f) "Goods" means all things which are treated as movable for the purposes of a contract of storage or transportation.

(g) "Issuer" means a bailee who issues a document except that in relation to an unaccepted delivery order it means the person who orders the possessor of goods to deliver. Issuer includes any person for whom an agent or employee purports to act in issuing a document if the agent or employee has real or apparent authority to issue documents, notwithstanding that the issuer received no goods or that the goods were misdescribed or that in any other respect the agent or employee violated his instructions.

(h) "Warehouseman" is a person engaged in the business of storing goods for hire.

(2) Other definitions applying to this Article or to specified Parts thereof, and the sections in which they appear are:

"Duly negotiate." Section 7-501.

"Person entitled under the document." Section 7-403(4).

(3) Definitions in other Articles applying to this Article and the sections in which they appear are:

"Contract for sale." Section 2-106.

"Overseas." Section 2-323.

"Receipt" of goods. Section 2-103.

(4) In addition, Article 1 contains general definitions and principles of construction and interpretation applicable throughout this Article.

Sec. 7-103.   Relation of Article to Treaty, Statute, Tariff, Classification, or Regulation

To the extent that any treaty or statute of the United States, regulatory statute of this State or tariff, classification or regulation filed or issued pursuant thereto is applicable, the provisions of this Article are subject thereto.

Sec. 7-104.   Negotiable and Nonnegotiable Warehouse Receipt, Bill of Lading, or Other Document of Title

(1) A warehouse receipt, bill of lading or other document of title is negotiable
   (a) if by its terms the goods are to be delivered to bearer or to the order of a named person; or
   (b) where recognized in overseas trade, if it runs to a named person or assigns.

(2) Any other document is nonnegotiable. A bill of lading in which it is stated that the goods are consigned to a named person is not made negotiable by a provision that the goods are to be delivered only against a written order signed by the same or another named person.

Sec. 7-105.   Construction Against Negative Implication

The omission from either Part 2 or Part 3 of this Article of a provision corresponding to a provision made in the other Part does not imply that a corresponding rule of law is not applicable.

PART 2   WAREHOUSE RECEIPTS: SPECIAL PROVISIONS

Sec. 7-201.   Who May Issue a Warehouse Receipt; Storage Under Government Bond

(1) A warehouse receipt may be issued by any warehouseman.

(2) Where goods including distilled spirits and agricultural commodities are stored under a statute requiring a bond against withdrawal or a license for the issuance of receipts in the nature of warehouse receipts, a receipt issued for the goods has like effect as a warehouse receipt even though issued by a person who is the owner of the goods and is not a warehouseman.

Sec. 7-202.   Form of Warehouse Receipt, Essential Terms, Options Terms

(1) A warehouse Receipt need not be in any particular form.

(2) Unless a warehouse receipt embodies within its written or printed terms each of the following, the warehouseman is liable for damages caused by the omission to a person injured thereby:

   (a) the location of the warehouse where the goods are stored;

   (b) the date of issue of the receipt;

   (c) the consecutive number of the receipt;

   (d) a statement whether the goods received will be delivered to the bearer, to a specified person, or to a specified person or his order;

   (e) the rate of storage and handling charges, except that where goods are stored under a field warehousing arrangement a statement of that fact is sufficient on a nonnegotiable receipt;

   (f) a description of the goods or of the packages containing them;

   (g) the signature of the warehouseman, which may be made by his authorized agent;

   (h) if the receipt is issued for goods of which the warehouseman is owner, either solely or jointly or in common with others, the fact of such ownership; and

   (i) a statement of the amount of advances made and of liabilities incurred for which the warehouseman claims a lien or security interest (Section 7-209). If the precise amount of such advances made or of such liabilities incurred is, at the time of the issue of the receipt, unknown to the warehouseman or to his agent who issues it, a statement of the fact that advances have been made or liabilities incurred and the purpose thereof is sufficient.

(3) A warehouseman may insert in his receipt any other terms which are not contrary to the provisions of this Act and do not impair his obligation of delivery (Section 7-403) or his duty of care (Section 7-204). Any contrary provisions shall be ineffective.

Sec. 7-203.   Liability for Non-Receipt or Misdescription

A party to or purchaser for value in good faith of a document of title other than a bill of lading relying in either case upon the description therein of the goods may recover from the issuer damages caused by the non-receipt or misdescription of the goods, except to the extent that the document conspicuously indicates that the issuer does not know whether any part or all of the goods in fact were received or conform to the description as where the description is in terms of marks or labels or kind, quantity or condition, or the receipt or description is qualified by "contents, condition and quality unknown, "said to contain" or the like, if such indication be true, or the party or purchaser otherwise has notice.

Sec. 7-204. Duty of Care; Contractual Limitations of Warehouseman's Liability

(1) A warehouseman is liable for damages for loss of or injury to the goods caused by his failure to exercise such care in regard to them as a reasonably careful man would exercise under like circumstances but, unless otherwise agreed, he is not liable for damages which could not have been avoided by the exercise of such care.

(2) Damages may be limited by a term in the warehouse receipt or storage agreement limiting the amount of liability in case of loss or damage, and setting forth a specific liability per article or item, or value per unit of weight, beyond which the warehouseman shall not be liable; provided, however, that such liability may on written request of the bailor at the time of signing such storage agreement or within a reasonable time after receipt of the warehouse receipt be increased on part or all of the goods thereunder, in which event increased rates may be charged based on such increased valuation, but that no such increase shall be permitted contrary to a lawful limitation of liability contained in the warehouseman's tariff, if any. No such limitation is effective with respect to the warehouseman's liability for conversion to his own use.

(3) Reasonable provisions as to the time and manner of presenting claims and instituting actions based on the bailment may be included in the warehouse receipt or tariff.

(4) This section does not impair or repeal . . .

Note: Insert in subsection (4) a reference to any statute which imposes a higher responsibility upon the warehouseman or invalidates contractual limitations which would be permissible under this Article.

Sec. 7-205. Title Under Warehouse Receipt Defeated in Certain Cases

A buyer in the ordinary course of business of fungible goods sold and delivered by a warehouseman who is also in the business of buying and selling such goods takes free of any claim under a warehouse receipt even though it has been duly negotiated.

Sec. 7-206. Termination of Storage at Warehouseman's Option

(1) A warehouseman may, on notifying the person on whose account the goods are held and any other person known to claim an interest in the goods, require payment of any charges and removal of the goods from the warehouse at the termination of the period of storage fixed by the document, or, if no period is fixed, within a stated period not less than thirty days after the notification. If the goods are not removed before the date specified in the notification, the warehouseman may sell them in accordance with the provisions of the section on enforcement of a warehouseman's lien (Section 7-210).

(2) If a warehouseman in good faith believes that the goods are about to deteriorate or decline in value to less than the amount of his lien within the time prescribed in subsection (1) for notification, advertisement and sale, the warehouseman may specify in the notification any reasonable shorter time for removal of the goods and in case the goods are not removed, may sell them at public sale held not less than one week after a single advertisement or posting.

(3) If as a result of a quality or condition of the goods of which the warehouseman had no notice at the time of deposit, the goods are a hazard to other property or to the warehouse or to persons, the warehouseman may sell the goods at public or private sale without advertisement on reasonable notification to all persons known to claim an interest in the goods. If the warehouseman after a reasonable effort is unable to sell the goods, he may dispose of them in any lawful manner and shall incur no liability by reason of such disposition.

(4) The warehouseman must deliver the goods to any person entitled to them under this Article upon due demand made at any time prior to sale or other disposition under this section.

(5) The warehouseman may satisfy his lien from the proceeds of any sale or disposition under this section but must hold the balance for delivery on the demand of any person to whom he would have been bound to deliver the goods.

Sec. 7-207. Goods Must Be Kept Separate; Fungible Goods

(1) Unless the warehouse receipt otherwise provides, a warehouseman must keep separate the goods covered by each receipt so as to permit at all times identification and delivery of those goods, except that different lots of fungible goods may be commingled.

(2) Fungible goods so commingled are owned in common by the persons entitled thereto, and the warehouseman is severally liable to each owner for that owner's share. Where because of overissue a mass of fungible goods is insufficient to meet all the receipts which the warehouseman has issued against it, the persons entitled include all holders to whom overissued receipts have been duly negotiated.

Sec. 7-208. Altered Warehouse Receipts

Where a blank in a negotiable warehouse receipt has been filled in without authority, a purchaser for value and without notice of the want of authority may treat the insertion as authorized. Any other unauthorized alteration leaves any receipt enforceable against the issuer according to its original tenor.

Sec. 7-209. Lien of Warehouseman

(1) A warehouseman has a lien against the bailor on the goods covered by a warehouse receipt or on the proceeds thereof in his possession for charges for storage or transportation (including demurrage and terminal charges) insurance, labor, or charges present or future in relation to the goods, and for expenses necessary for preservation of the goods or reasonably incurred in their sale pursuant to law. If the person on whose account the goods are held is liable for like charges or

expenses in relation to other goods whenever deposited and it is stated in the receipt that a lien is claimed for charges and expenses in relation to other goods, the warehouseman also has a lien against him for such charges and expenses whether or not the other goods have been delivered by the warehouseman. But against a person to whom a negotiable warehouse receipt is duly negotiated, a warehouseman's lien is limited to charges in an amount or at a rate specified on the receipt or if no charges are so specified then to a reasonable charge for storage of the goods covered by the receipt subsequent to the date of the receipt.

(2) The warehouseman may also reserve a security interest against the bailor for a maximum amount specified on the receipt for charges other than those specified in subsection (1), such as for money advanced and interest. Such a security interest is governed by the Article on Secured Transactions (Article 9).

(3) (a) A warehouseman's lien for charges and expenses under subsection (1) or a security interest under subsection (2) is also effective against any person who so entrusted the bailor with possession of the goods that a pledge of them by him to a good faith purchaser for value would have been valid but is not effective against a person as to whom the document confers no right in the goods covered by it under Section 7-503.

   (b) A warehouseman's lien on household goods for charges and expenses in relation to the goods under subsection (1) is also effective against all persons if the depositor was the legal possessor of the goods at time of deposit. "Household goods" means furniture, furnishings and personal effects used by the depositor in a dwelling.

(4) A warehouseman loses his lien on any goods which he voluntarily delivers or which he unjustifiably refuses to deliver.

Sec. 7-210. Enforcement of Warehouseman's Lien

(1) Except as provided in subsection (2), a warehouseman's lien may be enforced by public or private sale of the goods in block or in parcels, at any time or place and on any terms which are commercially reasonable, after notifying all persons known to claim an interest in the goods. Such notification must include a statement of the amount due, the nature of the proposed sale and the time and place of any public sale. The fact that a better price could have been obtained by a sale at a different time or in a different method from that selected by the warehouseman is not of itself sufficient to establish that the sale was not made in a commercially reasonable manner. If the warehouseman either sells the goods in the usual manner in any recognized market therefor, or if he sells at the price current in such market at the time of his sale, or if he has otherwise sold in conformity with commercially reasonable practices among dealers in the type of goods sold, he has sold in a commercially reasonable manner. A sale of more goods than apparently necessary to be offered to insure satisfaction of the obligation is not commercially reasonable except in cases covered by the preceding sentence.

(2) A warehouseman's lien on goods other than goods stored by a merchant in the course of his business may been forced only as follows:

(a) All persons known to claim an interest in the goods must be notified.

(b) The notification must be delivered in person or sent by registered or certified letter to the last known address of any person to be notified.

(c) The notification must include an itemized statement of the claim, a description of the goods subject to the lien, a demand for payment within a specified time not less than ten days after receipt of the notification, and a conspicuous statement that unless the claim is paid within that time the goods will be advertised for sale and sold by auction at a specified time and place.

(d) The sale must conform to the terms of the notification.

(e) The sale must be held at the nearest suitable place to that where the goods are held or stored.

(f) After the expiration of the time given in the notification, an advertisement of the sale must be published once a week for two weeks consecutively in a newspaper of general circulation where the sale is to be held. The advertisement must include a description of the goods, the name of the person on whose account they are being held, and the time and place of the sale. The sale must take place at least fifteen days after the first publication. If there is no newspaper of general circulation where the sale is to be held, the advertisement must be posted at least ten days before the sale in not less than six conspicuous places in the neighborhood of the proposed sale.

(3) Before any sale pursuant to this section, any person claiming a right in the goods may pay the amount necessary to satisfy the lien and the reasonable expenses incurred under this section. In that event, the goods must not be sold but must be retained by the warehouseman subject to the terms of the receipt and this Article.

(4) The warehouseman may buy at any public sale pursuant to this section.

(5) A purchaser in good faith of goods sold to enforce a warehouseman's lien takes the goods free of any rights of persons against whom the lien was valid, despite non-compliance by the warehouseman with the requirements of this section.

(6) The warehouseman may satisfy his lien from the proceeds of any sale pursuant to this section but must hold the balance, if any, for delivery on demand to any person to whom he would have been bound to deliver the goods.

(7) The rights provided by this section shall be in addition to all other rights allowed by law to a creditor against his debtor.

(8) Where a lien is on goods stored by a merchant in the course of his business, the lien may be enforced in accordance with either subsection (1) or (2).

(9) The warehouseman is liable for damages caused by failure to comply with the requirements for sale under this section and, in case of willful violation, is liable for conversion.

PART 3   BILLS OF LADING: SPECIAL PROVISIONS

Sec. 7-301.   Liability for Non-Receipt or Misdescription, "Said to Contain," "Shipper's Load and Count," Improper Handling

(1) A consignee of a non-negotiable bill who has given value in good faith or a holder to whom a negotiable bill has been duly negotiated relying in either case upon the

description therein of the goods, or upon the date therein shown, may recover from the issuer damages caused by the misdating of the bill or the nonreceipt or misdescription of the goods, except to the extent that the document indicates that the issuer does not know whether any part or all of the goods in fact were received or conform to the description, as where the description is in terms of marks or labels or kind, quantity, or condition of the receipt or description is qualified by "contents or condition of contents of packages unknown," "said to contain," "shipper's weight, load and count" or the like, if such indication be true.

(2) When goods are loaded by an issuer who is a common carrier, the issuer must count the packages of goods if package freight and ascertain the kind and quantity if bulk freight. In such cases "shipper's weight, load and count" or other words indicating that the description was made by the shipper are ineffective except as to freight concealed by packages.

(3) When bulk freight is loaded by a shipper who makes available to the issuer adequate facilities for weighing such freight, an issuer who is a common carrier must ascertain the kind and quantity within a reasonable time after receiving the written request of the shipper to do so. In such cases "shipper's weight" or other words of like purport are ineffective.

(4) The issuer may by inserting in the bill the words "shipper's weight, load and count" or other words of like purport indicate that the goods were loaded by the shipper; and if such statement be true the issuer shall not be liable for damages caused by the improper loading. But their omission does not imply liability for such damages.

(5) The shipper shall be deemed to have guaranteed to the issuer the accuracy at the time of shipment of the description, marks, labels, number, kind, quantity, condition and weight, as furnished by him; and the shipper shall indemnify the issuer against damage caused by inaccuracies in such particulars. The right of the issuer to such indemnity shall in no way limit his responsibility and liability under the contract of carriage to any person other than the shipper.

Sec. 7-302. Through Bills of Lading and Similar Documents

(1) The issuer of a through bill of lading or other document embodying an undertaking to be performed in part by persons acting as it agents or by connecting carriers is liable to anyone entitled to recover on the document for any breach by such other persons or by a connecting carrier of its obligation under the document but to the extent that the bill covers an undertaking to be performed overseas or in territory not contiguous to the continental United States or an undertaking including matters other than transportation this liability may be varied by agreement of the parties.

(2) Where goods covered by a through bill of lading or other document embodying an undertaking to be performed in part by persons other than the issuer are received by any such person, he is subject with respect to his own performance while the goods are in his possession to the obligation of the issuer. His obligation is discharged by delivery of the goods to another such person pursuant to the document, and does not include liability for breach by any other such persons or by the issuer.

(3) The issuer of such through bill of lading or other document shall be entitled to recover from the connecting carrier or such other person in possession of the goods

when the breach of the obligation under the document occurred, the amount it may be required to pay to anyone entitled to recover on the document therefor, as may be evidenced by any receipt, judgment, or transcript thereof, and the amount of any expense reasonably incurred by it in defending any action brought by anyone entitled to recover on the document therefor.

Sec. 7-303.   Diversion, Reconsignment, Change of Instructions

(1) Unless the bill of lading otherwise provides, the carrier may deliver the goods to a person or destination other than that stated in the bill or may otherwise dispose of the goods on instructions from
   (a) the holder of a negotiable bill; or
   (b) the consignor on a non-negotiable bill notwithstanding contrary instructions from the consignee; or
   (c) the consignee on a non-negotiable bill in the absence of contrary instructions from the consignor, if the goods have arrived at the billed destination or if the consignee is in possession of the bill; or
   (d) The consignee on a non-negotiable bill if he is entitled as against the consignor to dispose of them.
(2) Unless such instructions are noted on a negotiable bill of lading, a person to whom the bill is duly negotiated can hold the bailee according to the original terms.

Sec. 7-304.   Bills of Lading in a Set

(1) Except where customary in overseas transportation, a bill of lading must not be issued in a set of parts. The issuer is liable for damages caused by violation of this subsection.
(2) Where a bill of lading is lawfully drawn in a set of parts, each of which is numbered and expressed to be valid only if the goods have not been delivered against any other part, the whole of the parts constitute one bill.
(3) Where a bill of lading is lawfully issued in a set of parts and different parts are negotiated to different persons, the title of the holder to whom the first due negotiation is made prevails as to both the document and the goods, even though any later holder may have received the goods from the carrier in good faith and discharged the carrier's obligation by surrender of his part.
(4) Any person who negotiates or transfers a single part of a bill of lading drawn in a set is liable to holders of that part as if it were the whole set.
(5) The bailee is obliged to deliver in accordance with Part 4 of this Article against the first presented part of a bill of lading lawfully drawn in a set. Such delivery discharges the bailee's obligation on the whole bill.

Sec. 7-305.   Destination Bills

(1) Instead of issuing a bill of lading to the consignor at the place of shipment, a carrier may at the request of the consignor procure the bill to be issued at destination or at any other place designated in the request.

(2) Upon request of anyone entitled as against the carrier to control the goods while in transit and on surrender of any outstanding bill of lading or other receipt covering such goods, the issuer may procure a substitute bill to be issued at any place designated in the request.

Sec. 7-306.   Altered Bills of Lading

(1) An unauthorized alteration or filling of a blank in a bill of lading leaves the bill enforceable according to its original tenor.

Sec. 7-306.   Lien of Carrier

(1) A carrier has a lien on the goods covered by a bill of lading for charges subsequent to the date of its receipt of the goods for storage or transportation (including demurrage and terminal charges) and for expenses necessary for preservation of the goods incident to their transportation or reasonably incurred in their sale pursuant to law. But against a purchaser for value of a negotiable bill of lading a carrier's lien is limited to charges stated in the bill or the applicable tariffs, or if no charges are stated then to a reasonable charge.

(2) A lien for charges and expenses under subsection (1) on goods which the carrier was required by law to receive for transportation is effective against the consignor or any person entitled to the goods unless the carrier had notice that the consignor lacked authority to subject the goods to such charges and expenses. Any other lien under subsection (1) is effective against the consignor and any person who permitted the bailor to have control or possession of the goods unless the carrier had notice that the bailor lacked such authority.

(3) A carrier loses his lien on any goods which he voluntarily delivers or which he unjustifiably refuses to deliver.

Sec. 7-308.   Enforcement of Carrier's Lien

(1) A carrier's lien may be enforced by public or private sale of the goods, in bloc or in parcels, at any time or place and on any terms which are commercially reasonable, after notifying all persons known to claim an interest in the goods. Such notification must include a statement of the amount due, the nature of the proposed sale and the time and place of any public sale. The fact that a better price could have been obtained by a sale at a different time or in a different method from that selected by the carrier is not of itself sufficient to establish that the sale was not made in a commercially reasonable manner. If the carrier either sells the goods in the usual manner in any recognized market therefor or if he sells at the price current in such market at the time of his sale or if he has otherwise sold in conformity with commercially reasonable practices among dealers in the type of goods sold, he has sold in a commercially reasonable manner. A sale of more goods than apparently necessary to be offered to ensure satisfaction of the obligation is not commercially reasonable except in cases covered by the preceding sentence.

(2) Before any sale pursuant to this section any person claiming a right in the goods may pay the amount necessary to satisfy the lien and the reasonable expenses incurred under this section. In that event the goods must not be sold, but must be retained by the carrier subject to the terms of the bill and this Article.

(3) The carrier may buy at any public sale pursuant to this section.

(4) A purchaser in good faith of goods sold to enforce a carrier's lien takes the goods free of any rights of persons against whom the lien was valid, despite non-compliance by the carrier with the requirements of this section.

(5) The carrier may satisfy his lien from the proceeds of any sale pursuant to this section but must hold the balance, if any, for delivery on demand to any person to whom he would have been bound to deliver the goods.

(6) The rights provided by this section shall be in addition to all other rights allowed by law to a creditor against his debtor.

(7) A carrier's lien may be enforced in accordance with either subsection (1) or the procedure set forth in subsection (2) of Section 7-210.

(8) The carrier is liable for damages caused by failure to comply with the requirements for sale under this section and in case of willful violation is liable for conversion.

Sec. 7-309. Duty of Care, Contractual Limitation of Carrier's Liability

(1) A carrier who issues a bill of lading, whether negotiable or non-negotiable, must exercise the degree of care in relation to the goods which a reasonable careful man would exercise under like circumstances. This subsection does not repeal or change any law or rule of law which imposes liability upon a common carrier for damages not caused by its negligence.

(2) Damages may be limited by a provision that the carrier's liability shall not exceed a value stated in the document if the carrier's rates are dependent upon value and the consignor by the carrier's tariff is afforded an opportunity to declare a higher value or a value as lawfully provided in the tariff, or, where no tariff is filed, he is otherwise advised of such opportunity; but no such limitation is effective with respect to the carrier's liability for conversion to its own use.

(3) Reasonable provisions as to the time and manner of presenting claims and instituting actions based on the shipment may be included in a bill of lading or tariff.

PART 4 WAREHOUSE RECEIPTS AND BILLS OF LADING GENERAL OBLIGATIONS

Sec. 7-401. Irregularities in Issue of Receipt or Bill or Conduct of Issue

The obligations imposed by this Article on an issuer apply to a document of title regardless of the fact that

(a) the document may not comply with the requirements of this Article or of any other law or regulation regarding its issue, form or content; or

(b) the issuer may have violated laws regulating the conduct of his business; or

(c) The goods covered by the document were owned by the bailee at the time the document was issued; or

(d) the person issuing the document does not come with-in the definition of warehouseman, if it purports to be a warehouse receipt.

Sec. 7-402. Duplicate Receipt or Bill; Overissue

Neither a duplicate nor any other document of title purporting to cover goods already represented by an outstanding document of the same issuer confers any right in the goods, except as provided in the case of bills in a set, overissue of documents for fungible goods and substitutes for lost, stolen or destroyed documents. But the issuer is liable for damages caused by his overissue or failure to identify a duplicate document as such by conspicuous notation on its face.

Sec. 7-403. Obligation of Warehouseman or Carrier to Deliver, Excuse

(1) The bailee must deliver the goods to a person entitled under the document who complies with subsection (2) and (3), unless and to the extent that the bailee establishes any of the following.

    (a) delivery of the goods to a person whose receipt was rightful as against the claimant;

    (b) damage to or delay, loss or destruction of the goods for which the bailee is not liable [but the burden of establishing negligence in such cases is on the person entitled under the document];

Note: The brackets in (1) (b) indicate that State enactments may differ on this point without serious damage to the principle of uniformity.

    (c) previous sale or other disposition of the goods in lawful enforcement of a lien or on warehouseman's lawful termination of storage);

    (d) the exercise by a seller of his right to stop de-livery pursuant to the provisions of the Article on Sales (Section 2-7050);

    (e) A diversion, reconsignment or other disposition pursuant to the provisions of this Article (Section 7-303) or tariff regulating such right;

    (f) release, satisfaction or any other fact affording a personal defense against the claimant;

    (g) any other lawful excuse.

(2) A person claiming goods covered by a document of title must satisfy the bailee's lien where the bailee so requests or where the bailee is prohibited by law from delivering the goods until the charges are paid.

(3) Unless the person claiming is one against whom the document confers no right under Sec. 7-503 (1), he must surrender for cancellation or notation of partial deliveries any outstanding negotiable document covering the goods, and the bailee must cancel the document or conspicuously note the partial delivery thereon or be liable to any person to whom the document is duly negotiated.

(4) "Person entitled under the document" means holder in the case of a negotiable document, or the person to whom delivery is to be made by the terms of or pursuant to written instructions under a non-negotiable document.

Sec. 7-404. No Liability for Good Faith Delivery Pursuant to Receipt or Bill

A bailee who in good faith including observance of reasonable commercial standards has received goods and delivered or otherwise disposed of them according to the terms of the document of title or pursuant to this Article is not liable therefor. This rule applies even though the person from whom he received the goods had no authority to procure the document or to dispose of the goods and even though the person to whom he delivered the goods had no authority to receive them.

PART 5   WAREHOUSE RECEIPTS AND BILLS OF LADING: NEGOTIATION AND TRANSFER

Sec. 7-501. Form of Negotiation and Requirements of "Due Negotiation"

(1) A negotiable document of title running to the order of a named person is negotiated by his endorsement and delivery. After his endorsement in blank or to bearer any person can negotiate it by delivery alone.
(2) (a) A negotiable document of title is also negotiated by delivery alone when by its original terms it runs to bearer.
   (b) When a document running to the order of a named person is delivered to him, the effect is the document had been negotiated.
(3) Negotiation of a negotiable document of title after it has been endorsed to a specified person requires indorsement by the special endorsee as well as delivery.
(4) A negotiable document of title is "duly negotiated" when it is negotiated in the manner stated in this section to a holder who purchases it in good faith without notice of any defense against or claim to it on the part of any person and for value, unless its established that the negotiation is not in the regular course of business or financing or involves receiving the document in settlement or payment of a money obligation.
(5) Endorsement of a non-negotiable document neither makes it negotiable nor adds to the transferee's rights.
(6) The naming in a negotiable bill of a person to be notified of the arrival of the goods does not limit the negotiability of the bill nor constitute notice to a purchaser thereof of any interest of such person in the goods.

Sec. 7-502. Rights Acquired by Due Negotiation

(1) Subject to the following section and to the provisions of Section 7-205 on fungible goods, a holder to whom a negotiable document of title has been duly negotiated acquires thereby:

(a) title to the document;

(b) title to the goods;

(c) all rights accruing under the law of agency or estoppel, including rights to goods delivered to the bailee after the document was issued; and

(d) the direct obligation of the issuer to hold or deliver the goods according to the terms of the document free of any defense or claim by him except those arising under the terms of the document or under this Article. In the case of a delivery order the bailee's obligation accrued only upon acceptance and the obligation acquired by the holder is that the issuer and any endorser will procure the acceptance of the bailee.

(2) Subject to the following section, title and rights acquired are not defeated by any stoppage of the goods represented by the document or by surrender of such goods by the bailee, and are not impaired even though the negotiation or any prior negotiation constituted a breach of duty or even though any person has been deprived of possession of the document by misrepresentation, fraud, accident, mistake, duress, loss, theft or conversion, or even though a previous sale or other transfer of the goods has been made to a third person.

Sec. 7-503.   Documents of Title to Goods Defeated in Certain Cases

(1) A document of title confers no right in goods against a person who before issuance of the document had a legal interest or a perfected security interest in them and who neither

(a) delivered or entrusted them or any document of title covering them to the bailor or his nominee with actual or apparent authority to ship, store or sell or with power to obtain delivery under this Article (Section 7-403) or with power of disposition under this Act (Sections 2-403 and 9-307) or other statute or rule of law; nor

(b) acquiesced in the procurement by the bailor or his nominee of any document of title.

(2) Title to goods based upon an unaccepted delivery order is subject to the rights of anyone to whom a negotiable warehouse receipt or bill of lading covering the goods has been duly negotiated. Such a title may be defeated under the next section to the same extent as the rights of the issuer or a transferee from the issuer.

(3) Title to goods based upon a bill of lading issued to a freight forwarder is subject to the rights of anyone to whom a bill issued by the freight forwarder is duly negotiated; but delivery by the carrier in accordance with Part 4 of this Article pursuant to its own bill of lading discharges the carrier's obligation to deliver.

Sec. 7-504.   Rights Acquired in the Absence of Due Negotiation; Effect of Diversion; Seller's Stoppage of Delivery

(1) A transferee of a document, whether negotiable or non-negotiable, to whom the document has been delivered but not duly negotiated, acquires the title and rights which his transferor had or had actual authority to convey.

(2) In the case of a non-negotiable document, until but not after the bailee receives notification of the transfer, the rights of the transferee may be defeated.

    (a) by those creditors of the transferor who could treat the sale as void under Section 2-402; or

    (b) by a buyer from the transferor in ordinary course of business if the bailee has delivered the goods to the buyer or received notification of his rights; or

    (c) as against the bailee by good faith dealings of the bailee with the transferor.

(3) A diversion or other change of shipping instructions by the consignor in a non-negotiable bill of lading which causes the bailee not to deliver to the consignee defeats the consignee's title to the goods if they have been delivered to a buyer in ordinary course of business and in any event defeats the consignee's rights against the bailee.

(4) Delivery pursuant to a non-negotiable document may be stopped by a seller under Section 2-705, and subject to the requirement of due notification there provided. A bailee honoring the seller's instructions is entitled to be indemnified by the seller against any resulting loss or expense.

Sec. 7-505. Endorser Not a Guarantor for Other Parties

The endorsement of a document of title issued by a bailee does not make the endorser liable for any default by the bailee or by previous endorsers.

Sec. 7-506. Delivery Without Endorsement: Right to Compel Endorsement

The transferee of a negotiable document of title has a specifically enforceable right to have his transferor supply any necessary endorsement but the transfer becomes a negotiation only as of the time the endorsement is supplied.

Sec. 7-507. Warranties on Negotiation or Transfer of Receipt or Bill

Where a person negotiates or transfers a document of title for value otherwise than as a mere intermediary under the next following section, then unless otherwise agreed he warrants to his immediate purchaser only, in addition to any warranty made in selling the goods,

    (a) that the document is genuine; and

    (b) that he has no knowledge of any fact which would impair its validity or worth; and

    (c) that his negotiation or transfer is rightful and fully effective with respect to the title to the document and the goods it represents.

Sec. 7-508. Warranties of Collecting Bank as to Documents

A collecting bank or other intermediary known to be entrusted with documents on behalf of another or with collection of a draft or other claim against delivery of documents warrants by such delivery of the documents only its own good faith and authority. This rule applies even though the intermediary has purchased or made advances against the claim or draft to be collected.

Sec. 7-509.   Receipt or Bill: When Adequate Compliance with Commercial Contract

The question whether a document is adequate to fulfill the obligations of a contract for sale or the conditions of a credit is governed by the Articles on Sales (Article 2) and on Letters of Credit (Article 5).

PART 6   WAREHOUSE RECEIPTS AND BILLS OF LADING: MISCELLANEOUS PROVISIONS

Sec. 7-601.   Loss and Missing Documents

(1) If a document has been lost, stolen or destroyed, a court may order delivery of the goods or issuance of a substitute document and the bailee may without liability to any person comply with such order. If the document was negotiable the claimant must post security approved by the court to indemnify any person who may suffer loss as a result of non-surrender of the document. If the document was not negotiable, such security may be required at the discretion of the court. The court may also in its discretion order payment of the bailee's reasonable costs and counsel fees.

(2) A bailee who without court order delivers goods to a person claiming under a missing negotiable document is liable to any person injured thereby, and if the delivery is not in good faith becomes liable for conversion. Delivery in good faith is not conversion if made in accordance with a filed classification or tariff or, where no classification or tariff is filed, if the claimant posts security with the bailee in an amount at least double the value of the goods at the time of posting to indemnify any person injured by the delivery who files a notice of claim within one year after the delivery.

Sec. 7-602.   Attachment of Goods Covered by a Negotiable Document

Except where the document was originally issued upon delivery of the goods by a person who had no power to dispose of them, no lien attaches by virtue of any judicial process to goods in the possession of a bailee for which a negotiable document of title is outstanding unless the document be first surrendered to the bailee or its negotiation enjoined, and the bailee shall not be compelled to deliver the goods pursuant to process until the document is surrendered to him or impounded by the court. One who purchases the document for value without notice of the process or injunction takes free of the lien imposed by judicial process.

Sec. 7-603.   Conflicting Claims, Interpleader

If more than one person claims title or possession of the goods, the bailee is excused from delivery until he has had a reasonable time to ascertain the validity of the adverse claims or to bring an action to compel all claimants to interplead and may compel such interpleader, either in defending an action for non-delivery of the goods, or by original action, whichever is appropriate.

INDEX

Y